The National Young Leadership Cabinet

"Lead with Inspiration"

2006-2007

THE GENESIS OF
LEADERSHIP

Jewish Lights books by Nathan Laufer

The Genesis of Leadership: What the Bible Teaches Us about Vision, Values and Leading Change

Leading the Passover Journey: The Seder's Meaning Revealed, the Haggadah's Story Retold

THE GENESIS OF LEADERSHIP

What the Bible
Teaches Us about
Vision, Values and
Leading Change

Nathan Laufer

Foreword by **Senator Joseph I. Lieberman**

Preface by **Dr. Michael Hammer**,
author of *Reengineering the Corporation*

For People of All Faiths, All Backgrounds

JEWISH LIGHTS Publishing
Woodstock, Vermont

The Genesis of Leadership:
What the Bible Teaches Us about Vision, Values and Leading Change

2006 First Printing
© 2006 by Nathan Laufer
Foreword © 2006 by Joseph I. Lieberman
Preface © 2006 by Michael Hammer

Library of Congress Cataloging-in-Publication Data
Laufer, Nathan, 1957–
The genesis of leadership : what the Bible teaches us about vision, values, and leading change / Nathan Laufer ; foreword by Joseph I. Lieberman ; preface by Michael Hammer.
p. cm.
Includes bibliographical references.
ISBN-13: 978-1-58023-241-8 (hardcover)
ISBN-10: 1-58023-241-8 (hardcover)
1. Leadership—Biblical teaching. 2. Bible. O.T.—Criticism, interpretation, etc. 3. Bible. O.T. Genesis—Criticism, interpretation, etc. 4. Leadership—Religious aspects—Judaism. I. Title.
BS1199.L4L38 2006
296.6'1—dc22
2006014154

10 9 8 7 6 5 4 3 2 1

Manufactured in the United States of America
Jacket Design: Sara Dismukes

For People of All Faiths, All Backgrounds
Published by Jewish Lights Publishing
A Division of LongHill Partners, Inc.
Sunset Farm Offices, Route 4, P.O. Box 237
Woodstock, VT 05091
Tel: (802) 457-4000   Fax: (802) 457-4004
www.jewishlights.com

To Sharon,
for standing by my side

Contents

Book II: The Ten Guiding Principles of Leadership 83

Foreword

SENATOR JOSEPH I. LIEBERMAN

What does it take to make a great leader? Vision, creativity, charisma, a way with people, courage, opportunity, and luck all play a role in forming a leader and enabling success. Still, the bedrock of leadership is found in character and values. This is the lesson of the very special book that lies before you.

In the United States of America there is currently much debate and some confusion about the proper role for religion and values in public life and leadership. This confusion stems from our history. The founding generations of Americans separated church and state in order to achieve full equality among its citizens with their many faiths and denominational backgrounds. In recent decades, some have argued that political leaders should not draw upon religious values for fear they will impose their particular faith's principles on others. The regrettable result is the often-heard claim that religion should not be a factor in the societal conversation or in the formulation of public policy. But creating such a vacuum would weaken one of the strongest foundations of democratic values and human dignity: the faith that undergirds democracy and strengthens conscience. Those values are one of the best ways leaders link the people to one and other in community and inspire action to achieve public purposes, such as protecting our natural environment.

The inner link between leader and values, between the character of the leader and the leadership role, is superbly illuminated in this book. Rabbi Nathan Laufer has brilliantly spelled out the Bible's portraits of leadership as tools meant to inspire us to elevate ourselves and reach for the biblical standards of responsibility. Thanks to his role in shaping and guiding the Wexner Heritage programs in Jewish community leadership, Rabbi Laufer is one of the important Jewish educators of our time. In this book, Rabbi Laufer expands his personal teachings from the Wexner Heritage program to forge a book of deep insights into the nature of leadership and how character drives—or blinds—leaders to the tasks before them. He sketches the three concentric circles of responsibility that every person must accept to become a good leader. The innermost circle is to take responsibility for our own actions (or inactions) toward others, and the consequences of those actions. The second circle of responsibility involves the welfare of those with whom we have relationships—family, friends, colleagues, and coworkers. The outermost circle of responsibility is for all who cross our path or whose lives are touched by our leadership role. Laufer argues—and illustrates—that according to the Bible, taking responsibility is the most important value for leaders to learn and practice. In the end, he argues, leaders are ultimately responsible for the success and failure of their followers.

This message should not be misinterpreted as leaders' dominance over their followers. Just as the Bible teaches that perfecting the world is the outcome of a partnership between God and humanity, so is leadership—political, economic, and spiritual—the outcome of a partnership between leaders and followers. Great achievements and a better world are the outcome of such a partnership when it works. Accomplishments come from a harmony between values and policies, and the interaction of character and opportunity.

Rabbi Laufer also makes clear that the true measure of a leader's greatness is not success or failure. He offers an unforgettable portrait of the greatest Jewish leader of all time, Moses—of his character, of his growth, and of his failure to create a free people out of a cohort of emancipated slaves. He shows how Moses's inability to achieve entry into the promised land is the personal outcome of his life. His falling short stands side by side and is interactive with his extraordinary liberation of a people and creation of a life-affirming tradition. Laufer has accomplished an act of leadership himself in his portrait—distilled from the Bible—of God as leader and teacher of Israel.

Reading this book will enrich lovers of the Bible with an understanding of its guidelines for leaders. This writing will equally excite students of leadership with its feast of Biblical teachings and life's wisdom.

I want to add a word of personal testimony. In my years as a public servant, I found myself irresistibly drawn to the wells of my tradition for guidance and inspiration. My faith has offered a sustaining moral anchor and inner gyroscope. My wife, Hadassah, has added the dimension of meaning and values exemplified by survivors of the Holocaust and their children. These values, drawn out of the fire of suffering, as well as this character forged on the anvil of the Holocaust, were unbreakable. Through success and defeat, by helping us face down the temptations to sell out or run away from our commitments, this faith helped us come to the realization that the biblical promise is true: Those whose character cleaves steadfastly to the Lord and to eternal values are drawn to the side of life. They find the strength to lead and to rise above defeat and hopefully lead again.

We all owe a debt to Rabbi Nathan Laufer for opening the doors to wisdom for all willing to enter and learn. This is a gift for life, for living, and for leadership.

Preface

DR. MICHAEL HAMMER

Leadership has never been so badly needed as it is today, nor has it ever been in such short supply. I spend much of my time talking with frontline personnel and middle managers in organizations of all sizes, and the most common lament that I hear from them is "We aren't getting the leadership that we need." Despite the endless seminars on the topic, despite the numerous leadership development programs, despite the constant stream of leadership tomes seemingly published every day (here Eccles. 12:12 comes to mind, "Of making many books there is no end"), we are nonetheless suffering from a leadership crisis. Why?

The reason is that we are living in a period of extraordinary and unprecedented change. While change may not be new, its current pace certainly is. Long-standing assumptions and beliefs now crumble virtually overnight, while concepts and issues that would have been unintelligible just yesterday dominate today's agenda. As I write this, the newspapers are full of speculation about General Motors entering bankruptcy, about the impending collapse of the housing bubble, about the rise of social websites like MySpace, about the effect of very light jets on the aviation system. Not so long ago these notions would have been laughable or incomprehensible. Ask yourself what two characteristics the following items have in common: outsourcing and offshoring, hybrid cars, reality television, Internet blogs, and cloning. The first is that they are all important contemporary phenomena, shaping our lives and transforming major industries. The other is that almost no one had heard of any them as little as five years ago. And five years hence, they will be replaced by a set of concerns to which we are oblivious today. When issues can go from off the radar screen to the top of our concerns in so little time, then we are not living in Auden's Age of Anxiety but in an Age of Change.

The primary underlying cause of this change is, of course, the continuous advancement in our scientific and technological knowledge base. Science is a cumulative discipline; each practitioner builds on the results of all preceding ones. And since the number of scientists and engineers keeps growing (one estimate is that 90 percent of all those who ever worked in these fields are alive today), the amount of scientific and technological knowledge increases exponentially. The fruits of this knowledge do not take long to move from the laboratory to the marketplace and into our homes and lives. My cell phone has more computing power than the first mainframe I used in the 1960s, and its functionality (digital camera, hands-free operation, Internet access) surpasses the imagination of the science-fiction writers of my youth. Combine this basic driver of change with a culture that valorizes novelty (we view with suspicion not the newfangled but anything that isn't the latest) and a communications infrastructure that enables the rapid diffusion of innovations, and we have a perfect incubator of relentless change.

Change may be fun and exciting, but change also means that organizations and enterprises—large and small, public and private, manufacturing and service—must adapt to it or they will not survive. The landscape is littered with the remains of enterprises that did not adapt to drastically changed circumstances. How did Wal-Mart overtake Sears, why did the American automakers lose ground to their Japanese competitors, how did Microsoft elbow aside the leaders of the computing industry? Because established companies did not respond to changes in their environments. They stuck to the tried and true, to business as usual, which is now not prudence but a guarantee of disaster. And what is the essential prerequisite, the indispensable ingredient, if an enterprise is to rise to the challenge of overwhelming change? The answer is leadership.

The new leadership agenda is to redefine the enterprise for a radically new world, to develop a vision of how the organization will thrive in novel circumstances, and to formulate and execute a plan for getting there. While such leadership must start at the top of the enterprise, it cannot be confined there. People throughout the organization must form a leadership network that creates enthusiasm for change and influences everyone to contribute to it. None of this is easy to do because most people are terrified by change. Change requires them to let go of what they know, to relinquish familiar patterns of work and behavior, and to embrace not just the new but the unknown, to embark on a journey whose destination cannot yet be seen. Persuading people, motivating them, inspiring them to take such a leap is the modern leadership challenge. Yet few, if any, people in an enterprise—even (or perhaps especially) those at the top—know how to exercise such leadership for change. They have come of age working in or leading enterprises through periods that look stable compared to what we face today. They are adept at continuity, at stewardship, at solving problems in a familiar context. They are ill-prepared by their experiences to face down huge change and rally their people to master it. It is therefore fortunate that Nathan Laufer's book now appears because it offers people at all levels of an organization a powerful resource and tool for navigating their way through change.

There is no better case study of leadership through change than Moses's leadership of the Israelites from the land of Egypt to the Promised Land. At the beginning of the story, the Israelites find themselves in captivity in the land of Egypt, suffering at the hands of slave masters and oppressors—a suitable metaphor for enterprises beleaguered by more nimble competitors and demanding customers. At the end of the story they are in a land flowing with milk and honey—financial and organizational success. While it might seem that moving from one to the other would be an easy thing to do, we need to remember that to the Israelites in Egypt, the promised land of Canaan seemed like a distant fantasy, not a realistic destination. Even worse, between Egypt and Canaan lay the desert—a wilderness that possessed neither the virtues of Canaan nor the familiarity of Egypt. The desert is a perfect emblem of the experience of change, and it was through this wilderness that Moses somehow managed to lead his fearful, recalcitrant, and confused charges—in turn, perfectly representative of any group of people in any enterprise experiencing massive change. The lessons that Nathan Laufer extracts from this protean saga, and the principles and challenges that he enumerates, are universal and timeless and relevant to any person trying to exercise leadership and help those around him or her survive disorienting change.

As adults we learn far better from stories than from abstractions; human narratives engage us far better than dry generalities. There is no more powerful set of narratives than those in the Bible. They have captivated people of all ages and backgrounds for thousands of years; they clearly speak to something essential in human nature. The biblical narrative,

whether one interprets it historically or symbolically or mythically or in
literary terms, offers extraordinary material for the interpretive art. Nathan
Laufer helps us see the stories of the journey from Egypt to Canaan in new
ways, he turns them into universal paradigms that relate to situations we
all face every day, and he distills his insights into practical and powerful
guidelines. There is no algorithm for leadership, no cookbook recipe, but
it is hard to imagine a leader at any level of an enterprise whose capabili-
ties will not be enhanced by studying this book. It is somehow comforting
that help in coping with the dislocations of our modern technological age
can be found in one of our most ancient of texts. To cite Ecclesiastes again,
"There is nothing new under the sun" (1:9). The problems are eternal,
the lessons are all there to be learned—it is our responsibility to understand them and apply them anew.

Acknowledgments

Twenty years ago, I began working for a foundation, established by Mr. Leslie H. Wexner, chairman and founder of Limited Brands Inc., that educated philanthropic leaders in the North American Jewish community. I found the work fascinating and challenging. As part of my learning process in dealing with the foundation's constituents, I began to read everything I could get my hands on about leadership. I soon realized that, unlike the fields of law and theology in which I held advanced degrees, the field of leadership was still in the process of formation and had not yet congealed into an agreed-upon discipline. Everything from New Age spirituality to learning how to decipher algorithms seemed to fall under the rubric of "leadership education." There was a lot of sifting in order to evaluate what had true value for leaders and what was just a passing fad.

After several years of working with our growing membership and alumni on their leadership challenges and getting my arms around the diverse literature, I began to think about what the Bible, the bedrock of my own spiritual tradition, might have to say about leadership. Tentatively at first, but then with increasing confidence, I began to speak about what we, at the foundation, thought of as biblical or Mosaic leadership. Soon enough, by word of mouth, people all around the country began hearing our message and then inviting us to share our thoughts on biblical leadership. "How refreshingly clear!" I kept hearing over and over from my listeners. "That's the best single presentation on leadership that I have ever heard!" Ivy League MBA graduates told me. "You really must publish your insights in a book."

The positive feedback was very gratifying. But as the president and CEO of the foundation, traveling more than a hundred days every year and working sixty to seventy hours a week on behalf of the foundation, I found it impossible to invest the necessary time to turn out a quality manuscript. Fortunately, thanks to the graciousness of Leslie and Abigail

Wexner, I was able to travel to Israel to research and write this volume. I am very grateful to Les and Abigail for the opportunity to serve my community for almost two decades and for enabling me to share my scholarship now with a broader audience. I want to especially thank Les for encouraging me to attend the Leadership Educator Program at the John F. Kennedy School of Government at Harvard University. Many of the theories of leadership that found their way into this volume were born during my discussions with colleagues and faculty in that program.

Rabbi Herbert A. Friedman, founding president emeritus of Wexner Heritage, hired me and served as my professional mentor for many years; much of what I know about the practical side of leadership I learned from him. He was my Moses. I owe a good deal of my success at the foundation to the support of my professional colleagues, both staff and faculty, who collaborated with me in building an outstanding institution of leadership education. Together, we formed a guiding coalition that added value and enriched the leadership skills of our members and alumni. In the spirit of my tradition's spiritual sages, I learned much from my teachers and mentors, even more from my colleagues and friends but most of all from my students, the thirteen hundred members and alumni of the Wexner Heritage program whom I had the privilege of educating. It is their passionate and devoted leadership that inspired me and continues to do so.

Once in Israel, I was the beneficiary of a generous senior fellowship from the Shalem Center, a Jerusalem think tank addressing social, religious, and political issues of leadership in Israel and in the world. I was privileged to write this manuscript in their beautiful facility. I am especially grateful to my colleagues Dr. Daniel Polisar, the president of the center, and Dr. Yoram Hazony, its founder, for their moral and financial backing, intellectual insights, and commitment to this project's completion. This book would not have come to fruition without their foresight, support, and encouragement.

This book is seeing the light of day thanks to the incisive editorial efforts of Elisheva Urbas, with whom I have consulted every step along the way. Art Kleiner provided a second level of editorial input that proved very helpful in clarifying the text and contextualizing the Bible within the framework of current management thinking. The staff at Jewish Lights has been, now for the second time, a pleasure to work with. I especially want to thank Stuart M. Matlins, publisher, for believing in me and in this manuscript, and my working partners at Jewish Lights, Emily Wichland, Sarah McBride, and Tim Holtz for their unstinting professionalism.

One of the conclusions that I draw in this book from the experience of Moses is the importance that leaders be "held," that is, unconditionally supported, by a partner or mate, in order for them to "hold" others successfully through the challenges of leadership. My wife of twenty years, Sharon Fliss Laufer, has been my supportive partner and mate through the thick and thin of my professional and communal leadership. My achievements are hers. It is therefore to Sharon that *The Genesis of Leadership* is dedicated.

Nathan Laufer
Jerusalem, Israel

Introduction

The contemporary field of leadership as an academic discipline is only half a century old.[1] It is only in the past twenty-five years or so that the field has seen an explosion of public interest and a plethora of books published. However, long before books about leadership began to abound like the proverbial "waters that fill the seas,"[2] the Book of books—that is, the Bible—contained within its narrative a complete and sophisticated paradigm of leadership—one as relevant to leaders today as when the Bible was written and edited millennia ago. It is that biblical leadership model, particularly the one embedded within the "Five Books of Moses," beginning with the book of Genesis, that will be the focus of this volume. Hence, this book's title: *The Genesis of Leadership*.

In the Hebrew Bible, the Five Books of Moses are also known as the Torah, meaning "teaching." Indeed, the point of embedding a leadership model in the Torah was to teach leaders in subsequent generations what values and attitudes, skills and strategies, and perilous pitfalls are endemic to leadership. This book will follow the order of the first biblical books in laying out thematically what the biblical narrative has to teach us about leadership. We will begin by focusing on the values of relationship and responsibility underlying the leadership narrative in the Bible's first book, the book of Genesis. With those family-based values serving as a foundation we will then spiral up one level to the ten principles of effective leadership woven into the Bible's second book, the book of Exodus. We will then confront the potential stumbling blocks that leaders often confront in applying those values and principles to the real world: the eight recurring challenges of leadership embedded in the narrative of the Bible's fourth book, the book of Numbers. Finally, we will extrapolate the legacy of leadership and the importance of grooming a successor found in the Bible's fifth book, the book of Deuteronomy.[3]

The first common thread running throughout the Bible is that leadership is so challenging an endeavor that every leader, no matter how naturally charismatic and authoritative, must learn how to become more effective and successful. Indeed, as will be made clear throughout this volume, it is imperative that leaders learn how to be better leaders both from their own previous experiences as well as from the stories that comprise their cultural and religious traditions. In the Bible, even God is depicted as a leader who must learn how to lead successfully. Portraying God as a learning leader is the Bible's way of driving home to us that becoming a successful leader is neither an inborn certainty nor a mystical process but rather a learned art and a developed discipline.

If the Bible as a whole stands for anything, it stands for the proposition that people—including leaders—are capable of changing themselves and initiating change in others through the process of learning and teaching. Leaders are capable of and indeed are expected to draw the lessons of leadership from humanity's past if they are to be successful agents and models of change in the long term. The Bible (by making extensive use of narrative—that is, stories about the past) teaches by example what educational theorists have assumed ever since: that people learn and teach better through stories than through mere didactic instruction. Stories are a powerful platform for producing personal transformation and communal change.[4] As Noel Tichy, professor of organizational behavior and management at the University of Michigan's School of Business, puts it: "The basic cognitive form in which people organize their thinking is the narrative story.... Dramatic storytelling is the way people learn from, and connect with, one another."[5]

The Bible could have foregone its powerful storytelling style and been simply a dry book of law, ethical instruction, and ritual technique.[6] By weaving extensive narrative portions into its first five books, the Bible makes plain its intention to teach important yet accessible lessons with "take-home" value to its readers and leaders alike.

Several Words about "God"

In the Bible, "God" is a literary character who is portrayed as having something very much like a human personality. The twelfth-century philosopher Moses Maimonides, in the first section of his philosophic classic, *The Guide to the Perplexed*, recognized the problematic nature of the biblical description of God's humanness. That biblical description did not match what he believed to be true about God's ultimate perfection. Therefore, Maimonides did not read anthropomorphic descriptions of God's physical or emotional state in the Bible literally. Rather, he viewed and interpreted those descriptions metaphorically. To emphasize the yawning chasm between the Bible's very human description of God and our common understanding of God as the perfect, supreme, metaphysical being, Maimonides formulated a "negative theology" about God's essence that posited our inability to say anything positive about God in a metaphysical sense. For Maimonides, all that we can say about God's essence is what God is not—not like anything finite, limited, or definable in and of this world. God is totally transcendent, totally "other" from what human beings can think about, say, or even imagine. In contrast, Maimonides interpreted the anthropomorphic descriptions about God in the Bible as representative of the way people experience God's manifestations in the world, not as a literal description of God's being.

In fact, the Bible says many things about God and implies many others, many of which are inconsistent with what human beings generally believe to be true about God. Well before Maimonides, the spiritual masters of Judaism in the early centuries of the Common Era recognized this anomaly and coined the phrase "The Bible speaks in the language of human beings" to explain descriptions of God and biblical events that contradicted what they believed to be true. In effect, these sages were saying that God, in the Bible, is depicted in the image of human beings so that human beings could learn what to do and not to do. These spiritual masters continued this metaphoric process by describing God in the most anthropomorphic ways in their own biblical commentaries known as the Midrash.

In this book, I will not be analyzing God's unknowable and indescribable essence but rather the literary character of God, who is depicted in these very human terms. Specifically, I will focus on the biblical God's attempts to lead human beings, and their successes and failures in the biblical narrative. Like Maimonides and the sages preceding me, I assume that the narrative is "speaking in the language of human beings" to enable us, as readers, to learn important lessons from what transpired, not because these biblical stories convey literal truths or limitations, cognitive or otherwise, about God's essence. Like the sages who preceded me, I recognize my human limitation in understanding what God is "really" about. In the spirit of Maimonides' negative theology, I make no claims about God's essence from the anthropomorphic ways that God is described in the biblical text or by the critical way that I will be interpreting them. No matter how unflatteringly and flawed God is depicted in the biblical narrative, those descriptions do not detract from what I believe to be God's ultimate perfection, justice, and mastery of the universe. Rather, I view the biblical narrative as the conscious way the Bible chose to express itself to advance its teachings.

There were and are, of course, those who read and interpret the Bible differently. Some great scholars, such as the twelfth-century Rabad of Posquieries, who were highly critical of Maimonides' approach, read the biblical texts concerning God's physical and emotional attributes as conveying not a literary lesson but a literal truth. Such individuals would feel uncomfortable with my analysis and critique of "God's leadership" in the biblical narrative. I understand and respect their position but choose, with some trepidation to be sure, to follow a different approach in this volume—the path chosen by the Bible itself and by the spiritual masters of Judaism in the early centuries of the Common Era who employed similar anthropomorphic language to describe God in their biblical commentaries.[7]

For me, the two primary reasons that the Bible chose to speak about God and describe God's actions in such human terms was, first, because the Bible wanted to reinforce humanity's nobility as absolutely free beings created in the "image of God" and, second, because the Bible wanted us, its human readers, to understand and identify with God's character.

In my reading of the Bible, human freedom, the essence of being in the "image of God," is precisely what makes human history interesting to God and merits divine attention. If human beings were not godlike in the sense of being absolutely free, and if God in the biblical narrative knew and controlled everything that human beings were going to do before they did it, then humanity would be no more than a conglomeration of automatons, a boring lot, hardly worthy of divine attention and concern. Just as Adam, created in God's image, could not find fulfillment or companionship in naming and relating to the animal world, so God in the Bible would not find fulfillment in relating to a being that did not share with God the freedom to choose who to be and how to act. It is only because humanity shares with God the attribute of absolute free will that

God in the Bible is interested in initiating and sustaining the relationship with humankind and the people of Israel. For God, human beings were a worthy challenge to test God's own ability to educate and persuade without the use of force.

Second, while ennobling humanity, the Bible also wanted God, whose essence is invisible, indescribable, and transcendent, nevertheless to seem approachable, understandable, and accessible. Only by depicting God as having a human personality could God's leadership be a source of learning for us. Therefore, just like fallible human beings, God is portrayed in the Bible not as omniscient and perfect but as a God who learns by trial and error—God's initial failure in leading people teaches God what not to do, and God's subsequent successes teach God what to repeat and build upon in the future. Sometimes God in the Bible, like God's human look-alikes, evinces the same failed pattern of leadership more than once. God is presented as a character who gets disappointed and angry; who, in moments of rage, repeatedly threatens God's subjects without success; who lashes out at times, driving people away both literally and figuratively.[8] At the other end of the emotional spectrum, God is depicted as a personality who exhibits enthusiastic love, kindness, and patience, earning people's trust and devotion.[9] Indeed, part of the greatness of the Bible lies precisely in its graphic, humanlike descriptions of God's emotions and actions and in honestly describing the consequences that follow.

The Bible does not hide the learning curve of any of its literary heroes—not those of Abraham or Moses, and not even that of "God." The early flaws and later virtues of its literary characters are portrayed and exposed for all to see. In doing so, the Bible teaches the reader which attitudes and behaviors to emulate and which to avoid. If God in the Bible acts angrily or vindictively, out of all apparent proportion to people's misbehavior, resulting in massive death or destruction and the even further distancing of people from God, as happens in the middle of the book of Numbers, those leadership traits are obviously not to be emulated—not by ordinary people, and certainly not by leaders. The stories try to teach people, and leaders, what not to do, as God explicitly teaches in the legal sections of the Bible (Lev. 19:17–18). In contrast, if God acts justly, with encouragement, compassion, patience, and kindness, resulting in the uplifting of human life and the trusting devotion of God's people, then those are the traits the Bible wants us to admire and emulate. Those stories teach us what to do, as God again explicitly teaches in the legal sections of the Bible (Deut. 16:20, 24:17).

Moreover, by cataloging its heroes' mistakes—mistakes that may cause us to feel uncomfortable and conflicted because it is, after all, God who is committing them—the Bible teaches us something vitally important about leadership: no being—human or divine—is perfect. Every person and every leader makes mistakes, and must do so to learn and grow. Readers of the Bible can take heart in knowing that leaders far greater than they have made errors, often more than once, and yet have been largely successful in the end. The key to sustaining leadership, to developing resilience as a leader, is in not allowing our mistakes, no matter how egregious, to divert us from pursuing a positive, life-affirming vision for the future. We need to learn from our mistakes, even if we make the same mistake multiple times in different contexts, and then do our best to correct them and move on, incorporating that learning into our future leadership.

The Bible's truth in its narrative portions is embodied in its teaching of lessons that are true to human experience and essential to understanding the human condition: "The Bible speaks in the language of human beings." It is precisely because the Bible is so true and honest to what it means to be human that it is the ultimate bestseller and most read book of all time. Leaders are well served by learning the lessons it has to impart.[10]

A Final Note on Translating "God" in the Biblical Text

Unless otherwise noted, when I speak of the Bible I am referring to the Hebrew Bible. While relying primarily on the Jewish Publication Society translation of the Bible in this book, I have resorted to other translations when they better fit the context. What all translations share in common is a preference to refer to God in the masculine—a literal translation of the Hebrew text. In my own writing, however, I have used genderless language to refer to God, writing in the language of "human beings" rather than of "men" alone. In doing so, I have followed what I believe to be the human spirit if not the literal word of the biblical text.

Book I

IN THE BEGINNING ...

Relationships, Responsibility, and the Primacy of Values in Leadership

The book of Genesis, which is made up almost entirely of narrative, contains the foundational values and attitudes of successful leadership upon which the later narratives of the Bible build. Genesis is a primer on leadership. What are those basic values and attitudes? To explore them we first have to define what we mean by leadership.

Defining Leadership

Although there are many definitions of leadership, I define leadership as envisioning and initiating change, by persuading others to alter the status quo, in response to an urgent challenge and/or a compelling opportunity. Leadership is a type of relationship that has change as its essential goal.

In contrast, management may be defined as maintaining the status quo through the use of authority and control. Whereas the purpose of leadership is long-term, future-oriented change and its primary form of communication is encouragement and inspiration, the purpose of management is the very opposite: to maintain the smooth functioning of the status quo through policies and mechanisms of command and control. One might say, as John Kotter has, that "leadership, without change, equals management," or as Warren Bennis has pithily summed it up, "Managers do things right. But leaders do the right thing."[1]

Kotter, in an essay titled "Leadership at the Turn of the Century," goes to great lengths to distinguish leadership from management. He describes management as "keeping the current system operating through planning, budgeting, organizing, staffing, controlling, and problem solving." "Management," Kotter writes, "works through hierarchy and systems … the fundamental purpose of management is to keep the current system functioning." Later on, Kotter writes, "Management is about coping with complexity … Leadership, by contrast, is about coping with change."

The book of Genesis assumes that as soon as there are two person-
alities who are in a dynamic, changing relationship with one another,
there is the seed of leadership. Relationship is the fertile ground from
which leadership sprouts forth. Once there are two or more people, families, groups, clans, or nations in relationship, leadership opportunities
and crises will develop in which one party will lead—or fail to lead—and
one party will follow or refuse to do so. In some cases, one person may
lead, while in others, a different character will lead; there may be cases
where no one leads and cases where more than one side tries to lead. But
the point is that a leadership dynamic exists as soon as there is a bilateral
relationship with or without large numbers of people. Genesis is concerned primarily with these changing, microcosmic, family relationships.

The values and attitudes that emerge from the bilateral, and later
multilateral, family relationships in the book of Genesis serve as both
backdrop and prototype for the more fully developed relational and leadership issues that unfold in the books of Exodus and Numbers. For example, in the thirteenth chapter of Genesis, a family squabble arises between
the shepherds of Abraham and the shepherds of his nephew Lot. Their
tussle is prompted by the large flocks that both sets of shepherds are tend-
ing and the limited fields of pasture available in the immediate vicinity.
Abraham encourages his nephew to move away, despite their being
"brethren" who should presumably be able to live with each other peace-
fully. Through this act of separation, Abraham evades assuming responsibility for the well-being of his orphaned nephew, who chooses to move
and reside among the evil citizens of Sodom. When, shortly thereafter, Lot
and his family are taken as prisoners of war in a regional conflagration,
Abraham reverses his previous lack of responsibility for his nephew by
risking his life to "cross over" their competitive, economic divide and rescue his "brother" from captivity (Gen. 14).

This family conflict and its resolution serve as the backdrop and prototype for Moses's political decision at the end of the book of Numbers
to prevent two of the twelve tribes from separating from their "brethren."
Moses insists that they, too, "cross over" (the Jordan River) as a vanguard
force to aid their brethren in fighting for the Promised Land. There, too,
the tribes' request for the separation arose from the large flocks that those
tribes tended and their concern for grazing opportunities. But Moses
learned the importance of brethren looking out for each other from the

Abraham/Lot episodes and from the Israelites' early history, which is replete with conflict and sibling rivalry, and took a firm stand to keep the twelve tribes and their fighting forces united (Num. 32).

Genesis precedes Exodus and Numbers because it is essential that leaders develop responsibility and life-affirming values before they exercise their leadership skills and strategies. Otherwise, as we often witness in organizations today, their leadership is likely to result in destructive outcomes rather than constructive change. The multiple corporate abuses at Enron and Tyco are but two small examples of leaders failing to act responsibly and disregarding values such as trust and fair play.

In a developmental sense, the family relationships that are the focus of Genesis precede and parallel the relationships that leaders face in the larger world, such as those chronicled in Exodus and Numbers. The family is the womb in which a person's leadership potential is developed— or not. Leaders often recognize their families as the informal laboratories in which they experiment and discover what works and does not work in later persuading others to follow them. This early experimentation in their family context enables leaders to learn from their experiences and make adjustments in their subsequent leadership.

The entire range of family dynamics in the book of Genesis contains the core character issues of trust, responsibility, and fair play, which are the pivot points of successful and failed group leadership in the books of Exodus and Numbers, and in our own leadership lives today.

Leadership, Trust, and Responsibility

Individuals lead by projecting energy that attracts others. Once that energy is transmitted by a leader, and a follower tentatively or enthusiastically decides to join the leader, a potential leader-follower relationship is formed.

Yet being formed and being sustained are two different matters. Relationships—all relationships—have at their core the issues of trust and responsibility. For leadership purposes, I define *trust* from the perspective of the follower in the second person, negative: feeling a sense of security and reliance that the leader will not speak or act in a way that is harmful to my interests.[2] Trust implies that the followers believe that the leader will guide them to a better place and that the followers will feel valued and be treated respectfully by the leader in the process of getting there. On the flip side of the coin, I define *responsibility* from the perspective of the leader in the first person, positive: factoring in the consequences of my speech, actions, or inactions on those around me. Trust must be engendered in a leader's followers; responsibility must be assumed by the leader for the relationship to be sustained.

Three Circles of Responsibility

The bedrock of responsibility is freedom and choice. In the Bible, human beings are endowed with free will and are therefore held accountable by God for the choices they make and for their foreseeable consequences. The Bible assumes a high degree of foreseeability in assigning responsibility, more than many contemporary theorists may be willing to call reasonable. In the Bible, even unintended consequences, such as the accidental killing of another, carries with it the penalty of at least temporary exile (Exod. 21:13; Num. 35:11). This is partially because there is some degree of negligence assumed even in accidental circumstances.

There are three concentric circles of responsibility.[3] In the innermost circle, at the center, is my willingness to take responsibility for myself and my own actions or inactions in relationship to others. To take responsibility means to hold myself accountable not only for what I do or do not do but also for the consequences—intended or unintended—of those actions or inactions on those around me. Responsibility always assumes an "other," someone outside myself—whether God or human—to whom I respond. As we will soon examine in depth, Adam, Eve, and Cain's abdication of this first circle of responsibility can be fruitfully contrasted with Judah's willingness to assume responsibility for his actions, in betraying his daughter-in-law's trust, and their consequences (Gen. 38:26). When confronted with the evidence of his wrongdoing, Judah does not deny, offer excuses, or otherwise prevaricate; instead, he verbally admits his own irresponsibility[4] and changes his behavior from that moment forward, assuming responsibility for his actions and their consequences.[5]

The second circle of responsibility is for those with whom I am already in relationship and whom I am capable of affecting or influencing. This is an expansion of the first circle to include not merely accepting responsibility for the consequences of my own actions but also assuming responsibility for the welfare of others who are in my circle of influence: members of my family, employees and colleagues, friends and acquaintances. The closer my relationship is to others, the greater my responsibility is in protecting their well-being. As we will see, the first two circles of responsibility—or the lack thereof—were critical elements that were missing in the antediluvian biblical stories beginning with Adam and Eve and extending through Noah and his sons. In contrast, Abraham's courageous rescue of his estranged nephew Lot exemplifies the fulfillment of this second circle of responsibility.

The third circle of responsibility is toward those who enter into my orbit of concern: people with whom I may not have been in a substantive previous relationship but whom I can affect because of my position in life at this moment. For instance, rushing to the aid of a stranger in distress, colloquially known as being a "good Samaritan," is such a moment. Given the Bible's high standard of assigning responsibility, being a good Samaritan is not a charitable act in the Bible but rather a commanded act.

Because this third area of responsibility is not based on any close, preexisting relationship, this level of responsibility is rarely exhibited in human life. In the book of Genesis, Noah's failure to take responsibility for the members of his generation, who perished as a result in the Flood, is an early example of the failure to meet this level of responsibility. In contrast, Abraham's welcoming of the three strangers who were wandering in the desert and his heroic attempt to save the citizens of Sodom and Gomorrah from destruction in Genesis 18 are both examples of exercising this third circle of responsibility.[6] In more recent memory, the willingness of "righteous Gentiles" during World War II in Nazi-occupied Europe to risk their own lives to save Jews is another example of such heroic responsibility.

Without trust there is no basis for true relationship; without responsibility there is no hope of continuing relationship. I enter a relationship—be it business, friendship, or love—because I sense that the other person projects a positive energy that reflects my values and interests. I remain in a relationship because I come to believe that the other person is trustworthy and takes responsibility for his or her behavior and for the consequences of that behavior. If I come to believe that the other person is not "response-able," then my trust will diminish and I will begin to distance myself to protect myself and others from potential harm. My trust is dependent upon the other person assuming responsibility in our relationship.

If the first leadership thread that runs through the Bible is that leaders must learn and change to be successful, then the second thread in the Bible is that leaders must learn to assume responsibility. Taking responsibility is the biblical litmus test in life and in leadership. How leaders treat their followers is often an excellent indicator of the destination at which leaders will arrive. Those who act irresponsibly are likely to bring their followers to a place that is much worse than where they started. Those who act responsibly have the potential to actualize their vision and bring their followers to the proverbial Promised Land.

Because responsibility is the most important value that leaders must learn, I believe that leaders are ultimately responsible for the success or failure of their followers. This argument runs contrary to the way the Bible is usually understood. Traditional interpreters of the Bible have generally assumed that the failure of people to follow God's commands and live successful lives is primarily due to their own incorrigibility and the inherent flaws of the human condition. I believe that the Bible is telling us something quite different: leaders, whether human or divine, share a great deal of the responsibility, and ultimately are held accountable for the behaviors of their followers. This holds true for both success and failure. Leaders should be given far greater credit for their followers' successes and held to a much higher standard of responsibility for their followers' failures than is generally the case. The values and skills that leaders bring to their relationship with their followers are the crucial determinants of their followers' destinies.

God, Adam, and Eve

Right from the start, the Bible teaches us the importance of trust and responsibility through the leadership relationships of God, Adam, and Eve. The Bible tells us that after God creates the world and sets Adam and Eve down in the Garden of Eden, God begins to communicate with Adam: "And the Lord God commanded the man, saying, of every tree of the garden you may freely eat. But of the Tree of the Knowledge of Good and Evil, you shall not eat of it; for in the day that you eat of it you shall surely die" (Gen. 2:16–17).

God's first verbal communication to Adam is not only God's first act of relating to human beings but also God's first attempt at influencing their behavior and leading them. God is trying to lead Adam and Eve away from eating of the Tree of Knowledge of Good and Evil. God's method of persuasion is a threat: on the day that you eat it, you will die.

God's first attempt at leadership proves unsuccessful because what God is exercising is not inspirational leadership but heavy-handed management. Management, as I said earlier, is defined as maintaining the status quo through the mechanisms of authority and control. Here, God attempts to constrain Adam and Eve's actions through just that: command and control. Furthermore, while God tries to create a sense of urgency to impress upon Adam the seriousness of the command by threatening to terminate the offender, it appears, at least on the surface, to have been false urgency. Although God threatens immediate death, no one dies on that day. Why God's first attempt at management fails becomes even clearer when we compare it to Eve's successful attempt at leadership.

In contrast to God, Eve is attracted by the compelling opportunity involved in eating the fruit that God has forbade. She uses her imaginative vision to inspire herself and lead Adam to do the same:

> When the woman **saw** that the tree was good for food, and that it was **pleasant to the eyes,** and a tree to be desired to make one wise, she took of its fruit, and ate, and gave also to her husband with her; and he ate. [emphasis added] (Gen. 3:6)

Eve has a positive, compelling vision, which, as we will soon see, is a necessary attribute of leadership. She sees not only the beauty of the tree and the chance to satiate her appetite that the tree represents, but also the transformative opportunity to make herself as wise as God. By implication, she seems to also understand what she would be missing were she not to eat from the tree—the lack of wisdom, the missed opportunity to be like God, who knows good and evil. Despite God's death threat, she eats and leads Adam into eating from the tree as well.

Animating a person's imagination to visualize the positive rewards for following a certain path, as Eve does with Adam, is the starting point for successful leadership. The positive vision is understood by the person as an opportunity to actualize his or her creative "image of God" potential to choose freely, even when it violates a command issued by God directly. In response to the compelling opportunity to become more like God and the threatening challenge issued by God, Eve develops a leadership vision, takes the initiative, and persuades Adam to join her in changing the status quo.[7] And the status quo is changed: "Then the eyes of both of them were opened and they perceived that they were naked; and they sewed together fig leaves and made themselves loin cloths" (Gen. 3:7).

Knowing the difference between good and evil, Adam and Eve see themselves and each other differently than before. Later in the chapter, even God acknowledges the change in the status quo wrought by Eve's successful leadership:

> And the Lord God said, "Now that the human has become like one of us, knowing good and evil, what if the human should stretch out her/his hand and take also from the tree of life and eat, and live forever!" (Gen. 3:22)

There is an important leadership lesson in this first tale of human relationships. Eve's temptation thwarts God's threat because inspiring, visionary leadership trumps opaque, controlling, and dictatorial management. Consciously or unconsciously, people resent being arbitrarily "managed" by another, especially when the other uses the threat of negative consequences to keep people in line. When leaders communicate without explaining their rationale and by issuing threats, they violate the sense of autonomy, the human dignity of being created in the "image of God." Restraining a person's freedom without providing good cause violates the person's free will, even when the one doing the restraining is God, who endowed the person with free will in the first place.

This principle of leadership is similar to parental attempts to guide a child in learning right and wrong. Even though it is the parent who gave and sustains life for the child, the child will often resist the parent's verbal instruction, particularly when it is not accompanied by a genuine explanation. The child, who exercises control over her world through willful experimentation, will often ignore opaque parental warnings in order to satisfy her natural curiosity and desire to assert her freedom and independence.

Put simply, the use of threats to accomplish our ends is often experienced as a violation of trust in a relationship. Adam and Eve's trust in God, God's first human children in the biblical narrative, is violated by

God's use of a threat—and not just any threat, but the ultimate threat, the threat of death. Unfortunately, at this early point in the God-human relationship, God is not yet self-reflective. There is no awareness on God's part of how God's attempted use of coercion violates the dignity of the human "children" God created in God's own image. It will be a while before God, as depicted in the biblical story, grows into that awareness and becomes what all leaders must become to be successful: self-reflective leaders who take ownership of and learn from their failures.

God and the Human Condition

In speaking about the truth of the biblical narrative, we interpreted it to mean the truth about the human condition. But what is the Bible's understanding of the human condition? Put another way, what can leaders expect from their followers and followers from their leaders? Absent education and other civilizing influences, are human beings good (read: trustworthy and responsible) or evil (read: untrustworthy and irresponsible)?

After Adam and Eve eat from the tree, God is angry and disappointed. God had given them free run of the Garden. God had requested only that Adam and Eve respect one tree in the Garden that God was not prepared to share. Yet despite having the entire Garden's fruits at their disposal, Eve and Adam trespass God's boundaries. What further upsets God is Adam and Eve's failure to own up to and take responsibility for their actions:

> And the Lord God called to Adam, and said to him, "Where are you?" And he said, "I heard your voice in the garden, and I was afraid, because I was naked; and I hid myself." And He said, "Who told you that you were naked? Have you eaten of the tree, which I commanded you that you should not eat?" And the man said, "The woman whom you gave to be with me, she gave me of the tree, and I ate." And the Lord God said to the woman, "What is this that you have done?" And the woman said, "The serpent beguiled me, and I ate." (Gen. 3:9–13)

God's question of "Where are you?" is, as all commentators point out, not asked to seek geographical information as to Adam's whereabouts. God is addressing Adam, so God obviously knows where Adam is. Rather,

God is posing an existential query to Adam and Eve—not where are you literally, but who are you existentially? Do the two of you have the character and courage to stand up tall and respond straightforwardly, taking responsibility for your actions? Or are you fearful beings who hide behind rationalizations and excuses in order to shift responsibility and accountability away from yourselves and onto others?

When Eve is confronted with the revelation of her actions, she shifts responsibility to the serpent that influenced her to eat from the tree:

> *And the Lord God said to the woman, "What is this you have done!"*
> *The woman replied, "The serpent beguiled me, and I ate.*
> *(Gen. 3:13)*

Although it is true that the serpent did play a provocative role in challenging God's threat, we read in the text that it was also Eve's own imagination that played a pivotal role in her decision to eat the fruit. Eve could have chosen to ignore temptation. She had the capacity to respond (to be "response-able") to God other than the way that she did. Yet she makes no mention of her own role in coming to her decision and leading Adam to do the same; rather she focuses the entire blame on that which is outside of her. Like God, who does not take responsibility for the impact of God's own words on the subsequent actions of God's creations, Eve projects blame onto the other without reflecting on her own responsibility.

Adam's behavior is in a sense even more egregious from God's perspective. Not only does he shift blame to the woman for handing him the fruit to eat, but he also goes back one step in the chain of events by blaming God for providing the woman to him as a companion in the first place:

> *The man said, "The woman that **you** put at my side—**she** gave me*
> *of the tree, and I ate." [emphasis added] (Gen. 3:12)*

Adam shifts responsibility for what he did both sideways to Eve and upward to God. Like Eve, he too had the option of refusing to follow, or at the very least resisting, his mate's overture to partake of the fruit, but instead he obligingly followed her example.

Unintentionally, Adam answers God's query with the truth regarding his character: "… I was afraid … and I hid myself." Adam tells God that he is a fearful being, one who seeks to hide behind rationalizations rather than confront God or Eve and take responsibility for his actions. Adam lacks courage, and without courage there is no responsibility, not to God and not to Eve. Adam and Eve betray God's trust by violating God's word, trespassing on God's "space," and then shirking responsibility for their actions.

This is not a recipe for a healthy relationship, and much less so for leadership. What follows is an attempt by God to teach Adam and Eve through their own experience what it means to work and create. If the relationship between God and people is to be developed, then people need to understand and come to identify with God's perspective just as God eventually will have to better understand and empathize with the human perspective (see Gen. 8:21). The great effort that God put into creation, and the great hope that God invested in humanity, must be reenacted by humans through childbearing and productive work so that they and God might share a common reference point and live together in greater trust and harmony:

> To the woman He said, "I will greatly multiply the pain of your child-bearing; in sorrow you shall bring forth children; and your desire shall be to your husband, and he shall rule over you." And to Adam He said, "Because you have listened to the voice of your wife, and have eaten of the tree, of which I commanded you, saying, 'You shall not eat of it,' cursed is the ground for your sake; in sorrow shall you eat of it all the days of your life; Thorns also and thistles shall it bring forth to you; and you shall eat the herb of the field; Through the sweat of your brow shall you eat bread, till you return to the ground; for out of it you were taken; for dust you are, and to dust shall you return." (Gen. 3:16–19)

Until human beings learn to take responsibility for their own actions and are trustworthy in their relationships, God is anxious about allowing them to live in the Garden in such close proximity to God and God's treasures:

> And the Lord God said, "Behold, the man has become like one of us, knowing good and evil; and now, what if he puts forth his hand, and takes also from the tree of life, and eats, and lives forever?" So the Lord God sent him out from the Garden of Eden, to till the

ground from where he was taken. So he drove out the man; and he placed Cherubim at the east of the Garden of Eden, and a flaming sword which turned every way, to guard the way of the tree of life. (Gen. 3:22–24)

The irony is that just as Adam—who is created in God's image—is afraid of God's power, "God"—who is the prototype of humanity—is afraid of human beings' freedom. Hence God exiles Adam and Eve from the Garden. Yet placing the cherubim with their twirling, flaming swords at the entrance to the Garden is not the same as locking up the Garden and throwing away the key. Presumably, the angel that God appoints to guard the Garden can be recalled once God is satisfied that human beings have achieved the maturity to live with God again in trust and responsibility. Until then, we are left with the Bible's first evidence of the human condition: human beings who, from God's perspective, have not yet proven themselves to be trustworthy or responsible for their own actions or for those with whom they are in close relationship.

The violation of trust and the failure of responsibility that marked the first generation of God's relationship with human beings reemerges in the second generation.

The saga of Cain and Abel starts out quite hopefully. Cain, apparently, is seeking a way to reenter the Garden, to restore the fractured relationship with God. As a tiller of the soil (Gen. 4:2), Cain is impacted by God's cursing of the soil as a result of his parents' eating from the tree (Gen. 3:17–19). He offers God a gift of fruits, a symbolic returning of the fruit that his parents took; so far, so good. But when his brother Abel follows Cain's lead and offers the first and best of his "fruits," the flocks that he has been shepherding, and God responds favorably only to Abel's offering, not to Cain's, Cain feels angered and humiliated. He is crestfallen because his act of reconciliation has, in effect, been rejected. God's response, to the effect of "do better next time and you'll earn my favor, but I caution you, watch that temper or it will get the better of you," is not simply unhelpful; it also aggravates the intense feeling of self-consciousness and self-loathing that Cain feels after his gift is rejected.

As in the story of Adam and Eve in the Garden of Eden, God again fails to be self-reflective. God does not take into account the effect of God's own words or actions on those with whom God seeks to be in relationship. To favor Abel and totally disregard Cain is bad for leadership and awful for relationships. The one who is ignored loses face, and the one who is favored feels uncomfortable because he realizes, if only on an unconscious level, how poorly the other has been treated. At the outset of the biblical story, God is a novice at relationships and leadership, and it shows.

As God learns later on, leaders must encourage and inspire their followers, not abuse them while they are down. Being judgmental, as God is with Cain, is not the way of leadership; it is, in the best of circumstances, sometimes a limited, necessary tool of management. Criticism, if constructive and given in small doses, can be productive. But what constitutes the proper dose can only be ascertained on a case-by-case basis. God overplays God's hand here, and the result is fatal.

As we will see later in the book of Numbers, favoritism undermines morale; fairness enhances it. By not responding in any positive measure to Cain's offering and then by preaching to him, God has eroded the trust that Cain had tentatively demonstrated in initiating his gift of fruits to God in the first place. The sequence of events that follows is hardly surprising:

> Cain said to his brother Abel, [Ancient versions, including the Targum, add: "Come, let us go out into the field."] ... and when they were in the field, Cain set upon his brother Abel and killed him. The Lord said to Cain, "Where is your brother Abel?" And he said, "I do not know. Am I my brother's keeper?" (Gen. 4:8–9)

Cain, the leader in proactively offering a gift to God, now takes the lead again, initiating a conversation with Abel, perhaps leading, or rather misleading, him out into the field, and then striking him down with a lethal blow. As with God's question to Adam, God does not ask a geographic question regarding Abel's whereabouts but an existential question to ascertain whether Cain is prepared to take responsibility for his actions and for their fatal result. Cain, like his parents, attempts to shift blame away from himself.

There can be no trust and therefore no basis for an intimate relationship between God and Cain. God has violated Cain's trust by rejecting Cain's offering, and Cain has violated God's trust as well as his brother's right to life. God has failed to lead Cain; Cain has successfully led his brother into the grave. The net result is the death of Abel and the further rupturing of the relationship between God and humanity.

And God said, "What have you done? The voice of your brother's
blood cries to me from the ground! And now you are cursed from
the earth, which has opened her mouth to receive your brother's blood
from your hand; when you till the ground, it shall not henceforth
yield to you her strength; a fugitive and a wanderer shall you be in
the earth." (Gen. 4:10–12)

God grants Cain what he wanted, what he perhaps envisioned, but with
an unanticipated set of consequences. Cain wanted to be alone, not to
have to compete with his brother, Abel, whom Cain perceived as his
usurper. God grants him his wish. He will forever be alone. He will never
establish enduring, trustworthy relationships with other human beings
because he will always be a wanderer. He will also never have his brother's
assistance as he struggles to eke out a living by tilling the soil—the curse
of his father, carried over and magnified in the son. Cain is an effective
leader, yet his vision is only partial and his leadership, like Eve and Adam's
previous behavior, is irresponsible, both toward his brother and toward
God, bringing with it painful results.

With the story of Cain and Abel, the Bible tells us that the apple does
not fall far from the tree. Lacking trustworthiness and failing to take
responsibility are apparently intrinsic, not incidental, to the human condition. If the first two generations of humankind are a reliable indicator of
what future generations of humanity are going to be like, then human
beings by nature are apparently neither trustworthy nor responsible. As
God finally concludes after the Flood: "The Lord said in His heart, 'I will
not again curse the ground any more for man's sake; for the inclination
of man's heart is evil from his youth'" (Gen. 8:21). It is the extremely rare
individual for whom this is not so. The great educational challenge for
humanity and for leaders of human organizations is to make it so.

Know Where You Are Going: The Importance of Foreseeing the Consequences of Your Leadership

Eve and Cain's effective leadership, which nevertheless leads to less than
optimal results, reinforces the lesson that leadership is value neutral. To be
an effective leader does not mean that we lead our followers to a better
place. Effective leadership simply means leading change—guiding ourselves and our followers away from the status quo to something or some-

place different. But the different place, the change initiated by the leader, may not be for the better. Leaders often persuade their followers to join them on a journey whose destination turns out to be a far worse place than where the leader and follower started out. Such negative, unintended consequences often occur when a leader has only partial vision, seeing the immediate rewards but being blind to the long-term, larger picture. The grass may indeed be greener on the other side of the fence, but the toil necessary to make it so may be infinitely greater than expected or imagined. For better and for worse, Eve and Cain irrevocably lead themselves into existential and geographic exile.

Where leaders take their followers is no less important than their ability to take them somewhere in the first place. This is a common theme in contemporary writing about leadership, but it is often forgotten amid the day-to-day urgencies that exist for leaders of both profit and nonprofit organizations. It is not enough for leaders to exercise their charismatic capacity and finely honed leadership skills. They must also have a positive destination that is worth the risk and the energy invested in the leadership enterprise, and the more carefully thought through and long term the strategy, the better. In the Bible, the long-term reliability of a thing or a process is equivalent to its being true.[8] When leaders guide their followers to an "untrue" destination—that is, to seductive, short-term gains that have long-term aversive consequences—then their leadership becomes an exercise of bolstering the leader's ego rather than improving the followers' lot. That type of short-term, self-serving leadership, one that does not take responsibility for the potential negative consequences of the leadership action, does not meet the Bible's standard of what true leadership ought to be.

Two contemporary examples, one from the for-profit and one from the nonprofit sector, bring this point home. In the for-profit sector, CEOs, under pressure from stockholders often focus on the short-term market price of their stock rather than the long-term vision and strategy of the corporation. They often give their shareholders an immediate windfall by skewing the organization in strategically unsound and sometimes illegal manners; witness, again, the Enron scandal. In the nonprofit sector, boards' obsessive emphasis on the fund-raising prowess and accomplishments of their CEOs to the exclusion of their vision and authenticity in leadership reflects this same short-sighted tendency. Leaders who lack a deep commitment to the values of responsibility and do not keep their focus on the long-term vision inevitably succumb to transient, day-to-day pressures and fail the Bible's standard of true leadership. That is why the values and attitudes that a leader embodies and that shape the leader's goals come before and are at least as important as his or her leadership skills.

From a process point of view, the crucial attitude that leaders must embody and inculcate in others is the ability to acknowledge and learn from their mistakes, and then change. Some of the most evil people in history, from Pharaoh in the Bible to Adolf Hitler and Joseph Stalin in the twentieth century, were for a period of time effective, even successful, leaders, whose evil values and refusal to acknowledge and change their pernicious ways ultimately led their followers and much of their countries to destruction. Indeed, the meta-leadership lesson of the Bible may very well be "Do not become Pharaoh."[9]

The Bible consciously chooses as its first two examples of human leadership people who have natural leadership ability yet lead themselves and their followers to a worse place. It does so to stress the need for leaders to internalize an attitude of trustworthiness and responsibility and inculcate positive, life-affirming values before they lead themselves and their followers anywhere.

At the same time, the Bible teaches the need for leaders to possess effective leadership skills. It does this through how it depicts God's failed attempts to influence human behavior and lead at the beginning of human history. Instead of uplifting and inspiring through an upbeat, energetic, and confidence-enhancing message, God tries to suppress and repress human initiative and imagination. Thus, the Bible teaches us that leaders need to develop both good values and good leadership skills if they are to guide their followers effectively from the present to a better, more fulfilling future.

Heroes Who Fail to Lead: The Case of Noah

As humanity continues to generate biologically and degenerate behaviorally in the first five chapters of the book of Genesis, we come to the next major figure in the book—Noah. Noah builds a trusting relationship with God, a definite improvement over God's failed relationships with Adam,

Eve, and Cain: "Noah found favor with the Lord ... Noah was a righteous man; he was blameless in his age; Noah walked with God" (Gen. 6:8–9). When God tells Noah to build an ark to save himself, his family, and representative animals from the Flood, he does exactly as God says (Gen. 6:22). In fact, Noah's obedience saves the entire animal kingdom and the human race from extinction. He is certainly a hero in the biblical annals of human history.

What Noah does not do, however, is feel a sense of responsibility for the rest of humanity, which is doomed to death by the impending calamity. He does not pray or argue with God to spare the rest of humanity, as Abraham does when God reveals God's intention to destroy the evil city of Sodom (Gen. 18) or as Moses does when God plans to annihilate the Israelites (Exod. 32, 33; Num. 14). Nor do we find Noah alerting the people of the coming catastrophe and warning them to repent in order to save themselves, as the later biblical prophet Jonah ultimately does with the inhabitants of the Assyrian city of Nineveh. Noah takes care of himself and his immediate family but takes no responsibility for any other people in the orbit of his influence or concern. Noah's relationship with humanity prior to the Flood is less than inspiring. He is the paradigm of the hero who, because he lacks either caring or courage, fails to lead.

Noah's behavior toward people after the Flood is also less than exemplary. God tells him to leave the ark with his wife, and for his sons to leave the ark with their wives, to repopulate and fill the earth. Instead, Noah leaves the ark with his sons, and his wife leaves with their daughters-in-laws, a separation of the sexes that does not bode well for the future fecundity of humanity (Gen. 8:16–18). Far from presenting a regenerative role model and developing a hopeful vision with which to lead his family into their brave new world, Noah is unnerved by the devastation around him. Apparently, he is afraid to bring more human beings onto such a dangerous planet; shortly thereafter, he gets depressingly, rip-roaringly drunk: "And Noah began to be a farmer, and he planted a vineyard; and he drank of the wine, and became drunk; and he lay uncovered inside his tent" (Gen. 9:20–21).

It is plausible to assume that Noah is feeling a type of survivor's guilt at not having done all that he might have been able to do before the Flood to save his friends, relatives, and acquaintances from the global holocaust that God wrought. His drunken stupor is his way of numbing his conscience and anesthetizing his sense of guilt. Yet his failure to lead, at a moment in time when life-affirming leadership was desperately needed, brings with it unforeseen consequences.

Noah's vulnerability as a result of his drunkenness leads to his being sodomized by his youngest son, Ham. Ham, like Eve and Cain before him, has the instincts of a leader but abuses them to violate others: "And Ham, the father of Canaan, 'saw the nakedness of his father,' [a euphemism for sexual exploitation], and told his two brothers outside" (Gen. 9:22).

With the men and women living separately, Ham's actions, although disgraceful and despicable, are not all that surprising and were, perhaps, even predictable. After being pent up in the enclosed ark for a year's time and, plausibly, having his spouse unavailable to him afterward because of his father's ascetic choices, Ham channels his sexual energy in an abusive way against the person he holds responsible for his frustration.

Ham has vision; with his father drunk in his tent, he sees an opportunity for his own sexual gratification and perhaps for usurping his father's authority. But his vision, like those of Eve and Cain before him, is partial and narcissistic. Ham communicates with his brothers in the hope of persuading them to join him but Shem and Japheth, exercising their sense of respect and responsibility toward their father, refuse his overtures. Instead:

> Shem and Japheth took a garment, laid it upon both their shoulders, walked backward, and covered the nakedness of their father; their faces were backward and they did not see their father's nakedness. (Gen. 9:23)

In response to the paraphrased question that God asks Cain, and which hovers in the background of the entire Bible, "Are you your brother's [or, in this case, father's] keeper?" Ham would answer: "No, I am my father's sodomist." Only Japheth and Shem, who act with respect and responsibility, come out of the story blessed:

> And Noah awoke from his wine, and knew what his younger son had done to him. And he said, "Cursed be Canaan; a slave of slaves shall he be to his brothers." And he said, "Blessed be the Lord God of Shem; and Canaan shall be his slave. God shall enlarge Japheth, and he shall live in the tents of Shem; and Canaan shall be his slave." (Gen. 9:24–27)

Upon realizing what his son has done to him, Noah lashes out and condemns his youngest son's progeny to servitude and a destiny of inferiority. Noah, like the God "with whom he walks," fails to reflect on his own role in Ham's shameful behavior. Leaving a vacuum of leadership and wallowing in his own self-pity, Noah has set the stage for Ham to fill that vacuum with his ignoble attempt at forcefully asserting his leadership. One of the few for whom Noah took responsibility during the Flood are now cast out of his orbit of concern—a result of his failure to take responsibility for those in his orbit of concern both before and after the cataclysmic event.

Noah's failure to lead teaches us that refusing to take on the responsibility of leadership is not a morally neutral choice. Whether because of a lack of caring, courage, or both, failing to lead when our leadership is desperately needed often results in disastrous consequences. As happened in Noah's time, and which will happen again after the sin of the spies in the book of Numbers, the failure to lead can result in the loss of an entire generation and in deleterious consequences for generations to come.

Collectively, the stories of Eve, Cain, and Ham also teach us another important lesson of leadership. Leadership cannot be forcefully seized by violating another: not the other's property (Eve taking the fruit), not the other's life (Cain taking Abel's life), and not the other's bodily or personal dignity (Ham sodomizing his father). Leadership, like relationship, can only be established through trustworthiness and responsibility. In the Bible, leadership can only be earned through a history of reliable and virtuous actions that build the leader's credibility and results in a better world.

We will see later in Book II of this book that the sixth, seventh, and eighth commandments of the Ten Commandments deal precisely with these three issues: the unlawful taking of life (murder), the unlawful taking of property (theft), and the unlawful taking of another's bodily integrity (adultery). Ultimately, it is not just leaders but all human beings who must learn to take responsibility for others. But leaders, through their behavior, have disproportionate influence on their followers, who trail in their footsteps and emulate their gait.

Self-Reflective Leadership: God and the Flood

Prior to the Flood, God is still trying to manage rather than lead. God gives Noah detailed instructions on how to build the ark, how many animals to load onto the ark, and so forth. These are the types of details for a complex project that a good project manager would oversee. But there is little that is rousing or inspiring in God's vision. The lack of inspiration may stem from God's gloomy mood. Like Noah after the Flood, God, prior to the Flood, was sad, one might even say depressed:

> *And God saw that the wickedness of man was great in the earth, and that every imagination of the thoughts of his heart was only evil continually. And the Lord repented that God had made man on the earth, and it grieved God's heart. And the Lord said, "I will destroy man whom I have created from the face of the earth; both man, and beast, and the creeping thing, and the birds of the air; for I repent that I have made them." (Gen. 6:5–7)*

God's great moment of insight and of self-reflective growth takes place only after bringing the Flood that destroys the world:

> *The Lord said in his heart, "I will not again curse the ground anymore for man's sake; for the imagination of man's heart is evil from his youth; nor will I again destroy every living thing, as I have done. While the earth remains, seed time and harvest, and cold and heat, and summer and winter, and day and night shall not cease." (Gen. 8:21–22)*

After generating a planetary cataclysm, God realizes that the human being, created in God's own image, is aggressive and violent by nature. As a consequence of this realization, God vows never to destroy the world again. How does God come to this new insight and commitment to self-restraint? Perhaps, I would suggest, by reflecting on God's own expression of aggressive violence by destroying the world in the Flood. Humans, who are created in God's image and who were animated into life by God's own soul-breath, can be no better than God. If God's nature is violent, then humans must have a similar aggressive tendency built into their genetic predispositions. God must therefore learn to exercise self-control if humans are to have any chance of doing the same.

It is only once God has exercised self-control that God codifies commandments against aggressive behavior and spells out the consequences for violence:

"I require a reckoning for human life, of every man for that of his fellow man! Whoever sheds the blood of man, by man shall his blood be shed, for in God's image did God make man." (Gen. 9:5–6)

Once God learns to control God's own aggressive impulses, God can then demand that human beings do so as well. Thus, God empowers human beings with the explicit knowledge of what is right and wrong and grants them the power to enforce these laws, thereby matching their responsibility with the requisite authority to succeed.

The lesson for leaders of God's evolution is clear: self-reflection and self-transformation are key ingredients of successful leadership. The unreflective life is not worth living, and the unreflective leader is incapable of sustained, successful leadership. After unleashing the world-destroying Flood, God recognizes God's own role in the unfolding of human nature, learns the pertinent lessons for the future, and grows as a leader. That growth is later reflected in God's restrained response to the building of the Tower of Babel and in God's patience with Abraham, who emerges from the Tower's abandonment.

Misguided Leaders: Babel's Builders

The story of the attempted construction of the Tower of Babel, which follows the Flood, is one of the more puzzling narratives in the Bible. Without understanding the centrality of God's relationship to humanity, it is difficult to understand why God disrupts their monumental undertaking in the land that was later to become the Babylonian Empire, modern-day Iraq:

And the whole earth was of one language, and of one speech. And it came to pass, as they journeyed from the east, that they found a valley in the land of Shinar; and they lived there. And they said one to another, "Come, let us make bricks, and burn them thoroughly." And they used brick instead of stone, and slime for mortar. And they said, "Come, let us build us a city and a tower, whose top may reach to heaven, and let us make us a name for ourselves, lest we be scattered abroad upon the face of the whole earth." (Gen. 11:1–4)

The Tower of Babel story begins with people communicating with one another. They speak the same language and move forward with a single-minded focus. On the surface, there is no evidence of violence or corruption, which the Bible tells us was prevalent in the period leading up to the Flood. Like Noah, these leaders have a vision of what they want to accomplish and are engaged in an ambitious construction project to implement that vision. So what is the problem?

A closer examination reveals the problem. Unlike Noah, who "walks with God," who builds the ark upon God's request, and who offers sacrificial gifts of gratitude to God after surviving the Flood, the builders of the Tower are not engaged in a project meant to serve others—human or divine. Rather, they are engaged in a narcissist, self-aggrandizing project to *make a name for themselves.* This is leadership all right, but leadership that is egotistic and misguided—animated by an edifice complex in which followers obsequiously worship their leaders and leaders "worship the product of their own hands."[10] This is akin to King Nevuchadnezzar, a later leader of Babylon, who ruled the then-known civilized world and who ordered a huge golden obelisk in a Babylonian valley to be built and worshipped.[11]

In the modern world, as for much of human history, this self-aggrandizing edifice complex is often the norm rather than the exception when it comes to leadership. Many of today's technological and architectural towers of achievement are, like the Tower of Babel and the ancient Egyptian pyramids, attempts of business and political leaders to make a name for themselves, rather than serve the real needs of their constituents. These egotistical monuments often reflect as well an attempt to deny the leaders' own mortality. For contemporary leaders, the Tower of Babel is best understood as a metaphor for the human penchant toward hubris.[12]

Aside from the Tower of Babel's vain attempt to achieve immortality, one could say that the entire project was simply misguided. Like the generals who proverbially prepare to fight the last war rather than imaginatively prepare their troops for the next one, the leaders of the Tower of Babel project were apparently trying to build a safe and dry haven to which they could escape when the next flood came along, despite the fact that God had vowed never to bring such a destructive flood again. Rather than be subject to natural disasters or what they perceived as divine whims, the builders used man-made materials (bricks instead of stones, tar instead of mortar), to build a man-made structure that would, in their own minds, let them control their destiny and ensure their survival. They attempt to neutralize God, and make God irrelevant, as is apparent by the omission of God's name in the first four verses of the text that describes the builders' vision.

God intervenes because, in the biblical story, God does not create the world in order to abandon it and its inhabitants to their own devices. The biblical character of God cares about human beings and yearns for the same in return. God seeks a relationship with the world and particularly with humanity, whom God created in God's own image. Like humans for whom it is "not good to be alone," God, apparently, also does not wish to be alone. Such a God, who tells Moses in Exodus 34 that "God is a jealous being," will not permit human leaders to follow in Eve's footsteps by disregarding and usurping God's power.

> *And the Lord came down to see the city and the tower, which the sons of men built.*
>
> *And the Lord said, "Behold, the people are one, and they have all one language; and this they begin to do; and now nothing will be restrained from them, which they have schemed to do. Come, let us go down, and there confuse their language, that they may not understand one another's speech." So the Lord scattered them abroad from there upon the face of all the earth and they left off the building of the city. Therefore is the name of it called Babel; because the Lord did there confuse the language of all the earth; and from there did the Lord scatter them abroad upon the face of all the earth. (Gen. 11:5–9)*

In contemporary language, the Tower of Babel teaches leaders that an organization that is all about work and lacks a humanistic or spiritual dimension is a meaningless one, and one that will not endure. The work that organizations do must be made meaningful—that is, it must have some noble or socially redeeming purpose that motivates others to want to follow. Without such motivation, the effort is likely to disintegrate.[13]

In the post-Flood world, God acts in a far more restrained manner. God issues no painful punishments, as with Adam and Eve, stamps no mark of Cain, and brings no cataclysmic natural disasters. Instead, God confuses the builders' language for the same reason that God sends Adam and Eve, and later Cain, into exile: to teach the experience of utter aloneness. God's hope is that as human beings feel alone, they will reach out to God and serve not merely their own interests but also those of other human beings. Since, as I posited at the outset, relationship is the foundation of leadership, enabling those relationships makes genuine human leadership possible.

However, making something possible does not ensure fulfillment. Thus far, no one—not God, nor any human being—has successfully mastered the art of responsible leadership. Those failures make the evolution of Abraham, whose story follows, all the more important and remarkable.

Leaders Are Made, Not Born: The Story of Abraham

The person who might be described as the paragon of leadership in the book of Genesis does not seem to start out that way. Abraham begins as something of a follower. It is God who apparently learns something from Eve's "playbook" and tries a different leadership strategy, one that meets with initial success:

> And the Lord had said to Abram, "Get out from your country, and from your family, and from your father's house, to a land that I will show you; And I will make of you a great nation, and I will bless you, and make your name great; and you shall be a blessing;
> "And I will bless those who bless you, and curse him who curses you; and in you shall all families of the earth be blessed." So Abram departed, as the Lord had spoken to him…. (Gen. 12:1–4)

The God who created human beings in God's own image and who immediately, and intuitively, understood that "it is not good for man to be alone" reaches out in relationship to Abraham. God invites Abraham to come dwell with God in the "land that God will show him." To persuade Abraham to come along, God does not issue threats or speak judgmentally or condescendingly, strategies that met with utter failure in the cases of Adam and Cain; rather, God puts forth a positive, hopeful, redemptive vision of all that Abraham desires and has not yet been able to achieve: descendants, fame, and fortune.

Having recognized the opportunity, Abraham responds as God had hoped, journeying toward God's land and persuading his family and household to come along. Once there, he traverses the land, builds altars to God, and calls out in God's name. God has promised to make

Abraham's name great, and Abraham apparently reciprocates by doing the same:

> *And Abram took Sarai his wife, and Lot his brother's son, and all their possessions that they had gathered, and the souls that they had made in Haran; and they went forth to go to the land of Canaan; and to the land of Canaan they came … And the Lord appeared to Abram, and said, "To your seed will I give this land"; and there he built an altar to the Lord, who appeared to him. And he moved from there to a mountain in the east of Beth-El, and pitched his tent … and there he built an altar to the Lord, and proclaimed the name of the Lord. (Gen. 12:5–8)*

This is not the narcissistic attitude of Babel's builders, who ignored God and sought to generate their own fame and security. Abraham craves a relationship with God and understands what it takes to build such a relationship, responding to God's invitation to join God in the land. He builds a modest monument to God made of natural stone rather than man-made bricks and proclaims his understanding of God ("God's name") to the native inhabitants of the land. God enthusiastically responds to Abraham's overtures by appearing to Abraham and promising to give Abraham's descendants the land. Abraham seems to have the instincts to build relationships and forge a leadership path. Moreover, as is often the case in loving, intimate relationships, Abraham brings out the best in God as well.

Abraham has something else: he has vision. The first calling that brought him to the land, and God's subsequent "appearance" to Abraham at Beth-El, together form the first of seven visions that Abraham will have in the course of the biblical narrative—more than any biblical character other than Moses. The twentieth-century biblical scholar and philosopher Martin Buber, in his book of essays titled *On the Bible,* points to this seven-fold vision in characterizing Abraham as "Abraham the Seer." It could not be otherwise. The man who, it turns out, will be the founding father of a multitude of nations, including the nation upon which the Bible focuses its attention, the Israelites, must be a visionary, someone who is able "to persuade others to follow him in changing the status quo in response to a great opportunity." Because that vision is to bring blessing to the world, that people's mission will be the same as that of their founding father: to be a visionary, leadership nation in God's land, teaching the world to change for the better and thereby infusing the world with blessing.

But Abraham's innate qualities are insufficient, by themselves, to make him into a great leader. In fact, not long after arriving in the land, Abraham confronts adversity, veers away from his vision of the land full of promise, and descends from the path of responding to God just as swiftly as he embarked upon it.

> *And Abram journeyed, going on still toward the Negev. And there was a famine in the land; and Abram descended to Egypt to sojourn there; for the famine was severe in the land. (Gen. 12:9–10)*

Abraham leaves the Promised Land—and with the land, presumably God, whose presence is manifest there, to seek sustenance in Egypt. On the way down to Egypt, Abraham acts in a way that casts further doubt on his trustworthiness and future leadership potential:

> *And it came to pass, when he came near to enter to Egypt, that he said to Sarai, his wife, "Behold now, I know that you are a pretty woman to look upon. Therefore it shall come to pass, when the Egyptians shall see you, that they shall say, 'This is his wife'; and they will kill me, but you they will keep alive. Say, I beg you, that you are my sister that it may be well with me for your sake and my soul shall live because of you." And it came to pass, that, when Abram came to Egypt, the Egyptians saw the woman that she was very pretty. The princes of Pharaoh also saw her, and praised her to Pharaoh; and the woman was taken to Pharaoh's palace. (Gen. 12:11–15)*

Rather than be his "sister's keeper," Abraham ends up exposing Sarah to possible sexual exploitation in Pharaoh's harem to acquire wealth and to ensure his safety.[14] And wealthy Abraham becomes. Abraham succeeds in garnering wealth but fails utterly in his responsibility to protect the welfare of his wife. Fortunately for Sarah, what Abraham is willing to compromise on, God is not:

> *And the Lord plagued Pharaoh and his house with great plagues because of Sarai, Abram's wife. And Pharaoh called Abram, and said, "What is this that you have done to me? Why did you not tell me that she was your wife? Why did you say, 'She is my sister,' so I*

might have taken her for my wife?; now therefore behold your wife,
take her, and go your way." And Pharaoh commanded his men con-
cerning him; and they sent him away, and his wife, and all that he
had. (Gen. 12:17–20)

Abraham began his leadership journey on the right foot, following God's
vision to the Promised Land. Once there, he continued to develop that
relationship by building modest monuments to God and proclaiming
God's message to the local inhabitants. Yet soon thereafter he abandoned
God and constructively abandoned his wife. Nor does Abraham act appre-
ciably better once he leaves Egypt and returns to God's land. Once again,
Egypt and its wealth have jaded Abraham's priorities and his commitment
to keeping the integrity of his family intact:

And Abram went up from Egypt, he, and his wife, and all that he
had, and Lot with him, to the Negev. And Abram was very rich in
cattle, in silver, and in gold ... And Lot also, who went with Abram,
had flocks, and herds, and tents. And the land was not able to bear
them, that they might live together; for their possessions were great,
so that they could not live together. And there was strife between the
herdsmen of Abram's cattle and the herdsmen of Lot's cattle ... And
Abram said to Lot, "Let there be no strife, I beg you, between me
and you, and between my herdsmen and your herdsmen, for we are
brothers. Is not the whole land before you? Separate yourself, I beg
you, from me; if you will take the left hand, then I will go to the right;
or if you depart to the right hand, then I will go to the left." And
Lot lifted up his eyes, and saw the valley of the Jordan, that it was
well watered everywhere, before the Lord destroyed Sodom and
Gomorrah, like the garden of the Lord, like the land of Egypt ... So
Lot chose for himself the valley of the Jordan; and Lot journeyed
east, and they separated themselves, one from the other. Abram lived
in the land of Canaan, and Lot lived in the cities of the plain, and
pitched his tent toward Sodom, whose people were exceedingly wicked
and sinners before the Lord. (Gen. 13:1–13)

As we saw in the introduction, Lot, Abraham's nephew and dependent,
whom Abraham has raised after the death of Lot's father, Haran (Gen. 11:28),
and who has accompanied Abraham on his journeys, is urged by Abraham
to separate from him even though it means Lot's choosing to reside in an evil

and corrupt society. Sodom may be as fertile as Egypt, but it is also as promiscuous and depraved. To send Lot off to dwell in that region is in effect to expose him to the same danger of debased moral values that Abraham dreaded in advance of his entrance to Egypt. Yet Abraham closes his eyes to the danger to protect his own and Lot's burgeoning wealth. Rather than taking responsibility for his nephew, he treats him as if he were expendable.

Abraham refers to their relationship as one of brothers, a reference that should have heightened his sense of responsibility toward Lot rather than diminish it. Yet diminish it he does. Separation may not be immoral, but it is amoral. It may be the way of prudent management, but it is not the way of responsible leadership. When faced with adversity, Abraham has scored a trifecta of irresponsibility: abandoning God, his wife/"sister," and now his nephew/"brother."

Clearly, Abraham has some damage control to attend to. Fortunately, God, who is learning how to be a leader, displays uncharacteristic patience with Abraham. Rather than punish or criticize Abraham, God, appreciative of Abraham's rejoining God in the land, reiterates and expands upon the promising vision that motivated Abraham to come to God's land in the first place:

> And the Lord said to Abram, after Lot was separated from him, "Lift up, please, your eyes, and look from the place where you are to the north, and to the south, and to the east, and to the west; For all the land which you see, to you will I give it, and to your seed forever. And I will make your seed as the dust of the earth; so that if a man can count the dust of the earth, then shall your seed also be counted." (Gen. 13:14–16)

Having achieved in Egypt the great wealth that God had promised him, Abraham refocuses his vision and returns to his relationship with God. In the leadership turning point in the book of Genesis, he is about to achieve God's promises of fame and blessing as well.

The Advent of True Leadership: Becoming Your Brother's Keeper

Up to this point, the Bible has described the journeys of Abraham and his family. The biblical text surprises us by suddenly veering off in another direction that, at first, seems to have nothing to do with previous events.

The Bible tells us of an ongoing regional war between four kings and five kings, with the four kings emerging victorious. The level of detail, and the length (fourteen years) and breadth of the conflict (a total of nine kings, with a tenth to appear soon thereafter), are clear indicators that the text is setting the reader up for a tale of epic proportions. The Bible conveys a major conflagration, the ancient Middle Eastern equivalent of a world war, which unexpectedly draws in Abraham along the way.

In the course of the war, the four kings take Lot and his family as prisoners of war. Until this point, we have not yet seen an instance of one person taking responsibility for the welfare of another. Unexpectedly, Abraham does just that for his estranged "brother":

> *And there came one who had escaped, and told Abram the Hebrew ...*
> *And when Abram heard that his brother was taken captive, he armed*
> *his trained servants, born in his own house, three hundred and eight-*
> *een, and pursued them to Dan. And he divided himself against them,*
> *he and his servants, by night, and defeated them, and pursued them*
> *to Hobah, which is north of Damascus. And he brought back all the*
> *goods, and also brought again his brother Lot, and his goods, and the*
> *women also, and the rest of the people. (Gen. 14:13–16)*

In taking responsibility for his "brother," Abraham is the first biblical character to answer in the affirmative Cain's rhetorical question to God: "Am I my brother's keeper?" Abraham risks his own life, and the lives of his allies and members of his household, to rescue Lot from captivity. "Risks" is an understatement; doing battle with a ragtag army of just 318 people against four battle-hardened kings and their military forces is not exactly prescribed military doctrine. Yet Abraham prevails and does so without any obvious aid from God, who has not even been mentioned up to this point in the chapter.

For the first time, Abraham is given a surname in the biblical text: *Haivri,* "the one who crosses over." *Ivri,* "Hebrew," which becomes the name for the Israelites, is not used here for any obvious reason. This leads the spiritual masters of early Judaism, in a commentary on the Bible, to suggest a homiletic interpretation for its sudden appearance here: "all the world was on one side and Abraham crossed over to the other side." The masters suggest that everyone in biblical history, until this point in time, acted without taking responsibility for the welfare of other people;

Abraham is the first to take responsibility for his "brother," even though this "brother" was only a nephew with whom he had most recently had an unpleasant altercation. Abram becomes a Hebrew when he takes responsibility for another, when he becomes "his brother's keeper."[15]

It is also important to note that there is a classical act of leadership taking place. Abraham is "initiating change, by persuading others to join him in response to an urgent threat." He sees the threat, envisions a way of responding to that threat, and succeeds in persuading his friends, allies, and members of his household to follow him on a dangerous mission. Not only does Abraham demonstrate caring, courage, and responsibility, as well as effective leadership skills, but he also leads toward a constructive, life-affirming goal—the rescue of his family and the recovery of their seized property.[16]

Lest this act of life-affirming leadership be seen as a cover for merely acquiring the spoils of war, a much less noble aim, the Bible tells us what transpires immediately following the completion of Abraham's rescue mission:

> And the king of Sodom went out to meet him after his return … And the king of Sodom said to Abram, "Give me the persons, and take the goods for yourself." And Abram said to the king of Sodom, "I swear to the Lord, the most high God, the possessor of heaven and earth, that I will not take from a thread to a sandal strap, and that I will not take anything that is yours, lest you should say, 'I have made Abram rich.' Save only that which the young men have eaten, and the share of the men who went with me, Aner, Eshkol, and Mamre; let them take their share." (Gen. 14:17, 21–24)

The king of Sodom, the sovereign of a selfish, materialistic culture, reasoned that Abraham must have rescued Lot out of naked self-interest, to gain the spoils of war. Thus the king initiates negotiations with Abraham, and, as an opening gambit, offers him all the captured property so that he might retain control over the citizens of his kingdom. Abraham flatly turns down the king's offer. He will not even take a thread for himself. But he does not prevent his allies, who were perhaps less altruistically motivated than he was, from taking their fair share.

Leaders like Abraham, who make deposits in their follower's "trust accounts"—or in this case, bank accounts—and are prepared to sacrifice

the accretion of their own, make enormous strides in building their credibility.[17] This is the case here, where, as we will soon see, even God seems
totally taken by the combination of altruistic caring and death-defying
courage that Abraham displays.

A tenth king appears, not previously mentioned in the narrative,
but a king whom the Bible describes as being God's representative on
earth:

> *And Melchizedek, king of Shalem, brought forth bread and wine; and
> he was the priest of the most high God. And he blessed him, and said,
> "Blessed be Abram of the most high God, possessor of heaven and earth;
> And blessed be God the Most High, who has delivered your enemies
> into your hand." And he gave him a tenth of all. (Gen. 14:18–20)*

From his extraordinary act of responsibility, leadership, and selflessness,
Abraham has brought fame and blessings upon himself and fame and
blessings upon God. In a reversal of his earlier abandonment of his "sister," Sarah, and his "brother," Lot, because of his quest for riches, Abraham now renounces his entire share of the wealth and instead assigns a
tenth of the booty to God's earthly representative. By rescuing his
"brother," renouncing personal economic gain, and freely giving some of
the spoils to God, Abraham demonstrates that he is his brother's keeper
and God's keeper as well.

In one fell swoop, Abraham begins to correct the two glaring faults
that had previously characterized humanity in the Bible: disregard for God
and disregard for one's "brother." It is not surprising that God is moved by
Abraham's actions and seeks to institutionalize their relationship in the
following chapter, the mysterious covenant of the pieces.

The Long-Term Rewards of Leadership

For all the fleeting glory that is involved, leadership is still a difficult and
risky business. Because it involves change and upsetting the status quo,
leadership breeds the enmity of those invested in things remaining the
same; frequently, it gives rise to fantasies of revenge among those who
have been displaced by the change effort. Even when the leader has done
the right thing in the right way and has been hailed as a hero, as Abraham was, the leader has legitimate cause for concern.

After rescuing Lot by routing the four kings, Abraham is apparently anxious that those whom he defeated or their progeny may seek to avenge their military loss. He seeks reassurance from God, by some accessible, "low-hanging fruit," some tangible reward, that his righteousness will not go unnoticed. God, who anticipates Abraham's anxiety, first seeks to reassure him: "After these things the word of the Lord came to Abram in a vision, saying, 'Fear not, Abram; I am your shield, your reward will be very great'" (Gen. 15:1).

Abraham is reassured in the short term. But the vagueness of God's words still leaves Abraham questioning and uncertain. Abraham wants something discernible, something he can see, feel, or touch. Perhaps Abraham senses, or at least hopes, that now may be the time when God's remaining unfulfilled promises will come to pass: that God will build a great and numerous nation from him and give him and his descendants the Promised Land. First, Abraham seeks divine reassurance regarding to God's promise of progeny:

> But Abram said, "O Lord God, what can You give me, seeing that I shall die childless, and the one in charge of my household is Eliezer of Damascus!" Abram said further, "Since You have granted me no offspring, my steward will be my heir." The word of the ever-present God came to him in reply, "That one shall not be your heir; none but your very own issue shall be your heir." He took him outside and said, "Look toward heaven and count the stars, if you are able to count them." And He added, "So shall your offspring be." And because he put his trust in the ever-present God, God reckoned it to his merit. (Gen. 15:2–6)

God makes Abraham a literally unbelievable promise. At this point, Abraham is probably in his late seventies or early eighties, and God promises him future descendants as numerous as the stars in the sky. Although this is not something material that Abraham can hold on to, at least he has a visual image of how enormous his reward will be. So rather than question God further about this by citing evidence of his current childlessness, Abraham lets the matter rest. But Abraham still wants reassurance regarding the remaining unfulfilled promise: his, and his unborn progeny's, possession of the land, part of which he has just conquered in the course of rescuing his nephew. Abraham may be hoping that, having conquered a portion of the Promised Land, he might now, or at least shortly, take legal possession of it.

God, in response, choreographs a fire-and-brimstone ceremony in which God grants Abraham the right to the land, albeit with an unexpected clause:

> And He said to him, "I am the Lord who brought you out of Ur of the Chaldeans, to give you this land to inherit it." And he said, "Lord God, how shall I know that I shall inherit it?" … When the sun was going down, a deep sleep fell upon Abram; and, a fear of great darkness fell upon him. And God said to Abram, "Know, surely know, that your descendants shall be a stranger in a land that is not theirs, and shall serve and be afflicted there for four hundred years; But that nation whom they shall serve, will I judge; and afterward shall they come out with great wealth. And you shall go to your fathers in peace; you shall be buried in a good old age. In the fourth generation they shall return here again; for the iniquity of the Amorites is not yet full" … In the same day the Lord made a covenant with Abram, saying, "To your descendants have I given this land, from the river of Egypt to the great river, the river Euphrates." (Gen. 15: 7–19)

God cuts a covenantal deal, the equivalent of an ancient contract, with Abraham. The contract has good news and bad news in it. The good news is that his descendants will indeed possess this land. The bad news is that it will take four hundred years of alienation and slavery before they will be able to possess it. Abraham has scored a stunning victory over the four kings and achieved his immediate objective of freeing his nephew from captivity. His being endowed with biological heirs will take somewhat longer to accomplish. His heirs' permanent possession of the land will take even longer—much longer.

The Bible delivers a sobering lesson on leadership. Leadership, no matter how noble or noteworthy, does not necessarily bring with it instant gratification. Although God offers Abraham a symbolic small victory, becoming manifest to him in a pillar of fire and smoke to assure him of God's presence and promise, the goals of numerous progeny and territorial sovereignty will take far longer than Abraham expected. Often it takes a lifetime of work, and sometimes many lifetimes, to reach or have one's descendants reach the actual or proverbial "promised land."

As was the case here, the situation may not yet be ripe enough for radical change to occur and for the long-term vision to be achieved. Still, to say that things may take a long time, and be fraught with difficulty and sacrifice, is not to renounce hope of its ultimate attainment. Much of what is worthwhile in life and in leadership takes place only after a long and bitter struggle. The very difficulty of achieving a long-term vision makes it all the more precious and valuable once it is attained. This is true of Abraham's, and later Rebecca's and Rachel's, quest for children, as well as for Abraham's vision of possessing the land. It will also be true of Moses's later challenges, and it is true of our own leadership struggles today.

Discerning Leadership

When Abraham went down to Egypt to escape the famine in the land of Canaan, he referred to his wife, Sarah, as his "sister." He did so because he was afraid that someone in Egypt would be attracted by Sarah's beauty and would eliminate him, Sarah's husband, in order to consort with her. That someone turned out to be no one less than the king of Egypt. As a result of Abraham's lack of courage at the time, Sarah was constructively abandoned by him to be exploited as part of Pharaoh's harem. In return for Sarah's potential services, Abraham received substantial wealth, including male and female servants from Pharaoh's coffers.

Now it is time for Abraham to learn from and make up for his constructive abandonment of Sarah by taking responsibility for her childless condition and giving her the opportunity to become the ancient equivalent of a surrogate mother. Although Sarah is not a prisoner of war who needs to be rescued from captivity, she is a prisoner of her body's infertility and needs to be rescued from the feelings of barren desperation that gnaw at her identity. When Sarah proposes that Abraham impregnate Sarah's maidservant, Hagar (apparently part of the dowry that Abraham received for his "sister's" services to Pharaoh), and that Sarah raise the resulting child as her own, Abraham readily agrees. When later on in the story Hagar mocks Sarah for her continued infertility, Abraham sides with Sarah and gives her a free hand in dealing with Hagar as she pleases, despite the fact that Hagar is carrying Abraham's long-awaited child. In doing so, Abraham takes responsibility for his "sister's" welfare, a quantum leap of responsibility from his abandonment of her in Egypt, albeit at the expense of Hagar, his concubine.[18]

By telling this story at this point in the narrative, the Bible is trying to show how Abraham's saving of Lot was not a single instance of Abraham learning to take responsibility, nor one that only recognizes life-threatening vulnerability but extends to his no less vulnerable wife as well. Different people have different needs. The sign of a wise leader is the ability to discern between different situations and respond accordingly.[19] Although Abraham had to fight a war to rescue Lot, he needs to listen sensitively to Sarah's pain to rescue her from the feelings of shame in being barren. Abraham, like God, is proving himself to be a discerning leader, one who uses his innate gifts to learn from previous mistakes and figure out how to lead more responsibly in the future.

The Sacrificial Element of Leadership

Following the Hagar episode, God asks Abraham to circumcise himself and the members of his household as an expression of the covenantal bond between God, Abraham, and Abraham's descendants. Marking the generative organ of Abraham and his descendants with circumcision symbolizes, in the flesh, the perpetual blood bond of God with Abraham's progeny. To God's leadership credit, God puts forward a three-fold promise to Abraham that will constitute the reward for his bodily sacrifice: the descent of many nations from his circumcised loins, his descendants' permanent possession of the land, and the birth of a son through his heretofore barren wife, Sarah. Nevertheless, circumcision at Abraham's advanced age of ninety-nine is a painful undertaking that could potentially undermine Abraham's male identity and fertility. Through the covenant of circumcision, God is apparently testing Abraham's degree of devotion—his willingness to be not only his brother's and sister's keepers but also God's keeper, as it were, not merely with words, money, and actions, but also in the painful folds of his flesh. Moreover, God is ascertaining whether Abraham is prepared to inflict this "covenant of flesh and blood" on his children and thereby bind future generations to this painful divine covenant.[20]

The act of circumcising the generative and pleasure-filled organ is the Bible's way of suggesting that leaders must be prepared to sacrifice the lure of immediate gratification and to discipline physical desires—carnal or otherwise—to achieve long-term values and fully embody the commitment to a cause. Leaders often must endure pain, sacrifice part of themselves, and ask similar sacrifices of others to accomplish their long-term vision. Leadership is not an easy road. But as God's three-fold promise indicates, being prepared to make the necessary sacrifices is the way to achieve lasting, significant results and outlive our mortality.

Abraham passes God's test of sacrificial leadership. Abraham thus proves himself to be his brother's keeper by rescuing Lot, his sister's keeper by helping Sarah achieve surrogate motherhood, and now God's keeper by sacrificing his body's flesh and blood. Through this rectification of his previous abandonments, Abraham demonstrates the caring and courage necessary to take responsibility for ever wider circles of his community. The next episodes will determine whether he is prepared to go where no human being has gone before in the Bible: to become the stranger's keeper as well.

Becoming the Stranger's Keeper

As Abraham is recuperating from his circumcision, he has a vision of three strangers standing opposite his tent. Rather than continue to convalesce quietly and leave the strangers to fend for themselves, Abraham acts on his vision, proactively inviting the three strangers into his home, hurrying to provide for their comfort, and treating them to a sumptuous meal:

> The Lord appeared to him by the terebinths of Mamre; he was sitting at the entrance of the tent as the day grew hot. Looking up, he saw three men standing near him. As soon as he saw them, he ran from the entrance of the tent to greet them and, bowing to the ground, he said, "My lords, if it please you, do not go on past your servant. Let a little water be brought; bathe your feet and recline under the tree. And let me fetch a morsel of bread that you may refresh yourselves; then go on—seeing that you have come your servant's way." They replied, "Do as you have said." Abraham hastened into the tent to Sarah, and said, "Quick, knead three portions of choice flour and make cakes!" Then Abraham ran to the herd, took a tender and choice calf, and gave it to the lad who hastened to prepare it. He took curds and milk and the calf that had been prepared and set

these before them; and he waited on them under the tree as they ate. They said to him, "Where is your wife Sarah?" And he replied, "There, in the tent." Then one said, "I will return to you next year and your wife Sarah shall have a son!" (Gen. 18:1–10)

Abraham's graciousness and hospitality to the three strangers stands in marked contrast to the selfish and abusive way that the people of Sodom will treat these strangers once they arrive in that city. In Sodom, it will be only Lot, Abraham's nephew, who learned from his uncle the value of extending hospitality to the stranger, who will care for the strangers and try to protect their well-being, even to a fault. Later on in Genesis, Abraham's servant will use the test of extending hospitality as the litmus test for finding the proper wife for Abraham's son Isaac. The life-affirming values of extending graciousness and hospitality to the stranger are central parts of Abraham's leadership vision and his followers' legacy. As the founding leader of the Israelites, he acts as a role model for the type of openness and graciousness toward the stranger that the Bible later extols in words. Abraham walks the walk of his people's ethics. The angels, in turn, share the news of Sarah's impending pregnancy.

It is precisely this value of caring for the stranger that makes the story that follows (Abraham's argument with God to save the cities of Sodom and Gomorrah from destruction) truly unique in the book of Genesis. This story of Abraham's encounter with God deals not merely with extending hospitality to a couple of distinguished-looking strangers but also with saving from deserved destruction a city of evil people who are truly estranged from Abraham's spiritual and moral values. The Sodomites, by their sickening behavior toward the strangers, whom they wish to gang-rape, and toward their fellow citizen Lot, whom they wish to harm for thwarting their evil intent, prove that they neither fear God nor respect other images of God (Gen. 19). Yet Abraham rushes to Sodom's defense, unlike his predecessor Noah, who allows the wicked of his generation to be washed away in the Flood without uttering a word of protest. Abraham takes on God as one might a legal adversary in an attempt to save the people of the city. That he fails in his efforts is less important than that he undertakes this audacious attempt in the first place:

Abraham came forward and said, "Will You sweep away the innocent along with the guilty? What if there should be fifty innocent within

*the city; will You then wipe out the place and not forgive it for the
sake of the innocent fifty who are in it? Far be it from You to do
such a thing, to bring death upon the innocent as well as the guilty,
so that innocent and guilty fare alike. Far be it from You! Shall not
the Judge of all the earth deal justly?" And the Lord answered, "If I
find within the city of Sodom fifty innocent ones, I will forgive the
whole place for their sake." Abraham spoke up, saying, "Here I venture to speak to my Lord, I who am but dust and ashes: What if the
fifty innocent should lack five? Will You destroy the whole city for
want of the five?" And He answered, "I will not destroy if I find forty-
five there." But he spoke to Him again, and said, "What if forty
should be found there?" And He answered, "I will not do it, for the
sake of the forty." And he said, "Let not my Lord be angry if I go on:
What if thirty should be found there?" And He answered, "I will
not do it if I find thirty there." And he said, "I venture again to speak
to my Lord: What if twenty should be found there?" And He
answered, "I will not destroy, for the sake of the twenty." And he said,
"Let not my Lord be angry if I speak but this last time: What if ten
should be found there?" And He answered, "I will not destroy, for the
sake of the ten."*

*When the Lord had finished speaking to Abraham, He
departed; and Abraham returned to his place. (Gen. 18:23–33)*

In this amazing dialogue, Abraham demonstrates a caring for the stranger,
for people who are literally estranged from Abraham's values as well as
geographically removed from his home. In so doing, he demonstrates a
willingness to take responsibility for a far larger circle of people than any
previous or subsequent character in Genesis. Abraham becomes the
"keeper of the stranger" in a way that will later be mandated repeatedly
in biblical law.[21]

Corporate and nonprofit leaders would do well to take a page from
Abraham's example in evincing concern for those other than their stakeholders. For instance, oil companies, who in the current energy shortage are
generating unprecedented revenues, would be well advised to invest some
significant portion of their profits to produce alternative energies. Although
the threat of global warming will have little effect on the demand for oil
in the foreseeable future, these companies, whose products are the key contributing factor to the greenhouse effect, need to look beyond their short-

term interests and do what they can to save the planet's inhabitants from long-term and potentially destructive, environmental changes. From the Bible's point of view, what goes around comes around.

Like Abraham, who learned to take responsibility first for his own "stakeholders" and then to act on behalf of those with whom he had no previous relationship, corporate leaders, especially those riding a wave of success, should consider following suit to improve the general state of mankind. The Bill and Melinda Gates Foundation, whose mission it is to promote health and learning around the world, is an example of a corporate leader who is following in Abraham's ways.

Leaders Make the Same Mistakes Twice

Over time, Abraham develops into an exemplary leader. As in all leaders' lives, however, there are setbacks, and Abraham experiences those, too. When Abraham migrates to Philistine territory, there seems to be a replay of the earlier sordid episode when Abraham went to Egypt because of the local famine. Only this time it is not at all clear why he journeys into Philistine territory, a place that he believes, like the just incinerated Sodom and Gomorrah, to be lacking in the fear of God.

Again, Abraham, fearing for his safety and welfare, refers to his wife as his sister and leaves her vulnerable to the approaches of a foreign monarch, King Abimelech. But this time, God comes to Abimelech in a dream and reveals Sarah's true identity, demanding that she be returned to Abraham unharmed (Gen. 20:2–8).

Although God's intervention assures that Sarah is not molested, nevertheless Abraham has made the same mistake twice—abandoning responsibility for his wife. To make matters worse, he is blatantly disingenuous in attempting to rationalize his deception to the king, who angrily confronts him:

> *And Abimelech said to Abraham, "What did you see, that you have done this thing?" And Abraham said, "Because I thought, surely the fear of God is not in this place; and they will slay me for my wife's sake. And yet indeed she is my sister; she is the daughter of my father, but not the daughter of my mother; and she became my wife. And it came to pass, when God caused me to wander from my father's house, that I said to her, 'This is your kindness which you shall show to me;*

at every place where we shall come, say of me, "He is my brother."'"
(Gen. 20:10–13)

Despite Abraham's claim, Sarah is not the daughter of his father. She is, at best, the granddaughter of his father.[22] Whatever their biological relationship, however, the point that Abimelech makes is that Abraham hid that Sarah was his wife. Abraham's attempt at evading responsibility is unbecoming.

This episode points up a truth about human nature that leaders would do well not to ignore. The propensity to regress and to make the same mistake twice—or more—is precisely one of the great pitfalls of life and leadership. The external circumstances and/or internal motivations that cause leaders to err in the first place are likely to cause them to err similarly again. Even small changes in context from the original learning situation to a second similar, but not identical, situation can seduce a leader to fall back on old patterns of behavior. Especially when the consequences of a leader's actions turn out to be ambivalent, as when Abraham acquired great wealth because of his deceptive ruse, the life lessons that leaders need to learn may not be internalized.[23]

Even God in the Bible exhibits the human tendency to make the same or similar leadership mistakes more than once. The same leadership issues with which God struggles in the early chapters of the book of Genesis come back to haunt God again in the first half of the book of Numbers. In both cases, God's idyllic expectations of human beings lead to God's disappointment and frustration with those who act contrary to God's expectations. In each case, the thwarting of those expectations results in God angrily dooming an entire generation; in both cases, God, after a period of reflection, realizes human beings are more resistant to following God's lead than God originally supposed.[24]

God must learn the same lesson twice because the lessons learned in Genesis about relating to individuals and to humanity as a whole are not automatically transferred to God's emotionally charged relationship with the Israelites in Numbers. From the Bible's point of view, leadership, like human life itself, is more of a challenge than anyone, even God, cares to admit.

To prevent themselves from making the same mistake multiple times, leaders need to develop a heightened awareness of their own character flaws so they can detect as early as possible situations that are likely to entrap them. Then leaders must do their utmost to avoid placing themselves in comparable ensnaring situations. They must learn to recognize the similarity of circumstances despite the changes in context in which they occur. Otherwise, they are likely to find themselves in increasingly uncomfortable positions with cascading consequences that undermine their ability to lead.[25]

In fact, mistakes, if not caught early on, can and often do perpetuate themselves from one leadership generation to the next because the older generation serves as negative role models for the younger generation. Thus, Isaac followed in his father's footsteps and also referred to his wife as his sister, bringing on a similar set of embarrassing circumstances (Gen. 26:6–10). The Bible is straightforward in making this point about human foibles, to its abiding credit.

Losing Focus as a Leader

The Bible makes another point in the story of Abraham's encounter with the Philistines.[26] Even leaders who make incredible progress in actualizing their vision may, at some point along the way, lose their visionary focus and begin to stray. When Abraham tells the king of the Philistines that God caused him to wander from his father's house, he is perhaps expressing an unconscious truth. Instead of being vision-directed, he seems to have lost his focus—he is wandering, spiritually and morally, lost in the land of the Philistines, a place he had no apparent reason for visiting, a place he thought was lacking in "the fear of God" and that he should have avoided. Not surprisingly, he has also regressed in his leadership responsibility toward his wife, Sarah, who is soon to bear Abraham's second child, Isaac, just as he abdicated responsibility for his concubine, Hagar, when she was carrying his first child, Ishmael. His wandering, and his abdication of responsibility for the women in his life and their unborn children, foreshadow the episodes that follow.

Taking Responsibility for the Next Generation

It is one thing to learn to be responsible for our contemporaries. One of the great challenges of leadership is to become responsible not only for the group's short-term present but also for the group's long-term future, for future generations of followers and leaders. Later in the Bible the issue is framed in terms of political succession; in Genesis, this responsibility for the future is embodied in assuming responsibility for our children and future heirs.[27] Abraham fails in this regard with his first son, Ishmael, and only at the last possible moment succeeds with his second son, Isaac.[28]

Abraham's failure to protect Ishmael is an outgrowth of his failure to protect Hagar, Ishmael's mother. Recall that in chapter 16 of Genesis, after being impregnated by Abraham, Hagar mocks her mistress, Sarah, apparently for being infertile:

> [Abraham] cohabited with Hagar and she conceived; and when she saw that she had conceived, her mistress was lowered in her esteem. And Sarai said to Abram, "The wrong done me is your fault! I myself put my maid in your bosom; now that she sees that she is pregnant, I am lowered in her esteem. The Lord judge between you and me!" Abram said to Sarai, "Your maid is in your hands. Deal with her as you think right." Then Sarai treated her harshly, and she ran away from her. (Gen. 16:4–6)

Rather than verbally reprimanding Hagar when she mocked Sarah's infertility, Abraham abdicated responsibility to his wife, who in turn physically abused her maidservant. Although Abraham was being responsive to his wife, a virtue that I pointed to earlier, he failed to assume responsibility for his concubine, who was carrying his child, and for the stability and harmonious relations within the household.

It is hardly surprising that the animosity between the mothers was transferred to the next generation and that Sarah's solution to that bitter rivalry is the banishment of Hagar and her son:

> And Sarah saw the son of Hagar the Egyptian, whom she had born to Abraham, mocking [presumably mocking Isaac, because of the use of the word metzachek, the same root word as Isaac]. And she said to Abraham, "Cast out this slave and her son, for the son of this slave shall not be heir with my son, with Isaac." And the thing was egregious in Abraham's sight because of his son. And God said to Abraham, "Let it not be egregious in your sight because of the lad and because of your slave; in all that Sarah has said to you, listen to her voice, for in Isaac shall your seed be called. And also of the son of the slave will I make a nation, because he [too] is your seed." (Gen. 21:9–13)

Although Abraham is troubled by the situation with his son and though he receives divine sanction for following Sarah's directive, he does not attempt to argue with God as he did to save the lives of the wicked residents of Sodom and Gomorrah. Moreover, his actions early the next morning are hard to fathom and even harder to justify:

> And Abraham rose up early in the morning, and took a loaf of bread, and a bottle of water, and gave it to Hagar, putting it on her shoulder, and the child, and sent her away; and she departed, and wandered in the wilderness of Beersheba. And the water was spent in the bottle, and she cast the child under one of the shrubs. And she went, and sat down opposite him a good way off, as it were a bowshot; for she said, Let me not see the death of the child. And she sat opposite him, and lifted up her voice, and wept. (Gen. 21:15–16)

By banishing Hagar and Ishmael to the vast and arid Negev desert with only the food that Hagar can carry on her shoulders, a single loaf of bread and a jug of water, Abraham has, in effect, failed to take responsibility for his future. Like Abraham, Hagar loses her way, and both she and Ishmael almost perish in the desert. Fortunately, God compassionately intervenes, sending Hagar a well of water that will save their lives, and saving Abraham from criminal neglect in the death of his concubine and son.

God has saved the day, but Abraham has failed to take responsibility for part of his family's future. Without a leader taking responsibility for the welfare of the next generation, there can be no sustained future for the group, whether that group be your nuclear family or a multinational corporation. For Abraham to be the founding father of God's people, he must learn to take responsibility for the future, no matter who tells him to do otherwise. He must also learn how to respond to multiple and conflicting responsibilities. Those lessons, that Abraham must learn and internalize, are embodied in the test of the sacrifice of Isaac that appears in the very next chapter:

> And it came to pass after these things, that God tested Abraham, and said to him, "Abraham"; and he said, "Behold, here I am." And he said, "Take now your son, your only son Isaac, whom you love, and go to the land of Moriah; and offer him there for a raised offering upon one of the mountains which I will tell you." And Abraham rose up early in the morning, and saddled his ass, and took two of his young men with him, and Isaac his son, and broke the wood for the offering, and rose up, and went to the place of which God had told him.

Then on the third day Abraham lifted up his eyes, and saw the place far away. And Abraham said to his young men, "Stay here with the ass; and I and the lad will go there and worship, and come back to you." And Abraham took the wood of the offering, and laid it upon Isaac his son; and he took the fire in his hand, and a knife; and they went both of them together. And Isaac spoke to Abraham his father, and said, "My father"; and he said, "Here I am, my son." And he said, "Behold the fire and the wood; but where is the lamb for a burnt offering?" And Abraham said, "My son, God will provide himself a lamb for a burnt offering"; so they both went together. And they came to the place which God had told him; and Abraham built an altar there, and laid the wood in order, and bound Isaac his son, and laid him on the altar upon the wood. And Abraham stretched out his hand, and took the knife to slay his son. (Gen. 22:1–10)

Abraham is about to make the same mistake with Isaac that he made with Ishmael, compounded by his failure to tell Sarah of his intentions. If Abraham goes through with slaughtering Isaac, as God has asked, he will have failed to take responsibility for his family's future. One can only imagine how Sarah would have reacted had Abraham gone through with killing her only child.[29] Fortunately, Abraham changes course with a little prodding from an angel (his conscience?) and saves the future of his family and people:

And the angel of the Lord called to him from heaven, and said, "Abraham, Abraham"; and he said, "Here I am." And he said, "Do not lay your hand upon the lad, nor do anything to him; for now I know that you fear God, seeing that you did not withhold your son, your only son from me." And Abraham lifted up his eyes, and looked, and beheld behind him a ram caught in a thicket by his horns; and Abraham went and took the ram, and offered him up for a burnt offering in place of his son. (Gen. 22:11–13)

Managing Conflict Responsibilities

In the case of his first son, Ishmael, Abraham seems unable to find a way of listening to Sarah, his wife, and God while at the same time taking responsibility for Ishmael and Hagar, his son's mother. Neither Sarah nor God told Abraham to sentence his son and concubine to a slow, painful death in the desert. Abraham, who by this time has amassed considerable wealth, could have sent Hagar and Ishmael away from his camp in a dignified manner, given them servants to guide and care for them, and enough wealth to support them for the rest of their days. That would have been the responsible thing to do.[30] His failure to do so necessitated divine intervention to save them.

God tests Abraham to see whether he is capable of making the adjustment in the case of his remaining son. By offering God his son on top of the altar but then slaughtering a male ram as a surrogate for his son, Abraham discovers a way both to follow God's command and to save the life of his son and the future of his family.[31]

The angel tells Abraham it is enough that he has not withheld his one remaining son from God. That is what God expected, nothing more. Although on the surface the angel's message seems to contradict God's command, Abraham is able to resolve the contradiction and pass God's test by placing Isaac on the altar but not harming him. Abraham has learned to take responsibility for God, to be "God's keeper," while at the same time taking responsibility for his son, his wife, and his family's future by becoming his "son's keeper."[32] Later, Abraham takes this obligation further by commissioning his servant to find a suitable spouse for his son, thus doing his part to help assure that there will be future generations after Isaac.

Initially in Genesis the issue of taking responsibility is fairly one-dimensional, but later the responsibility becomes more complex. When God asks Abraham to sacrifice Isaac, Abraham finds himself torn between two conflicting responsibilities—toward God on one hand and toward his son and wife on the other. In the next generation, the complexity and conflicts become even more pronounced: how does a parent act responsibly toward one son without abdicating responsibility for the second son? How does a child act responsibly toward one parent without abdicating responsibility for the other parent? These potentially conflicting responsibilities are often the stuff that makes leadership, quite literally, a no-win situation. In no-win situations, there is no single solution that satisfies all our constituencies. The best we can do in such circumstances is to manage the complexity rather than solve it.[33]

In complex situations where there are competing claims for a leader's attention, a leader must first manage the conflict by responding to the needs of each party while also acknowledging the needs of the other party. Then leaders must exercise creative imagination, thinking outside the either/or box. By paying careful attention to the environment, as Abraham did by noticing the ram stuck in the bushes behind him, leaders can find a third way, coming up with a vision that will at least minimally address the needs of both sides. Although these conflicting situations are often frustrating to American business and political leaders who have been led to believe by popular culture that all problems have quick solutions, not all dilemmas can be solved at the snap of a finger. A paradigmatic case study of the difficulties in managing competing claims is encased in the story of the generation that follows Abraham: Isaac's blessing of Jacob and Esau in Genesis 27.

Leadership by Deceit: Jacob and Esau

Shortly after the traumatic events of his near sacrifice, Isaac marries his cousin Rebecca. After enduring twenty years of childlessness, Rebecca suffers a difficult pregnancy. She does not content herself by coping with her physical discomfort but intuits that there is a spiritual meaning behind her condition. She initiates a query to God, who responds with more than she bargained for:

> The Lord answered her:
> "Two nations are in your womb,
> Two separate peoples shall issue from your body;
> One people shall be mightier than the other,
> And the older shall serve the younger." (Gen. 25:23)

Through her spiritual search, Rebecca acquires a long-term vision of the future, a vision that her husband, Isaac, seems to lack. Henceforth, she knows that her younger son, Jacob, is destined to rule over her older son, Esau. The Bible tells us that Isaac loves his older son because Esau brings him hunted game to feast upon, and Rebecca loves her younger son, Jacob (Gen. 25:28). Rebecca's visionary foreknowledge, along with the affection that she has cultivated for Jacob, is undoubtedly what prompts her to act on Jacob's behalf when she hears that Isaac is about to give his blessings of leadership to Esau:

Rebecca said to her son Jacob, "I overheard your father speaking to your brother Esau, saying, 'Bring me some game and prepare a dish for me to eat, that I may bless you, with the Lord's approval, before I die.' Now, my son, listen carefully as I instruct you. Go to the flock and fetch me two choice kids, and I will make of them a dish for your father, such as he likes. Then take it to your father to eat, in order that he may bless you before he dies." Jacob answered his mother Rebecca, "But my brother Esau is a hairy man and I am smooth-skinned. If my father touches me, I shall appear to him as a trickster and bring upon myself a curse, not a blessing." But his mother said to him, "Your curse, my son, be upon me! Just do as I say and go fetch them for me." (Gen. 27: 6–13)

Isaac has no vision. By persuading Jacob to impersonate Esau, Rebecca plays the pivotal role in deceiving her blind husband. As a result of her deceit, Isaac blesses Jacob with material wealth and bestows upon him the future leadership of the family. Rebecca has succeeded in manipulating a wonderful set of blessings for Jacob, but by substituting Jacob for Esau, she has deprived Esau of the same.[34]

Because leadership is value neutral, one might say that Rebecca's actions are a classical leadership act: she envisions and initiates change by persuading others (i.e., Jacob) to alter the status quo in response to a compelling opportunity (i.e., to have her younger son acquire Isaac's blessing) and/or an urgent challenge (i.e., having the wrong son given the blessing of dominance by her husband). Yet the way she goes about it is deceitful. It is leadership all right, but not responsible leadership. Like the snake that shrewdly persuades Eve and causes Adam to sin, Rebecca has shrewdly persuaded Jacob to cause Isaac to err. Rebecca has led, but because she has led by deceit, she gets a string of unintended and unwanted consequences: her younger son receives the blessings intended for Esau, but Esau vows to kill his brother for his role in the deception; Jacob must flee into exile, and Rebecca never sees him again in her lifetime; unlike Sarah, whose tent she inhabits, Rebecca's death is never explicitly recorded in the Bible, most likely a purposeful exiling because of her duplicitous act; and finally, Jacob must later return the fruits of his deceit to his brother to effect a reconciliation (Gen. 32:3–33:11).

The responsibility of a spouse like that of a brother, sister, parent, or son, is to be the other's keeper, to guard and shield them from harm—

certainly not to abet that harm. Rebecca, while taking responsibility for Jacob, has, at the same time, caused incredible pain to Esau and Isaac:

> *No sooner had Jacob left the presence of his father Isaac—after Isaac had finished blessing Jacob—than his brother Esau came back from his hunt. His father Isaac said to him, "Who are you?" And he said, "I am your son, Esau, your firstborn!" Isaac was seized with very violent trembling. "Who was it, then," he demanded, "that hunted game and brought it to me? Moreover, I ate of it before you came, and I blessed him; now he must remain blessed!" When Esau heard his father's words, he burst into wild and bitter sobbing, and said to his father, "Bless me too, Father!" (Gen. 27:30–34)*

As with the cases of Adam and Eve, Cain, the generation of Babel, and Ishmael, the failure to assume responsibility for significant others leads to their exile. In Rebecca's case, her son is exiled and the recording of her own death is exiled from the biblical text. This lesson of learning to take responsibility for all of one's family will recur in Jacob's life and in the lives of his children. It is a lesson that will have to be internalized before the book of Genesis can come to a conclusion.

What should Rebecca have done instead? She should have communicated her point of view directly to Isaac that she wanted Jacob, not Esau, to be blessed, as her mother-in-law, Sarah, did when it came to deciding who should be Abraham's heir. By failing to summon the courage to communicate straightforwardly with her husband, she undermined the trust necessary to be a responsible leader and caused needless enmity between her two sons.[35]

How do we know that Isaac would have listened to Rebecca had she leveled with him? We don't know for sure. However, when she pleads with Isaac to send Jacob to her homeland to find an appropriate spouse so that Jacob will not marry a Canaanite woman, Isaac complies without a rebuttal. Isaac also bestows upon Jacob additional covenantal blessings:

> *So Isaac sent for Jacob and blessed him. He instructed him, saying, "You shall not take a wife from among the Canaanite women. Go, and take yourself to Paddan-aram, to the house of Bethuel, your mother's father, and take a wife there from among the daughters of Laban, your mother's brother. May El Shaddai bless you, make you fertile and numerous, so that you become an assembly of peoples.*

*May He grant the blessing of Abraham to you and your offspring,
that you may possess the land where you are sojourning, which God
assigned to Abraham." (Gen. 28:1–4)*

When Rebecca dealt truthfully with her husband, the result was far better
than when she dealt deceitfully with him. Not only was Jacob blessed with
material wealth, but he also received the twin blessings of fertility and of
possession of the land, the blessings God bestowed upon Abraham in
the two covenants that God contracted with him (Gen. 15 and 17). Those
blessings, unlike the material blessings wrongfully taken from Esau, will
be kept by Jacob, who will in turn pass them on to his children, grandchildren, and all the future "children of Israel."

Even had Rebecca failed to persuade her husband to bestow the
blessings intended for Esau on Jacob, her attempt would have been a
noble and heroic one, and one for which the Bible would certainly have
given her great credit. Instead, her choice in acting deceptively brings to
mind Leo Strauss's famous maxim: "It is better to fail nobly than succeed
basely." Rebecca succeeded basely, and the consequences of that "success" follow.

The lesson for leaders is that gains won by deceit, like gains that are
attempted by force (see the story of Ham and Noah earlier), are gains
that are born in sin and that lead to adverse, unintended consequences.
Such gains are the result of short-term thinking and the seeking of immediate gratification. True leadership requires long-term vision and the ability to delay gratification, the type of vision and postponed gratification
that Abraham possessed but that Jacob had not yet developed. Having
the courage to confront unpleasant conversations is the way to build
respect and trust and to succeed in leadership and in life. How leaders
can develop that courage, long-term vision, and delayed gratification are
subjects we will take up later in this book.

The story of Jacob deceptively taking his brother's blessing was not
simply a matter of following his mother's orders. Like Adam before him,
Jacob could also have responded differently than he did. Despite his
mother's entreaties, he could have not merely resisted her urgings (which
he initially did, an improvement upon Adam's failure even to attempt to
resist Eve's urgings) but firmly, if respectfully, refused to cooperate with
her deceptive scheme. However, instead of steadfastly refusing to deceive
his father, Jacob went along with his mother's ruse and then, through his

own deceptive speech, led his father into bestowing upon him the blessing intended for his brother Esau:

> [Jacob] went to his father and said, "Father." And he said, "Yes,
> which of my sons are you?" Jacob said to his father, "I am Esau,
> your firstborn; I have done as you told me. Pray sit up and eat of my
> game, that you may give me your innermost blessing." Isaac said to
> his son, "How did you succeed so quickly, my son?" And he said,
> "Because the Lord your God granted me good fortune." Isaac said to
> Jacob, "Come closer that I may feel you, my son—whether you are
> really my son Esau or not." So Jacob drew close to his father Isaac,
> who felt him and wondered. "The voice is the voice of Jacob, yet the
> hands are the hands of Esau." He did not recognize him, because
> his hands were hairy like those of his brother Esau; and so he blessed
> him. He asked, "Are you really my son Esau?" And when he said, "I
> am," he said, "Serve me and let me eat of my son's game that I may
> give you my innermost blessing." (Gen. 27:18–25)

This wasn't the first instance of Jacob not taking responsibility for his brother's welfare, of not being his "brother's keeper." Earlier, Jacob took advantage of his brother's exhaustion to persuade him into selling him the rights of the firstborn for a bowl of lentil stew (Gen. 25:29–34):

> And Jacob cooked pottage; and Esau came from the field, and he was
> fatigued. And Esau said to Jacob, "Feed me, I beg you, with that same
> red pottage; for I am fatigued"; therefore was his name called Edom
> [Red]. And Jacob said, "Sell me this day your birthright." And Esau
> said, "Behold, I am at the point of death; so what profit shall this
> birthright be to me?" And Jacob said, "Swear to me this day"; and
> he swore to him; and he sold his birthright to Jacob. Then Jacob gave
> Esau bread and pottage of lentils; and ate, drank, rose up, and went
> on his way; thus Esau spurned his birthright. (Gen. 25:29–34)

Although the biblical text makes clear that Esau behaved less than admirably, Jacob's cunning and his manipulation of his brother's famished plight to his own advantage is disturbing as well. Esau realizes that in selling his birthright to Jacob for a bowl of soup he has been taken by his brother. Esau bears a grudge against Jacob and his feelings of ill will are reawakened by Jacob's deceptive taking of his father's blessing:

And he [Esau] said, "Is not he rightly named Jacob? For he has sup-
planted me these two times; he took away my birthright; and, behold,
now he has taken away my blessing" ... Now Esau harbored a grudge
against Jacob because of the blessing which his father had given
him, and Esau said to himself, "Let but the mourning period of my
father come, and I will kill my brother Jacob." (Gen. 27:36–41)

Taking something away from its rightful owner recalls the first human sin in the Bible—Eve and Adam's taking the fruit from God's Tree of Knowledge. As the Bible makes clear in its legal sections later on, what is taken away must be returned—and more. Punitive damages for misappropriation range from twice the value of the item misappropriated to four or five times its value, depending on the preciousness of the item wrongfully taken (e.g., Exod. 21:37). After Jacob is forced to flee from his enraged and vindictive brother, he spends the next twenty years of his life learning that lesson the hard way, as the disciple of his devious and wily uncle, Lavan. As Jacob deceived his father, Lavan deceives Jacob. On Jacob's wedding night no less, Lavan replaces Rachel, the daughter for whom Jacob has agreed to work for Lavan for seven years, with Leah, her older sister. When Jacob learns of the deception the next morning, Lavan pointedly says to him in obvious reference to Jacob's previous deception of his father: "It is not the practice in our place to give the younger before the older" (Gen. 29:26). Jacob compliantly, if resentfully, agrees to Lavan's new terms for marrying Rachel: working an additional seven years on her behalf.

Nor is it only in family relations that Jacob is deceived by Lavan. Repeatedly, Lavan switches the terms of their employment agreement in an attempt to deceive Jacob of his hard-earned wages. In their final encounter, after Jacob has slaved under Lavan for twenty years, he flees from Lavan's domain with Lavan in pursuit. As he approaches the border of the Promised Land, Jacob finally summons the courage to confront Lavan for his attempted malfeasance over the previous two decades:

"Of the twenty years that I spent in your household, I served you four-
teen years for your two daughters, and six years for your flocks; and
you changed my wages ten times! Had not the God of my father,
the God of Abraham, and the fear of Isaac, been with me, you would
have sent me away empty-handed. But God took notice of my plight

and the toil of my hands, and He rebuked you last night." (Gen.
31:41–42)

Having endured and survived the cunning deceit of his uncle Lavan, Jacob
learns the hard way what it feels like to be on the receiving end of deception by a close relative. Perhaps feeling remorse for what he did to his
brother, and certainly fearful of the consequences to him and his family
that may now ensue, Jacob concludes that if he is to end his exile and
return to his parents home, he must find a way to reconcile with his
brother Esau. That realization, and the struggle that Jacob must endure
to effect reconciliation, is brilliantly embodied in the story of Jacob's
struggle with the mysterious, anonymous man/angel the night before
encountering Esau:

> *Jacob was left alone. And a man wrestled with him until the break*
> *of dawn. When he saw that he had not prevailed against him, he*
> *wrenched Jacob's hip at its socket, so that the socket of his hip was*
> *strained as he wrestled with him. Then he said, "Let me go, for dawn*
> *is breaking." But he answered, "I will not let you go, unless you bless*
> *me." Said the other, "What is your name?" He replied, "Jacob."*
> *Said he, "Your name shall no longer be Jacob, but Israel, for you have*
> *striven with God and with men and have prevailed." (Gen.*
> *32:25–31)*

Jacob learns through this symbolic encounter with the unnamed man
(himself? an angelic substitute for his brother Esau?) that he must courageously confront his brother in a straightforward manner. He must also be
prepared to spend his physical resources and sacrificially humble his gait
if he is to transform himself from Jacob, "a follower," named so because
he was born holding onto Esau's heel, to Yisrael, meaning "struggler with"
or "prince of" God. For Jacob to regain the moral high ground, develop
into a leader, and go from being Esau's supplanter to Esau's moral equal,
Jacob must return to Esau what should have been Esau's in the first place:
the material fruits of his stolen blessings and the right to mastery over
his brother.

Upon crossing the border into the Promised Land and hearing Esau
is on his way to greet him with an entourage of four hundred men, Jacob
first returns the stolen goods:

*And Jacob sent messengers before him to Esau his brother to the land
of Seir, the country of Edom. And he commanded them, saying,
"Thus shall you speak to my lord Esau; Your servant Jacob said thus,
'I have sojourned with Lavan, and stayed there until now; And I have
oxen, and asses, flocks, and menservants, and women servants; and
I have sent these to my lord, that I may find favor in your sight ...'"
Jacob said, "I will appease him with the present that goes before me,
and afterward I will see his face; perhaps he will accept me." (Gen.
32:13–20)*

Returning the fruits of his duplicity to Esau, Jacob also symbolically
returns the blessing of lordship over his brother by addressing Esau as "my
lord," referring to himself as Esau's "servant," and prostrating himself
and his family before his older brother:

*And Jacob lifted up his eyes, and looked, and, behold, Esau came,
and with him four hundred men ... And he passed over before them,
and bowed to the ground seven times, until he came near to his
brother. And Esau ran to meet him, and embraced him, and fell on
his neck, and kissed him, and they wept....*

*Then the maids, with their children, came forward and bowed
low; next Leah, with her children, came forward and bowed
low; and last, Joseph and Rachel came forward and bowed low.
(Gen. 33:1, 3–7)*

Finally, Jacob persuades Esau to accept back the blessing itself, thus com-
pleting their reconciliation:

*And he [Esau] said, "What do you mean by all this drove which I
met?" And he [Jacob] said, "These are to find grace in the sight of my
lord." And Esau said, "I have enough, my brother; keep what you
have for yourself." And Jacob said, "No, I beg you, if now I have
found grace in your sight, then receive my present from my hand;
for seeing your face is as though I had seen the face of God, and you
were pleased with me. **Take,** I beg you, **my blessing** that is brought to
you; because God has dealt graciously with me, and because I have
enough." And he urged him, and he [Esau] took it. [emphasis
added] (Gen. 33:8–11)*

Jacob has returned to Esau the blessing that he misappropriated from him. By bowing down repeatedly, he confirms his older brother's dominance, and by sending him wave after wave of his flocks, he hands back the fruit of his deception. Through a long, painful, twenty-year lesson, Jacob has learned the futility of gaining leadership by deceit; conversely, he has learned the rewards of peaceful coexistence engendered by acting responsibly and being his brother's keeper.

In an age when corporate leaders are being indicted nearly every month for deceiving their stakeholders, it is hard to imagine a lesson more germane than this case study of leadership by deceit and repentance in Genesis.

The Sins of Leaders Visited Upon Their Successors: Jacob and His Family, Joseph and His Brothers

Despite all this, despite Jacob's maturation as his brother's keeper, and despite his self-assertion vis-à-vis Lavan and Lavan's family, Jacob has not yet learned himself, nor taught his household, how to be each other's keepers. Like his parents and grandparents, he has a fragmented sense of responsibility toward those in his immediate orbit, and this leads to the fragmentation, and nearly the permanent disintegration, of his own family.

Regarding his spouses, Jacob chooses to favor one of his spouses, Rachel, the apple of his eye, while relegating Leah, the product of his father-in-law's deception, to second-class status. Jacob has the same character flaw as his mother, who hovered over him. He favors one spouse over the other and brings misery to both. This favoritism strains the relationship between Rachel and Leah, leaving Leah feeling cast aside and inferior, even hated (Gen. 29:31, 33). As a corrective, God ends up favoring Leah with seven children, causing Rachel to grasp at increasingly desperate measures to bear children of her own.

When Rachel histrionically pleas that Jacob impregnate her, Jacob responds to her cries by angrily brushing her off: "Am I in God's place to withhold from you children?" (Gen. 30:2) he says, undoubtedly deepening her feelings of inadequacy and self-reproach. Rather than pray on her behalf as his father, Isaac, had done for his barren mother, Rebecca, Jacob pushes Rachel, the woman who has totally beguiled him with her beauty, into a proverbial corner. There, seeing no other viable options on the horizon, she offers her maid, Bilhah, to Jacob so that she, like Sarah, can become a surrogate mother of her maid's child.

Later on, Rachel, still childless, bargains away a night with her husband for her sister Leah's fertility flowers, degrading Jacob into a commodity to be bought and sold for mating purposes.[36] The last of Rachel's desperate acts—stealing her father's fertility idols—leads Jacob to unwittingly curse Rachel with death (Gen. 31:32) and leads to her premature demise while giving birth to Benjamin, her second son (Gen. 35:15ff.). Albeit unintentionally and indirectly, Jacob loses his beloved wife Rachel because he fails to take responsibility for her and for the feelings and welfare of his other wife, Leah.

Jacob's neglect of Leah apparently extends even to his and Leah's only daughter, Dinah. When, shortly after returning to the Promised Land, Dinah is raped by the local prince of Shechem, who holds her captive in his chambers, Jacob is passive and silent. Rather than express righteous indignation at the sexual abuse of his daughter, Jacob holds his own counsel and fails, outwardly at least, to assume responsibility for his daughter's welfare. In some sense, as Judah tells Joseph later on, the only person Jacob ever really considered to be his wife was Rachel, and the only children that Jacob really considers to be his children are Rachel's children (Gen. 44:27–29). Therefore, it is left to Dinah's brothers, Shimon and Levi, to take responsibility for their sister's welfare and free their sister from her rapist's grip. In the process, however, they go on a violent rampage, wiping out all the men of the town and taking all the women, children, and property as spoils of war. Their ransacking of the entire city and partaking of the town's booty besmirches their honorable intentions in freeing their sister. Jacob's passivity leads his children to unconscionable violence and plunder (Gen. 34).

Jacob's mistakes in leading his family continue. The pattern of his mistake is the same, only the names differ. In each case, Jacob shows responsibility to one (spouse, child) and does not express his responsibility toward the others (spouses, children). This pattern is destined to result in fateful consequences, not only for Jacob's immediate family but also for generations to follow.

After returning from his stint with Lavan and settling down in Canaan, Jacob chooses to favor Rachel's sons, Joseph and Benjamin, over the ten sons of his other wives, thereby setting up discord among the

brothers. Joseph feels superior and lords it over his brothers, while the
brothers, like their mothers, feel cast aside and purposely neglected by
their father:

> *At seventeen years of age, Joseph tended the flocks with his brothers
> … And Joseph brought bad reports of them to their father. Now Israel
> loved Joseph best of all his sons, for he was the child of his old age;
> and he had made him a coat of many colors. And when his brothers
> saw that their father loved him more than any of his brothers, they
> hated him so that they could not speak a friendly word to him. Once
> Joseph had a dream which he told to his brothers; and they hated him
> even more. He said to them, "Hear this dream which I have
> dreamed: There we were binding sheaves in the field, when sud-
> denly my sheaf stood up and remained upright; then your sheaves
> gathered around and bowed low to my sheaf." His brothers answered,
> "Do you mean to reign over us? Do you mean to rule over us?"
> And they hated him even more for his talk and for his dreams.
> (Gen. 37:2–8)*

Joseph betrays his brother's secrets to their father and flouts his chosen
status over them. Although he is blessed with future vision, an indication
that he has the potential to be a leader, he does not communicate that
vision in a way that his brothers can hear. They understand it as his desire
to rule them, and they resent him deeply for it. Perhaps they also fear that,
like Abraham who chose Isaac, and Isaac who chose Jacob, Jacob will
choose only one of the sons to be his heir to the covenantal promise. In
this context, the combination of Joseph's arrogant retelling of his dreams
and his tale-bearing of his brother's misdeeds is a powder keg waiting for
a spark to ignite it. With the stories of Cain and Abel, and Jacob and Esau
in the background, it is not long before this volatile mixture of hatred and
arrogance explodes in potential fratricide. As happened in the stories of
God and Abel, Rebecca and Jacob, and Jacob and Rachel, the favoring of
Joseph by Jacob in an attempt to forge a closer relationship between the
two, results paradoxically in the opposite: the distancing and loss of the
one who is unfairly favored.

> *And his brothers went to feed their father's flock in Shechem. And
> Israel said to Joseph, "Are not your brothers feeding the flock in
> Shechem? Come, and I will send you to them." And he said to him,*

"Here I am" ... And Joseph went after his brothers, and found them in Dothan. And when they saw him from far away, even before he came near to them, they conspired against him to slay him. And they said to one another, "Behold, this dreamer comes. Come now therefore, and let us slay him, and throw him into some pit, and we will say, some evil beast has devoured him; and we shall see what will become of his dreams." And Reuben heard it, and he saved him from their hands; and said, "Let us not kill him." And Reuben said to them, "Shed no blood, but throw him into this pit that is in the wilderness, and lay no hand upon him"; [Reuben] said so in order to save [Joseph] from their hands, to be able to return him to his father again. And it came to pass, when Joseph came to his brothers, that they stripped Joseph of his coat, his coat of many colors that was on him; And they took him, and threw him into a pit; and the pit was empty, there was no water in it. And they sat down to eat bread; and they lifted up their eyes and looked, and, behold, a company of Ishmaelite traders came from Gilead with their camels bearing gum, balm and myrrh, going to carry it down to Egypt. And Judah said to his brothers, "What profit is it if we slay our brother, and conceal his blood? Come, and let us sell him to the Ishmaelites, and let not our hand be upon him; for he is our brother and our flesh." And his brothers listened. Then there passed by Midianite merchants; and they drew and lifted up Joseph out from the pit, and sold Joseph to the Ishmaelite traders for twenty pieces of silver; and they brought Joseph to Egypt. (Gen 37:12–28)

Because of Joseph's favored status, his betrayal of his brothers' secrets, and his self-aggrandizing dreams, his brothers hate him. When their father sends Joseph out into the fields to find them, they kidnap him and contemplate killing him. Under Judah's influence they then sell him to a caravan of traders going down to Egypt where, under the normal course of events, he would be doomed to a lifetime of abject slavery (Gen. 37:12–28). Although this turns out not to be the case, Joseph does remain incommunicado from his father and brothers for twenty years.

Having rid themselves of their haughty brother, the brothers then proceed to cover up their actions (reminiscent of Adam and Eve hiding and then covering themselves with makeshift clothing, and of Jacob concealing his identity with Esau's clothing) by making it appear that Joseph has been mauled by a wild animal, thus bringing further grief upon their elderly father:

> *Then they took Joseph's coat, slaughtered a young goat, and dipped the coat in the blood. They had the coat of many colors taken to their father, and they said, "We found this. Please examine it; is it your son's coat or not?" He recognized it, and said, "My son's coat! A savage beast devoured him! Joseph was torn by a beast!" Jacob rent his clothes, put sackcloth on his loins, and observed mourning for his son many days. All his sons and daughters sought to comfort him; but he refused to be comforted, saying, "No, I will go down mourning to my son in Sheol." Thus his father bewailed him. (Gen. 37:31–35)*

The brothers' actions devastate their father, who feels responsible for his son's death. After all, it was Jacob who sent Joseph out to find his brothers; had he not done so, he must have thought to himself, nothing amiss would have befallen Joseph. Jacob's guilty conscience over Joseph's fate explains Jacob's otherwise irrational resistance twenty years later to sending Benjamin down to Egypt with his brothers when the family is starving from a regional famine. Even though the entire family, including Benjamin, is in danger of perishing, Jacob stubbornly refuses to release Benjamin until Judah stands up and vows to take responsibility for the safe return of his youngest half-brother.

Like the story of Jacob, the story of Joseph and his brothers is the story of brothers and young leaders who refused to be their brother's keepers. In his youth, Joseph did not take responsibility for his words and actions and did not seem to care about his brothers' welfare. He may have acted responsibly toward his father by keeping him informed of his brothers' doings, but he did not behave responsibly toward his brothers. The brothers act similarly: they deny their own responsibility for what happens to Joseph and are unconcerned about their brother's welfare. Rather than be his keeper, they are his kidnapper. Like their father Jacob, Joseph and his brothers must learn the lessons of responsibility. Because Judah was the leader in persuading his brothers to sell Joseph into slavery, he must learn this lesson first. He must become a reflective, learning leader if he, and the brothers whom he leads, are to fulfill their destiny as each other's keepers. As is often the case in Genesis and the beginning of Exodus, it is a woman who will teach Judah what he needs to learn and alter his family's destiny.

Leaders Need Mentors: Tamar and Judah

Immediately following the sale of Joseph, the narrative tells us of Judah's decline:

> And it came to pass at that time, that Judah went down from his brothers, and turned in to a certain Adullamite, whose name was Hirah. And Judah saw there a daughter of a certain Canaanite, whose name was Shuah; and he took her, and he came to her. (Gen. 38:1–2)

The Bible immediately signals the reader that Judah is in a process of decline by telling us he "went down" rather than that he simply went. It then tells us that he married a Canaanite woman, a decision not in accord with Abraham and Isaac's values, apparently because of the Canaanites' immoral and idolatrous tendencies.[37] Unlike three of the four matriarchs of the Israelites, for whom conceiving a child is difficult and therefore precious, Judah's Canaanite wife has no trouble conceiving and giving birth to three children in rapid succession. So easy do these pregnancies and childbirths come that Judah does not bother naming his second or third son, nor is he even present for the birth of his third son, an abdication of parental responsibility foreshadowing more of the same later on.

All seems fine until the children begin to marry. Then the questionable moral practices of their maternal Canaanite heritage begins to take their toll:

> And Judah took a wife for Er his firstborn, whose name was Tamar. And Er, Judah's firstborn, was wicked in the sight of the Lord; and the Lord slew him. And Judah said to Onan, "Come into your brother's wife, and marry her, and raise up seed to your brother." And Onan knew that the seed should not be his; and it came to pass, when he went in to his brother's wife, that he spilled it on the ground, lest that he should give seed to his brother. And the thing which he did was wicked in the sight of the Lord; therefore he slew him also. (Gen. 38:6–10)

Although the biblical text does not explicitly tell us what it was that Er and Onan did, both acts are considered "wicked in the sight of the Lord," so it is plausible to assume that they practiced the same sin. That sin was not simply masturbation. Rather, as the text makes explicit, the sin was the refusal to impregnate their wife, Tamar, an abdication of their responsibility to father a child with their wife, who desperately sought, as did the matriarchs of the Israelites, to achieve motherhood. So egregious are these omissions of responsibility that both of them meet an untimely end.

Judah, afraid that his daughter-in-law is bad luck for his family, indefinitely postpones his youngest son's marriage to her. However, instead of summoning the courage to confront his daughter-in-law with his misgivings, he instead deceives her into believing that he will give his youngest son in marriage to her once he matures a bit. In the meantime, he disingenuously recommends that she wait in her father's home: "Remain a widow at your father's house, till Shelah my son grows up; for he said, lest perhaps he die also, as his brothers did" (Gen. 38:11).

When Tamar sees that Judah has deceitfully led her to a dead end and is not keeping his promise, she, too, resorts to deceit to attain her vision of motherhood through his family. Disguising herself as a prostitute, Tamar seduces Judah without his knowing her identity. Moreover, she persuades him to part with the items that confirm his identity—his signet ring, cloak, and staff—as purported collateral for a young goat that he is to send her for her services. When Judah's friend, acting as his agent, tries to bring her the goat and retrieve the collateral from her, she is nowhere to be found. Three months later, it becomes apparent why Tamar made herself scarce: she needs the collateral to prove Judah's identity as the father of her child(ren), so that he might rescind the order to have her executed for alleged adultery:

> And it came to pass about three months after, that it was told Judah, saying, "Tamar your daughter-in-law has played the harlot; and also, behold, she is with child by harlotry." And Judah said, "Bring her out, and let her be burned." When she was brought out, she sent to her father-in-law, saying, "By the man whose these are, am I with child"; and she said, "Discern, I beg you, whose are these, the signet, and cloak, and staff." And Judah acknowledged them, and said, "She has been more righteous than I; because I did not give her to Shelah my son." And he knew her again no more. (Gen. 38:24–26)

Reflecting the Bible's underlying philosophy of "measure for measure," Tamar uses some of the same devices to deceive Judah that Judah and his brothers used to deceive their father regarding Joseph's fate. She, too, uses a young goat to cover up her plan, takes Judah's cloak as the brothers took Joseph's coat, and, like the brothers said to their father through a messenger, she says to Judah through a messenger: "Discern, I beg you, to whom these belong."

To Judah's credit, instead of going ahead with Tamar's execution and covering up his responsibility for her condition, he immediately acknowledges his role and admits to her superior moral righteousness in this case. He recognizes that his deception of her is responsible for her deception of him. As Lavan taught Jacob, Tamar, through deceit, has taught Judah what it feels like to be taken. She teaches him to assume responsibility for his actions and their consequences on the people around him. Being an outsider and not mired in the family's dysfunctionality enables Tamar to understand and teach what Judah, alone, could not recognize by himself. She and Judah are blessed with not one but two sons, who are born shortly thereafter (Gen. 38:27–30).

Because Tamar has shown Judah that he must take responsibility for those around him, the pivotal lesson of leadership in Genesis, Judah is now ready, after a twenty-year hiatus, to repent for his sin against Joseph and achieve reconciliation with his long-lost brother. In doing so, he follows Jacob's example of repenting and reconciling with his brother Esau after a similar twenty-year separation. By internalizing this lesson of leadership, Judah and his descendants will later be blessed with the leadership of his brothers and ultimately of the Israelite nation.

The Crucible of Leadership: Joseph in Egypt

While Judah is learning his lesson of taking responsibility back in the land of Canaan, Joseph is going through a parallel process in Egypt. It should be noted that God was totally absent from the stories of Joseph and his brothers and from the story of Judah and his rehabilitation as a leader. When brothers do not care and take responsibility for each other, God is nowhere to be found. It is only when Joseph is sold into slavery and learns to take responsibility for his actions and for the welfare of those around him that God reappears in the story as the one who aids Joseph in becoming successful.

Having been humbled by being sold into slavery, Joseph learns to be responsible in the household of Potiphar, his master, where he takes responsibility for all of his master's affairs and earns his trust for doing so:

When Joseph was taken down to Egypt, a certain Egyptian, Potiphar, a courtier of Pharaoh and his chief steward, bought him from the Ishmaelites who had brought him there. The Lord was with Joseph, and he was a successful man; and he stayed in the house of his Egyptian master. And when his master saw that the Lord was with him and that the Lord lent success to everything he undertook, he took a liking to Joseph. He made him his personal attendant and put him in charge of his household, placing in his hands all that he owned. And from the time that the Egyptian put him in charge of his household and of all that he owned, the Lord blessed his house for Joseph's sake, so that the blessing of the Lord was upon everything that he owned, in the house and outside. He left all that he had in Joseph's hands and, with him there, he paid attention to nothing save the food that he ate. (Gen. 39:1–6)

When Potiphar's wife tries to seduce Joseph and betray Joseph's loyalty to his master, Joseph exhibits greater self-control and willpower than his father Jacob had when his mother, Rebecca, urged to him to betray the trust of his father, Isaac. Joseph steadfastly refuses her overtures:

Now Joseph was well built and handsome. After a time, his master's wife cast her eyes upon Joseph and said, "Lie with me." But he refused. He said to his master's wife, "Look, with me here, my master gives no thought to anything in this house, and all that he owns he has placed in my hands. He wields no more authority in this house than I, and he has withheld nothing from me except yourself, since you are his wife. How then could I do this most wicked thing, and sin before God?" And much as she coaxed Joseph day after day, he did not yield to her request to lie beside her, to be with her. (Gen. 39:6–10)

Even with no one around to witness the betrayal, Joseph remains true to the trust that his master has in him: "One such day, he came into the house to do his work. None of the household being there inside, she caught hold of him by his garment and said, 'Lie with me!' But he left his garment in her hand, pulled away, and fled outside" (Gen. 39:11–12).

Still, as we noted after Abraham's victory over the four kings, taking a responsible stand often has short-term, negative consequences. Joseph's refusal to betray his master's trust gets him into trouble with Potiphar's wife, who feels spurned by Joseph:

> *When she saw that he had left it in her hand and had fled outside, she called out to her servants and said to them, "Look, he had to bring us a Hebrew to dally with us! This one came to lie with me; but I screamed loud. And when he heard me screaming at the top of my voice, he left his garment with me and got away and fled outside." ... When his master heard the story that his wife told him, namely, "Thus and so your slave did to me," he was furious. So Joseph's master had him put in prison. (Gen. 39:13–15, 19–20)*

Joseph has now become the victim of slander, the same behavior he engaged in earlier in his life with his brothers. He had brought back bad tales about them to his father, and now Potiphar's wife does likewise, with Joseph being the victim.

In the Bible, as in life, what goes around ultimately comes around. He has paid for his youthful indiscretions and arrogance toward his brothers through his humbling ordeal. God is again with him, and even in prison, by being conscientious and responsible, he again rises to the top of the heap:

> *But even while he was there in prison, the Lord was with Joseph: He extended kindness to him and disposed the chief jailer favorably toward him. The chief jailer put in Joseph's charge all the prisoners who were in that prison, and he was the one to carry out everything that was done there. The chief jailer did not supervise anything that was in Joseph's charge, because the Lord was with him, and whatever he did the Lord made successful. (Gen. 39:20–23)*

Although in prison, one would think that Joseph would not be in much of a position to lead, he does just that by caring about and responding to the depressed moods of Pharaoh's chief butler and baker, who are two of his charges. By interpreting their disturbing dreams insightfully, he builds credibility and trust with these two former officers. This will ultimately lead to a change in his circumstances, and he is brought before Pharaoh to interpret his disturbing dreams.

Joseph plays the consultant's role in Genesis that Jethro will later play in Exodus. Both interpret what they hear and see, and then prescribe a solution for the sovereigns' dilemmas. Both are offered the opportunity to go from outside consultant to internal manager. The key role that these consultants play points to its importance in leadership situations. By virtue of coming in from the outside and viewing the challenge with fresh eyes, the consultant is literally able to see what the insider can not.

Once standing before Pharaoh, Joseph's leadership ability finds full expression. Listening carefully to Pharaoh's retelling of his dreams, Joseph interprets the dreams and presents Pharaoh with a double vision. He tells Pharaoh that Egypt will have seven years of plenty, then seven years of famine. He then helps Pharaoh plan to avert the famine by storing surplus food during the years of plenty so that the population can be fed during the famine. Joseph persuades Pharaoh to appoint a minister to take charge of the surplus collection and storage program, and Pharaoh chooses Joseph to head the program. Having positioned himself with the requisite authority to get the job done, Joseph then implements the program and prepares Egypt for the oncoming famine.

When the famine hits and Joseph's brothers come down to Egypt to purchase food, Joseph is perfectly positioned to assert the dominance over his siblings that he twice dreamt about as a young man. Just as he was slanderously accused of having been brought to Egypt only to uncover his mistress's nakedness, he slanderously accuses his brothers of the same: "to see the nakedness of the land have you come." He imprisons them for three days, giving them all a very small taste of his own experience as a falsely accused prisoner in Egypt. He releases all except for one, the violence-prone Shimon, whom he keeps locked up until the other brothers return with his brother Benjamin. Will the brothers do what is necessary to free their brother from prison? Joseph tests them to see whether they care about their brother's welfare. In the meantime, he surreptitiously returns the money they have paid for their food before they depart for Canaan.

When the brother's food supply runs out again and they need to return to Egypt, Reuben, the eldest of Jacob's sons, tries in vain to persuade his father to send Benjamin with them in his care, so that they can purchase additional food from Joseph:

> *Then Reuben said to his father, "You may kill my two sons if I do*
> *not bring him back to you. Put him in my care, and I will return*
> *him to you." But he [Jacob] said, "My son must not go down with*
> *you, for his brother is dead and he alone is left. If he meets with dis-*
> *aster on the journey you are taking, you will send my white head*
> *down to Sheol in grief." (Gen. 42:37–38)*

As happened in the kidnapping and sale of Joseph, Reuben means well,
but he fails to persuade and lead. He lacks the courage to take personal
responsibility, and his argument that Jacob can kill his two sons, Jacob's
own grandsons, if he fails to return Benjamin is ludicrous.

It is Judah, who has learned from Tamar what it means to take personal
responsibility, who is able to step forward, persuade, and lead his family:

> *Then Judah said to his father, Israel, "Send the boy in my care, and*
> *let us be on our way, that we may live and not die—you and we and*
> *our children. I myself will be the collateral for him; you may hold*
> *me responsible: if I do not bring him back to you and set him before*
> *you, I shall stand guilty before you forever. For we could have been*
> *there and back twice if we had not dawdled." Then their father Israel*
> *said to them, "If it must be so ... take your brother and go back at*
> *once to the man." (Gen. 43:8–13)*

The brothers return to Egypt with Benjamin, Shimon is released from
prison, their food bags are refilled, and all seems well. Joseph, however,
is apparently still distrustful of his brothers. True, the brothers have done
what is necessary to free Shimon, Leah's son. But would they do the same
for Benjamin, Rachel's son? Or will they abandon their half-brother at
the first opportunity just as they rid themselves of Joseph twenty years earlier? To test whether they have truly been remorseful for their actions,
and to protect Benjamin from future possible harm, Joseph hatches a
plot to test the brother's sincerity and intentions. He has his aide surreptitiously place Joseph's silver goblet in Benjamin's food sack, then sends
his cavalry after the brothers and accuses them of stealing the cup.

Joseph does to his brothers precisely what God did to his great-
grandfather, Abraham, when God commanded him to sacrifice Isaac.
There, God tested Abraham after Abraham had sent off Isaac's older
brother, Ishmael, to die in the desert. God wanted to see whether
Abraham would abandon his other son, Isaac, simply because God told

him to do so. Abraham passes the test when he substitutes a ram for his younger son.

Here, Joseph tests his brothers to see whether they are prepared to abandon Benjamin, Joseph's younger brother, to a lifetime of slavery, just as they abandoned Joseph twenty years earlier. Like Abraham, who had the pretext of listening to God's command to sacrifice Isaac, the brothers have the pretext of listening to Joseph's command to abandon their brother in Egypt. Judah's offer to substitute himself for Benjamin enables the brothers to pass Joseph's test, just as Abraham's substitute of the ram for Isaac enabled Abraham to pass God's test.

Joseph's later assertion that he would not enslave his brother, asking, "Am I a substitute for God?" (Gen. 50:19), is given added irony because Joseph had assumed precisely God's role in testing the brothers.

> Then Judah went up to him and said, "Please, my lord, let your servant appeal to my lord, and do not be impatient with your servant, you who are the equal of Pharaoh.... Your servant, my father, said to us, 'As you know, my wife bore me two sons. But one is gone from me,' and I said: 'Alas, he was torn by a beast! And I have not seen him since. If you take this one from me, too, and he meets with disaster, you will send my white head down to Sheol in sorrow.' ... Now, if I come to your servant, my father, and the boy is not with us—since his own life is so bound up with his—when he sees that the boy is not with us, he will die, and your servants will send the white head of your servant, our father, down to Sheol in grief. Now your servant has pledged himself for the boy to my father, saying, 'If I do not bring him back to you, I shall stand guilty before my father forever.' Therefore, please let your servant remain as a slave to my lord instead of the boy, and let the boy go back with his brothers. For how can I go back to my father unless the boy is with me? Let me not be witness to the woe that would overtake my father." (Gen. 44:18, 30–34)

Joseph has led his brothers to change their behavior. With Judah literally in the lead, they are now prepared to be their brother's keeper rather than his kidnapper. They are willing to take responsibility for Benjamin and their father, despite Jacob's continued favoritism of Rachel's sons. Judah succeeded in leading his brothers to sell Joseph into slavery, succeeded in persuading his father to put Benjamin in his care for the journey to Egypt, and now by offering to sacrificially substitute himself for Benjamin, succeeds in persuading Joseph of the genuine change in their behavior.

With Judah having proven his responsible leadership to Joseph, it is now Joseph's turn to reconcile with his brothers and reunite the family for, perhaps, the first time:

> *Joseph could no longer control himself before all his attendants, and he cried out, "Have everyone withdraw from my presence!" So there was no one else about when Joseph made himself known to his brothers. His sobs were so loud that the Egyptians could hear, and so the news reached Pharaoh's palace. Joseph said to his brothers, "I am Joseph. Is my father still well?" But his brothers could not answer him, so dumbfounded were they on account of him. Then Joseph said to his brothers, "Come forward to me." And when they came forward, he said, "I am your brother Joseph, he whom you sold into Egypt. Now, do not be distressed or reproach yourselves because you sold me here; it was to save life that God sent me ahead of you. It is now two years that there has been famine in the land, and there are still five years to come in which there shall be no yield from tilling. God has sent me ahead of you to ensure your survival on earth, and to save your lives in an extraordinary deliverance. So, it was not you who sent me here, but God; and He has made me a father to Pharaoh, lord of all his household, and ruler over the whole land of Egypt. Now, hurry back to my father and say to him: 'Thus says your son Joseph, "God has made me lord of all Egypt; come down to me without delay. You will dwell in the region of Goshen, where you will be near me—you and your children and your grandchildren, your flocks and herds, and all that is yours. There I will provide for you—for there are yet five years of famine to come—that you and your household and all that is yours may not suffer want."'" (Gen. 45:1–11)*

Joseph and his brothers have apparently reconciled. They have learned the lesson of mutual responsibility and are now prepared, under Joseph's influence and protective sponsorship, to unite together as one family in the land of Goshen.

Judah and Joseph's learning to take responsibility for their brothers has a salutary effect on Jacob's leadership as well. After Jacob reunites with his long-lost son and as he approaches the end of his life, he finally internalizes the lesson of taking responsibility, not only for those he favors but also for his entire family.

Although Reuben, his eldest son, was a disappointment as a leader and even attempted to usurp the right to leadership succession by sleeping with one of Jacob's wives (Gen. 35:22), and Shimon and Levi, the next two in the birth order, wiped out an entire city and took its spoils, Jacob does not remove them from the family's covenantal legacy.[38] Jacob does find a way, however, to neutralize Shimon and Levi's violent streak but still keep them in the family.[39] By including all twelve of his sons in his blessings, despite the questionable behavior of the three oldest, Jacob breaks the pattern set by Abraham and Isaac of choosing only one son to carry on the heritage while excluding the others.

Jacob blesses all of the sons in each other's presence. He wants it to be clear that no one is left out, even if the blessings are not completely equal. Furthermore, in parceling out the blessings, he assigns the leadership of the brothers not to his favorite, Joseph, but to Judah, the accepted leader amongst the other brothers:

> You, O Judah, your brothers shall praise;
> Your hand shall be on the nape of your foes;
> Your father's sons shall bow low to you ...
> The scepter shall not depart from Judah,
> Nor the ruler's staff from between his feet;
> So that tribute shall come to him
> And the homage of peoples be his. (Gen. 49:8–10)

Jacob recognizes that, despite his love of Joseph, Joseph does not command the trust and loyalty of the brothers. How right he was. After Jacob's death, the brothers are afraid that Joseph will avenge their selling him into slavery by executing them, just as their uncle Esau vowed to kill his own brother, Jacob, once Isaac, their father, died. Their fears, however, prove to be groundless:

> When Joseph's brothers saw that their father was dead, they said, "What if Joseph still bears a grudge against us and pays us back for all the wrong that we did him?" So they sent this message to Joseph: "Before his death your father left this instruction: So shall you say to Joseph, 'Forgive, I urge you, the offense and guilt of your brothers who treated you so harshly.' Therefore, please forgive the offense of the

*servants of the God of your father." And Joseph was in tears as they
spoke to him. His brothers went to him themselves, flung themselves
before him, and said, "We are prepared to be your slaves." But Joseph
said to them, "Have no fear! Am I a substitute for God? Besides,
although you intended me harm, God intended it for good, so as to
bring about the present result—the survival of many people. And so,
fear not. I will sustain you and your children." Thus he reassured
them, speaking kindly to them. (Gen. 50:15–21)*

Joseph has truly internalized what it means to be his brother's keeper. He
is able to reframe the past so that all the brothers can share a common
future.

Jacob knew all his sons better than they realized. By choosing Judah
to be their future leader, he chooses the one whose followers, the other
brothers, trust. Despite his magnanimous gesture, Joseph cannot earn
their trust. At the most, he is able to earn their respect and gratitude. Jacob
fulfills the leader's task of grooming and appointing the correct successor
to his leadership.

It takes Jacob/Israel a lifetime to correct his mistakes and become
the responsible leader of his entire family. The Israelites are called the "children of Israel" because of their identification with Jacob's lifelong struggle
with learning how to be a leader. Jacob does not start out as a leader, and
when he does lead in his youth he often does so without being responsible.
He acts irresponsibly toward his father and brother when he leads his
father into bestowing the blessing intended for his brother on himself
instead. He fails to take responsibility for three of his four spouses, for ten
of his twelve sons, and for his sole daughter. He has to learn the hard way,
by not taking responsibility, what the consequences are for his failures. Yet
by the end of his life he learns from his own children how to take responsibility for his entire family. Jacob models the role of the leader who assures
not only his own and the next generation's leadership but the long-term
leadership of his nascent people. As such, he serves a role model for Moses
in the book of Numbers and for contemporary leaders to do the same.

The Abuse of Leadership: Joseph and His Egyptian Brethren

Although Joseph learned the lesson of taking responsibility for his biological family, in doing so he failed to take responsibility for his national

family, the people of Egypt. While protecting his brothers, Joseph abused his power over the Egyptian people. What may have been a rewarding short-term management tactic proved itself to be a short-sighted leadership strategy.

Where exactly did Joseph go wrong as a leader? After all, at the beginning he seemed to have done everything right! He demonstrated double vision, foreseeing the famine and its devastating consequences for Egypt. He persuasively communicated his vision to Pharaoh and established a position for himself so he could implement his plan to save Egypt from famine.

However, his leadership takes a wrong turn once the famine begins. Instead of handing out rations to the Egyptian people to get them through the famine, he sells the stored grain back to the Egyptian people at prices so exorbitant that within one year he has bankrupted the entire Egyptian economy.

> *Now there was no bread in all the world, for the famine was very severe; both the land of Egypt and the land of Canaan languished because of the famine. Joseph gathered in all the money that was to be found in the land of Egypt and in the land of Canaan, as payment for the rations that were being procured, and Joseph brought the money into Pharaoh's palace. (Gen. 47:13–14)*

Having achieved a monopoly over the money supply, Joseph then sells the grain for commodities, soon giving Pharaoh control over all the livestock of Egypt:

> *And when the money gave out in the land of Egypt and in the land of Canaan, all the Egyptians came to Joseph and said, "Give us bread, lest we die before your very eyes, for the money is gone!" And Joseph said, "Bring your livestock, and I will sell to you against your livestock, if the money is gone." So they brought their livestock to Joseph, and Joseph gave them bread in exchange for the horses, for the flocks of sheep and cattle, and the donkeys; thus he provided them with bread that year in exchange for all their livestock. (Gen. 47:15–17)*

By the end of the second year, Joseph gains control over all the real estate in the country and manipulates the population to sell themselves into slavery to Pharaoh:

> *And when that year was ended, they came to him the next year and said*
> *to him, "We cannot hide from my lord that, with all the money and*
> *flocks of animals consigned to my lord, nothing is left at my lord's dis-*
> *posal save our persons and our farmland. Let us not perish before your*
> *eyes, both we and our land. Take us and our land in exchange for bread,*
> *and we with our land will be slaves to Pharaoh; provide the seed, that*
> *we may live and not die, and that the land may not become a waste." So*
> *Joseph gained possession of all the farm land of Egypt for Pharaoh, every*
> *Egyptian having sold his field because the famine was too much for*
> *them; thus the land passed over to Pharaoh. (Gen. 47:18–20)*

More egregious still is that Joseph engages in massive population transfers thereby making the Egyptians strangers in their own land: "And he removed the population town by town, from one end of Egypt's border to the other" (Gen. 47:21). The only persons who were exempt from Joseph's draconian policies, aside from his Israelite family, were, interestingly enough, the priesthood. It should be remembered that Joseph's wife was the daughter of the priest of the sun god, On: "Only the land of the priests he did not take over, for the priests had an allotment from Pharaoh, and they lived off the allotment which Pharaoh had made to them; therefore they did not sell their land" (Gen. 47:22).

Having gained ownership over all of Egypt—money, livestock, real estate, and persons—he then adds insult to injury by imposing a 20 percent tax on crops, thereby ensuring a continuous stream of income into Pharaoh's coffers:

> *Then Joseph said to the people, "Whereas I have this day acquired*
> *you and your land for Pharaoh, here is seed for you to sow the land.*
> *And when harvest comes, you shall give one-fifth to Pharaoh, and*
> *four-fifths will be yours as seed for the fields and as food for you and*
> *those in your households, and as nourishment for your children."*
> *(Gen. 47:23–24)*

Joseph was so successful in subjugating the Egyptian natives that they actually expressed gratitude to him for saving their lives. In effect, they were thanking Joseph for making them into slaves. Joseph succeeds in exploiting, impoverishing, and enslaving the Egyptian people to the point where they internalize the identity of penniless slaves and do not realize the pernicious nature of Joseph's actions:

*And they said, "You have saved our lives! We are grateful to my
lord, and we will be slaves to Pharaoh." And Joseph made it into a
land law in Egypt, which is still valid, that a fifth should be
Pharaoh's; only the land of the priests did not become Pharaoh's.
(Gen. 47:25–26)*

What makes Joseph's actions all the more painful is that while he was enslaving the Egyptians he was unapologetically protecting his Israelite brethren in Goshen: "Thus Israel settled in the country of Egypt, in the region of Goshen; they acquired property there, were fertile and increased greatly" (Gen. 47:27). The Israelites were unaffected by the famine and Joseph's exploitative policies toward the Egyptian people. No wonder the Bible tells us both in Genesis and again at the outset of Exodus that the Israelites took hold of the land, were fertile, and increased greatly! They were living the good life while the Egyptians were surviving by the skin of their teeth.

Although it was not wrong for Joseph to take responsibility for the welfare of his extended biological family, it was wrong for him to do so while impoverishing and enslaving the people of Egypt. Had he been fair and benevolent with the Egyptians, his favoring of his own family would barely have been noticed. As it was, however, his nepotism must have stood out like a sore thumb. At the very least, it gave the appearance of impropriety, a leadership mistake that Moses will commit with his own brother in the book of Numbers. It took a later Pharaoh "who knew not Joseph," that is, who owed Joseph no allegiance for consolidating the monarchy's power, to capitalize on the pent-up rage that the Egyptians must have felt for their impoverished condition, directing their anger against the increasingly powerful Israelites.

Why does Joseph do this? Not for his own personal enrichment but for the benefit of his master, Pharaoh. Yet, in doing so, he benefits by reinforcing his political standing in Pharaoh's court. Unlike his great-grandfather Abraham, who tried to defend the wicked people of Sodom by speaking truth to power to the King of kings, Joseph fails to stand up for the Egyptian people when addressing Pharaoh. Rather, he ingratiates himself by instituting a policy that results in royal enrichment and empowerment while degrading and enslaving the Egyptian masses.

Joseph's failure to take responsibility for the Egyptian people caused the Israelites' subsequent enslavement in Egypt for hundreds of years.

The nearly omnipotent central government that Joseph empowered turns against his own people when Joseph passes on and a new Pharaoh rises in Egypt. Joseph's failure to actualize his potential and mission to become a "blessing to all the peoples of the earth" leads to the suffering and enslavement of his people for centuries afterward, the story of which we will examine from a leadership perspective in Book II.

Conclusion

The book of Genesis begins with the creation of one man and woman. The spiritual masters of early Judaism understood that by telling the story of humanity this way, the Bible teaches its readers that all of humanity has a single father and mother, that all human beings are, in fact, brothers and sisters. If there is a leadership lesson to be learned from the stories in the book of Genesis and from the Egyptian exile that follows in the book of Exodus, it is that brothers who do not watch over each other, or worse, harm each other, are doomed to a future of degradation and weakness. Brothers, whether biological or metaphorical, who don't safeguard the integrity of their families are destined to experience the ravages of exile. In contrast, brothers who do act responsibly toward each other are blessed and are a blessing to others.

The same is true for leaders of nations, communities, and organizations today. Leaders who do not take responsibility for others undermine the integrity and morale of their group. This failure ultimately leads to the group's dissolution. The other side of the story is that those who do have the caring and the courage to assume responsibility lead their organizations to true greatness—what the Bible refers to as abundant blessings. Everyone wins when leaders act responsibly and with life-affirming values.

In the book of Genesis we have seen examples of almost the entire gamut of leadership. Despite the generational ups and downs in each family setting, real progress has been made. But now the drama of the Israelites' national story and the systematic lessons of responsible leadership—lessons that will affect not just a family but an entire nation—are about to begin.

Book II

THE TEN GUIDING
PRINCIPLES OF
LEADERSHIP

Imagine being a senior executive at work one day and receiving a phone call from the chairman of your organization, summoning you to his or her office. You walk in, sit down, and, somewhat surprisingly, but perhaps not entirely so, are offered the challenging opportunity by the chairman to become the president and CEO. What would you do? Would you accept? You certainly might be tempted to. But what would happen if you felt unprepared, inadequate for the immensity of the position being offered to you, unsure that you really had what it takes to lead your company? You might then agonize over what to do and lean toward declining.

Let us say that the situation took another twist: it was made clear to you that you had almost no choice in the matter because there was simply no one else who could do the job except you. What would you do then? Would you still decline because you failed to summon the courage to go out front and lead? Or would you seize the opportunity, embrace the challenge of leadership by persuading others with complementary skills and resources to join and support you, and do yourself and your organization proud?

Moses, like our hypothetical executive, found himself at work one day when out of the blue he received a "call" from the "Chairman of the Board." Not just any board, mind you, but the board responsible for overseeing the operations of the universe! Moses was given the opportunity to take the CEO position of his long-abandoned people and lead them from abject slavery to redemptive freedom. At first, he felt unprepared and inadequate for the job and did his best to decline. When he was told there was no one else who could do the job, and was assured that he would receive leadership support from significant others, he ultimately agreed, despite deep personal misgivings, to step forward and assume the risk of leadership.

Moses and "the Chairman" collaborated together on an unabashedly honest record of that leadership challenge, which they faced together.

The narrative legacy of that record begins in the book of Exodus and concludes in the book of Deuteronomy. The biblical story of their leadership of the Israelites systematically develops what the book of Genesis introduced in a far more elementary fashion: a working template of what it takes to lead change successfully. In ten sequential guiding principles, the God and Moses leadership team shows us what is necessary to lead any group or organization from one place to the next, what leads to success, and what leads to failure.

The Ten Guiding Principles of Leadership

1. Create urgency by defining the threatening challenge and/or compelling opportunity (Exod. 1).
2. Care deeply and act courageously (Exod. 2).
3. Develop double vision; see the present clearly and envision a promising future (Exod. 3:1–10).
4. Recruit a guiding coalition by communicating the vision with conviction and perseverance to potential core leadership members who complement strengths and compensate weaknesses (Exod. 3–4).
5. Position oneself to secure the legitimacy and authority to lead. Build credibility and trust by promising and delivering (Exod. 5–14).
6. Communicate vision and mission with emotional passion to the larger group multiple times through multiple modalities (Exod. 15, 19, 24).
7. Implement the vision by:
    (a) generating small victories and building momentum (Exod. 15:22–17)
    (b) broadening governance and forming management hierarchies (Exod. 18).
8. Establish the vision by codifying the values, policies, and laws necessary to actualize the vision (Exod. 19–24).
9. Institutionalize the vision by building sacred space and carving out sacred times (Exod. 25–31, 35–40; Lev. 23; Num. 7).
10. Protect the vision by dealing decisively with detractors (Exod. 32–33).

Leading Change

As we saw in the Bible's earliest stories of relationship, leaders are proactive in generating change. The leader recognizes that something in the environment—whether a compelling opportunity or a threatening challenge—cries out for response or repair. To respond, the leader must engage others in a conversation both to recognize the urgency of the current situation and to join in seeking a solution. If the leader is able to convince others of the urgency and of the general direction that the response should take, then that person has, by definition, begun to play a leadership role in that particular project or organization.

In thinking about successfully leading change, Michael Hammer, author of *Reengineering the Corporation*, brilliantly noted that one of the great records of group change is found in the Bible's story of God and Moses leading the Israelite exodus from Egypt.[1] It is hard to imagine a more dramatic change than taking an inchoate rabble of dependent slaves and transforming them into an independent, self-reliant nation capable of fighting for and establishing their own sovereign country. We can learn a great deal about the process and perils of leading change by examining the story of Moses leading the Israelites.

Because leaders are called upon to drive change, the challenge of leadership is almost self-evident: how to get people to go along with and embrace that change. Michael Hammer states the challenge quite succinctly: "People experience all change as loss." Even *good* change is experienced as loss.[2]

Anyone who doubts the universal and personal applicability of this maxim need only witness the behavior of a prospective bride and groom in the weeks leading up to their wedding. Although both bride and groom presumably wish to marry each other and choose to do so out of their own volition, they nevertheless exhibit the symptoms of desperate anxiety and prospective loss, including, perhaps, hysterical crying bouts for the woman and raucous bachelor parties for the man. Apparently, although both the man and the woman wish to connect with each other, each is afraid of the loss of autonomy and freedom that accompanies long-term commitment.

The experiencing of "change as loss" is true for individuals, families, and organizations of whatever size and shape. Change, by its very

nature, is disorienting. In addition, when people are in some way dependent on the continuation of the status quo, then those advocating change
are seen as threats, even enemies.

Therefore, we have a paradox: while a leader's job is to initiate and
sustain change by persuading others of its necessity, people tend to resist
change at all costs. Leadership has built into it anxiety, tension, and the
potential for acute conflict; hence, the challenge of change.

If the dissonance between leader and followers becomes too great,
the leader will be unsuccessful and will likely suffer considerable personal
damage in the process. Therefore, leaders, in generating change, put
themselves at great risk. On a prosaic level, leaders who generate change
without "buy in" from their constituents may suddenly find themselves
losing crucial votes or their position of leadership. In more dire cases,
leaders may find themselves victims of ad hominem attacks and character assassinations designed to stop them from following through on their
goals. It is not unusual for this type of character assassination to dog
leaders in their future attempts at leadership for years to come. In the
worst case, leaders may come to physical harm as a result of their leadership efforts.

The 1981 assassination of Egypt's president, Anwar Sadat, and the
1995 slaying of Israeli's prime minister, Yitzchak Rabin, leaders who tried
to change the balance of war and peace in the Middle East, are two potent,
real-life examples of the very real dangers inherent in leading change.
Sadat and Rabin were not killed by terrorists of other nations; they were
gunned down by individuals from their own peoples who felt threatened
by the political changes each of them was leading. Going further back in
time, the reluctance of biblical prophets such as Moses and Jeremiah may
also be understood, at least in part, as coming from their awareness of
the dangers from their potential constituents.

If leaders almost always encounter resistance and, sometimes dangerous resistance to their change efforts, what motivates leaders to seek
change? As we noted briefly in Genesis and will now see more extensively in the opening chapters of the book of Exodus, the Bible teaches
us that four factors must be present: two external and two internal. The
external elements in the environment that prompt change are two different types of *urgency,* either threatening challenges and/or compelling
opportunities that motivate a leader to seek change. The internal quali-

ties that must be present in the individual who leads change are deep caring and uncommon courage, which together add up to the willingness to assume responsibility for the change effort.

Principle 1: Create Urgency! (Exod. 1)

The beginning of the book of Exodus, like the first verses in the book of Genesis, starts out positively, one might even say idyllically. Let us look back at the book of Genesis first.

Genesis begins with a story of creation in which each act is followed by "and God saw that it was good." When creating human beings, God blesses them to "be fruitful, multiply, fill the earth and achieve dominion over it" (Gen. 1:28). After their creation God sees that "everything was very good." The goodness of creation creates a benchmark for the way that the world "ought" to be, which stands in sharp contrast to the degeneration of God's world that follows. By the end of chapter 5 of Genesis, God sees that the good world has indeed become filled with humanity, but a human race set on evil and violence. God regrets having created the world in the first place and decides to destroy God's creation. The very future of the planet, not to mention, of its inhabitants, is put at stake. Thus, the Bible has set up the radical sense of urgency necessary to introduce the heroism of Noah and his life-saving ark on the earth's womb-like waters. It is there that human hope and human life will be reborn.

Similarly the first seven verses of Exodus begin with the Israelites fulfilling God's blessing for humanity, which is stated in the first chapter of the book of Genesis. Then the narrative proceeds to develop the urgency of their situation.

The early period of the Israelites' residence in Egypt, like the beginning of human life in the universe, is a good and blessed one. The nascent Israelite nation grows from seventy souls to hundreds of thousands of people. The land of Egypt is filled with them. They achieve great power and dominion. But as chapter 1 progresses, their very growth and success, the fulfillment of God's blessings, become a threat to Pharaoh and the Egyptians. Pharaoh therefore initiates a series of steps to stem their growth, each more severe than the previous one:

> *Therefore they did set over them taskmasters to afflict them with their burdens. And they built for Pharaoh treasure cities, Pithom and*

Raamses. But the more they afflicted them, the more they multiplied
and grew. And they were mortified because of the people of Israel.
And the Egyptians made the people of Israel serve with rigor; And
they made their lives bitter with hard slavery, in mortar, and in brick,
and in all kinds of service in the field; all their service, which they
made them serve, was with rigor. (Exod. 1:11–14)

First, Pharaoh drafts the Israelite males into an army of slave labor. He
hopes thereby to separate them from their spouses and drain them of their
virility. Paradoxically, however, the more the Israelites are oppressed, the
faster they seem to grow. Pharaoh's second plan is to clandestinely kill the
male infants at birth. Yet his evil plan is stymied by two simple, good-
hearted, God-fearing midwives. These midwives have a respect for human
life that he does not possess. This leads Pharaoh to take more nefarious
public action: "And Pharaoh charged all his people, saying, 'Every son
who is born you shall throw into the river, and every daughter you shall let
live'" (Exod. 1:22).

By the end of chapter 1 of Exodus, with Pharaoh's royal decree to
drown every Israelite baby boy, the future of the Israelites, a future that
had looked so blessed and promising, is put in grave peril. Exodus dramatically depicts an urgent life-or-death situation that serves to introduce the leadership of Moses and his small life-saving ark on the
womblike waters of Egypt's Nile River. There, the hope of the Israelite
nation will in effect be reborn.

By beginning with a backdrop of goodness and blessing and then
painting a foreground filled with evil and violence, both Genesis and Exodus create a yawning gap between the two realities and a sense of urgency
to which leaders in the subsequent chapters will respond.

The opening chapters of Genesis and Exodus teach us that the external prompt for the leaders to generate change requires a significant change
in the larger environment. If human beings in the book of Genesis had
been happily ensconced in God's presence in the Garden of Eden, there
would have been no need for Noah and his ark. Had the Israelites in the
book of Exodus still been a sheltered caste under Joseph's protective aus-
pices, there would be no need for the leadership of Moses and his miraculous staff. What prompted the need for Noah and Moses was a drastic
change for the worse in their respective environments. The redemptive
changes that Noah and Moses introduced were responses to the lethal

changes around them that the rest of the population was either unwilling to acknowledge or unable to respond.

John Kotter, professor of leadership at Harvard Business School, states that 50 percent of change efforts fail because of the leader's inability to generate a radical sense of urgency in the organization. Without that sense of urgency, the leader cannot rally those around him to join the change effort.[3] To use Michael Hammer's terminology, the leader must have both a wedge with which to dislodge the constituents from their complacency and a magnet with which to draw them to the new promised land. Therefore, it is essential that the Bible, in both Genesis and Exodus, begins the way that it does: first, by making the urgency clear (by depicting that the human/Israelite enterprise is at stake) and second, by creating the wedge for change (by graphically depicting the evil and violence into which the original goodness and blessing have degenerated). Each book begins with the benchmark of goodness, which serves as the magnet to which each book will seek to approximately return. I say "approximately" because there is no possibility of returning to the Garden of Eden or to the idyllic state of political protection, prosperity, and fertility that marked Joseph's reign in Egypt.[4]

Nevertheless, the hankering to return to a state of overflowing material abundance, which prosperity and fertility represent, and the sense of security, which the Garden of Eden and Joseph's stewardship of his people exemplified, becomes the defining future vision of both books. They are the subconscious meaning behind God's promise to bring the Israelites to a land dripping with milk and honey. There, all their material needs and questing for permanence will be provided for abundantly, not through the good will of the local authorities but through the benevolent kingship of God.

Pharaoh: Leadership without Values

What are we to make of Pharaoh's leadership? First, we notice that he is a keenly observant leader. He recognizes the shift in the balance of forces between the Israelite and Egyptian peoples. Thanks to Joseph's policies, the Israelites have indeed taken root in the land and grown numerically, financially, and politically. At the same time, the Egyptian nation has been reduced to penury and internal exile. Seeing this, Pharaoh articulates the situation to the Egyptians in urgent terms: "We must outwit them, lest they continue to grow, join with our enemies and eject us entirely from the land!" He also has a plan for how to reverse the Israelites' growth: first a labor tax, then oppressive slavery, then clandestine infanticide, and finally an executive order to murder the infant boys. The latter two are exceptionally clever ploys because, if successful, killing the male infants will eliminate future insurgents while allowing the infant girls to live will provide the native Egyptian population with sex slaves to reward them for their support of his policies. Clearly, Pharaoh has many of the skills that make for effective, if cunning, leadership.

What Pharaoh lacks is life-affirming leadership values. A despot, willing to murder innocent babes because of their ethnicity, does not meet the Bible's or any reasonable, humane standard of decent or successful leadership. As in the cases of Eve, Cain, and Ham in Genesis, Pharaoh's values, which make a mockery of human life, dignity, and property, will effectively lead his people to a place far worse than where they are now. Pharaoh, like the many tyrants of history who followed him, demonstrates clearly the fallacy of emphasizing leadership skills without leadership values.

Pharaoh's lack of values will ultimately undermine his leadership effectiveness in another way. As God and Moses begin to bring the ten plagues upon the Egyptians, Pharaoh, at several points in the narrative, verbally agrees to free the Israelites from bondage. Yet, as soon as the plagues pass, his "heart hardens" and he reneges on his word, thus bringing further destruction upon his people. His refusal to reflect on the consequences of his inhumane actions and his disingenuous words betray his self-centered ego, which prevents him from learning and changing. Pharaoh's refusal to assume responsibility for the consequences of his behavior and for the welfare of his citizens, the Bible's primary leadership value, bring ruin to him and all of Egypt.

Principle 2: Care Deeply and Act Courageously (Exod. 2)

There are many people who are perceptive enough to detect compelling opportunities or threatening challenges in their environments. They may even recognize and feel the urgency of those opportunities or challenges. Only a few, however, step forward and rally their group to respond to that urgency. What distinguishes the leaders from their followers is not merely the street smarts or the ability of the leader to notice the change in the environment and assess its urgency; it is the caring and courage to assume responsibility for the situation and risk doing something about it. In classic *Wizard of Oz* terms, a leader must have not only an intelligent brain but also a deeply caring heart with the courage to take action.

Dr. Elias Zerhouni, director of the National Institutes of Health (NIH), made a similar point about the necessary qualities of leadership in an interview with the *New York Times*. When asked what it takes to be a leader, he said, "I think it takes three things. First you have to have a big heart, because if you don't have a big heart you will never be able to lead. And a big heart means several things to me. You have to have a passion. You have to believe in some things that are your core values. The second is that you have to have a spine, which means stand up for what you think and take the risks that you think are important. And third and least important is brains. People often think that high intelligence is a prerequisite. I don't believe so. I think a big heart and a strong spine are more important than high intelligence."[5]

Having created a sense of urgency in chapter 1 of Exodus, the Bible proceeds in chapter 2 to tell a story that highlights the two fundamental, internal characteristics necessary for leadership: caring and courage. All of the episodes in this chapter swirl around the development of Moses's caring and courage. The chapter begins with Moses's father, Amram, boldly marrying[6] and parenting a child in defiance of Pharaoh's decree to drown all male infants. This is then followed by the fortitude of Yocheved, Moses's mother, in hiding the newborn infant and her resolute, protective placing of the child in a waterproofed straw basket among the reeds of the Nile. Courage and caring are transmitted to Moses's sister, Miriam, who fearlessly places herself in harm's way to watch over and then intervene on behalf of her younger brother—an extraordinary demonstration of courage and caring for a young child. Finally, Moses's adoptive mother—Pharaoh's daughter—compassionately and courageously saves the Hebrew baby boy, knowing full well that in doing so she is contradicting the edict of her father, perhaps the most powerful man in the ancient world.

> *And his sister stood at a distance, to see what would be done to him.*
> *The daughter of Pharaoh came down to wash herself at the river; and*
> *her maidens walked along by the river's side; and when she saw the*
> *ark among the reeds, she sent her maid to fetch it. And when she had*
> *opened it, she saw the child; and, behold, the baby wept. And she had*

compassion on him, and said, "This is one of the Hebrews' children."
Then his sister said to Pharaoh's daughter, "Shall I go and call for
you a nurse of the Hebrew women, that she may nurse the child for
you?" And Pharaoh's daughter said to her, "Go." And the girl went
and called the child's mother. And Pharaoh's daughter said to her:
"Take this child away, and nurse it for me, and I will give you your
wages." And the woman took the child, and nursed it. And the child
grew, and she brought him to Pharaoh's daughter, and he became her
son. And she called his name Moses; and she said, "Because I drew
him out of the water." (Exod. 2:4–10)

Moses is raised by these four caring and courageous individuals. All of
them recognize the urgency of the situation. While Moses's biological
family is motivated by the urgent threat that Pharaoh's decree poses to
their family and their people, Pharaoh's daughter's motive may have been
the compelling opportunity to raise the baby as her own child. All of them
are responding to a change in their environments. By acting proactively,
they change not merely the status quo of their own families but also the
course of history.

From the trilogy of stories about Moses that follows it is clear that
Moses's biological and adoptive families cultivate, and Moses imbibes,
these attributes of courage and caring. First, Moses bravely saves his
Hebrew "brother" from a fatal beating by an Egyptian taskmaster:

And it came to pass in those days, when Moses was grown, that he
went out to his brothers, and looked on their burdens; and he spied an
Egyptian beating a Hebrew, one of his brothers. And he looked this
way and that way, and when he saw that there was no man, he slew
the Egyptian, and hid him in the sand. (Exod. 2:11–12)

Although the text states that Moses looked both ways and saw that "there
was no man," from the fact that by the following day Moses's actions are
common knowledge, it is plausible that the text intends a figurative rather
than a literal reading: i.e., no man with the compassion and courage to
intervene and halt the assault. In this reading, the text underscores Moses's
unique courage among his enslaved brethren in intervening on their behalf.

One might also recall that the last time the words *brother* and *Hebrew*
are mentioned together is in Genesis 14, where Abraham rescues his
"brother" Lot in a daring nighttime raid. Moses, like Abraham, the

Israelites' founder, who is referred to in that pivotal story with the surname Ivri ("the one who crossed over"), is willing to "cross over" from his identity as an indifferent Egyptian prince to an empathetic, concerned Israelite who intervenes to rescue his "brother" from impending harm. Later in the book of Numbers,[7] Moses will demand the same of the tribes of Gad and Reuven: insisting that they "cross over" the Jordan to fight with their imperiled brethren during the military conquest of Canaan. All three cases are existential instances of identification, caring, and courage—the necessary internal attributes of biblical leadership.

As the story of Exodus continues, Moses's concern and courage prompt him the next day to intervene between two quarreling Israelites, an event that precipitates his flight to the backwater region of Midian as a fugitive from perverse Egyptian justice:

> *And when he went out the second day, behold, two men of the Hebrews struggled together; and he said to the one who did the wrong, "Why do you strike your fellow?" And he said, "Who made you a prince and a judge over us? Do you intend to kill me, as you killed the Egyptian?" And Moses feared, and said, "Certainly this thing is known." And when Pharaoh heard this matter, he sought to slay Moses. But Moses fled from the face of Pharaoh, and dwelt in the land of Midian; and he sat down by a well. (Exod. 2:13–15)*

No sooner does Moses arrive in Midian than he valiantly rescues the daughters of the priest of Midian, a man who will go on to become his father-in-law, from a group of bullying shepherds who were harassing the young girls. Moses's compassion in siding with the vulnerable against the aggressor and his courage in sticking his own neck out to protect the aggrieved victims of injustice are qualities that his future father-in-law, Jethro, immediately detects and values.

Not only is Jethro impressed by Moses's caring and courage; God as well seems to take the cue from Moses at the end of the chapter, evincing the same empathy for the Israelites as Moses's significant others—and Moses himself—exhibited earlier in the chapter:

> *And it came to pass in the process of time, that the king of Egypt died; and the people of Israel sighed because of the slavery, and they cried, and their cry came up to God because of the slavery. And God heard their groaning, and God remembered God's covenant with Abraham,*

with Isaac, and with Jacob. And God looked upon the people of Israel, and God knew [that it was time to fulfill God's covenantal promise]. (Exod. 2:23–25)[8]

The Bible includes this chapter, interrupting the narrative regarding the general state of the Israelites, to explain God's choosing Moses as the leader of the Exodus in chapter 3. Ironically, Moses later validates God's selection of him as leader by showing the caring and courage to challenge God for not alleviating the miserable plight of God's people. After Moses returns to Egypt and confronts Pharaoh, only to find that Pharaoh increases the workload of the Israelite slaves in response to Moses's intervention, Moses has the audacity to take God to task for worsening the situation of God's people. Reminiscent of Abraham's challenge to God before God's destruction of Sodom and Gomorrah: "Shall the Judge of all the earth not do justly?" (Gen. 18:25), Moses, out of a sense of deep empathy for the Israelites and profound outrage at the injustice of Pharaoh's actions, asks God:

"O Lord, why did You bring harm upon this people? Why did You send me? Ever since I came to Pharaoh to speak in Your name, he has dealt worse with this people; and still You have not delivered Your people!" (Exod. 5:22–23)

In fact, Moses's finest hour as the leader of his people comes when he has the nerve to issue God an ultimatum a year or so later, after the incident of the Golden Calf. When God offers to destroy the Israelites and begin a new people from Moses himself, Moses tells God that either God forgive the people or Moses will perish with them (Exod. 32:10, 32). In response, God relents. God is clearly taken by Moses's selfless sacrifice on behalf of his people (Exod. 33:17).

Throughout most of his life and leadership, Moses continued to display empathy and courage. When those feelings of empathy began to erode, and his heart hardened toward his constituents who were in need, he lost his credibility as a leader and was informed that it was time to step aside (Num. 20).

The Roots of Caring

It is worthwhile digressing here from the narrative of the text to examine the roots of caring and courage. What is caring? To care is to possess a feeling of empathy and a sense of responsibility toward one's world; caring presupposes a sense of identification with another. Budding leaders must develop enough of an empathetic character to be in touch with their feelings and the feelings of others. This character development can be the result of young potential leaders being exposed to the role modeling of adult significant others who act on their empathy by taking responsibility for the people around them who are in need. When young people witness those acts of empathy, even if they are just told vivid stories about them, they are inspired to emulate them in their own lives. The adage "kindness is contagious" is not a Pollyannish truism but an observable truth. Moses grew up in a nurturing, caring environment and developed into a caring leader as a result.

Whether or not they were born with it, leaders need to develop the capacity to identify with and feel empathy for other people, and the earlier in life, the better. Failure to develop the capacity for empathy has potentially severe repercussions for life and for leadership. Such uncaring leaders, while successful in the short term, will be shunned—or worse—in the long term. The chief American psychologist at the Nuremberg trials for Nazi war criminals after World War II noted that the common characteristic possessed by these German leaders convicted of war crimes was their inability to feel empathy for their victims.

Moses was fortunate enough to be raised by members of his biological and adoptive families who displayed strong feelings of empathy and caring toward him. He internalized those same feelings and acted upon them when he came of age and saw people being mistreated by others.

The Roots of Courage

What is it that makes leaders courageous? Some leaders may be endowed with a genetic predisposition toward risk-taking, or they may have courageous role models who inspire them. But more significantly, budding leaders must feel secure enough to make themselves vulnerable and be willing to bear the pain and assume the risks of leadership. This deep-seated feeling of security derives from leaders themselves being held, supported, and cared for by significant others. Ron Heifetz, director of the Leadership Project at the Kennedy School of Government at Harvard, borrows a term from psychotherapeutic literature to refer to this supportive nurturance as a "holding environment."[9]

While in Egypt, Moses was literally, not merely figuratively, held by two caring and courageous mothers. Even after fleeing from Egypt and being separated from his biological and adoptive families to live in Midian, Moses was fortunate enough to find a surrogate "holding environment." The household and mentorship of his father-in-law, Jethro, and the companionship of his spouse, Tziporah, restored his sense of inner security and bolstered his self-confidence. This enabled Moses to feel empathy and passionate concern for his tormented people, whom he had left behind in Egypt. Ultimately, the security of his home in Midian, along with the knowledge that his brother Aaron would be his partner, instilled sufficient courage in Moses to return to Egypt, confront Pharaoh, and lead his people to freedom.[10]

Peter Koestenbaum, a fugitive from Nazi Germany and later professor emeritus of philosophy at San Jose State University, sees courage in different terms—as an autonomous decision of individuals to tolerate maximum amounts of anxiety and uncertainty in the freely chosen pursuit of their convictions. Courage, to Koestenbaum, is the willingness to choose a painful path precisely because we are convinced that it is the only just thing to do. To enter a situation filled with tension, uncertainty, and risk and nevertheless to do what we believe is right is the very definition of courage.[11]

Two leaders in Genesis, prefiguring Moses, may embody this other definition of courage. Abraham's remarkable decision to risk his life and rescue his nephew Lot seems to fit precisely into Koestenbaum's paradigm. The same is true of Judah's decision to offer himself as a slave to free his younger brother Benjamin from a lifetime of servitude (Gen. 44:33).

By this definition, Moses and his parents act courageously throughout the second chapter of Exodus, primarily out of their individual decisions to do what is right and not necessarily because they feel held or otherwise supported. Using Koestenbaum's interpretive lens, Moses's residence in Jethro's household was a temporary respite before returning to the place of conflict, where he fulfilled his true destiny as a leader among his own people.

Courage and caring are seen by the Bible as the sine qua nons of leadership, regardless of their origin. They are the antithesis of the tyrannical leadership of Pharaoh, which relies on cunning, duplicity, and oppressive power to shape reality.

Principle 3: Develop Double Vision (Exod. 3:1–10)

Despite the urgent situation of the Israelites, and despite Moses's internalization and demonstration of caring and courage, it was not at all a foregone conclusion that Moses would become one of the most enduring and emulated leaders in human history.[12] After all, once he fled Egypt and settled down in Midian, Moses devolved from being a nascent leader of his people to becoming a meditative, bucolic shepherd of his father-in-law's flocks. For decades, he led a quiet, pastoral life far from the trials and tribulations of the Israelites. In addition, when asked by God to return to Egypt, he brought forth every excuse in the book to avoid doing so.

Why, then, did God choose Moses to be the leader of the Exodus from Egypt? What transformed Moses from the shy, bucolic shepherd into the fiery, passionate leader of the Israelites? What reignited his courage and gave him the inspiration to return to a people who had rejected him, confront a mighty king who wanted to murder him, and succeed in bringing his people out of slavery and to the cusp of the Promised Land? These verses provide the answer:

> And Moses shepherded the flock of Jethro his father-in-law, the priest of Midian; and he led the flock far away into the desert, and came to the mountain of God, to Horeb. And the angel of the Lord appeared to him in a flame of fire out of the midst of a bush; and he looked, and, behold, the bush burned with fire, and the bush was not consumed. And Moses said, "I will now turn aside, and see this great sight, why the bush is not burnt." And when the Lord saw that he turned aside to see, God called to him out of the midst of the bush, and said, "Moses, Moses." And he said, "Here am I." And he said, "Do not come any closer; take off your shoes from your feet, for the place on which you stand is holy ground." And he said, "I am the God of your father, the God of Abraham, the God of Isaac, and the God of Jacob." And Moses hid his face; for he was afraid to look upon God. And the Lord said, "I have surely seen the affliction of my people who are in Egypt, and have heard their cry because of their taskmasters; for I know their sorrows; And I have come down to save them from the hand of the Egyptians, and to bring them out of that land to a good and large land, to a land flowing with milk and

honey; to the place of the Canaanites, and the Hittites, and the
Amorites, and the Perizzites, and the Hivites, and the Jebusites. And
therefore, behold, the cry of the people of Israel has come to Me; and
I have also seen the oppression with which the Egyptians oppress
them. Come now therefore, and I will send you to Pharaoh, that you
may bring forth My people the children of Israel out of Egypt."
(Exod. 3:1–10)

The transformative event in Moses's life was his "double vision" at the burning bush. Moses saw a small, bare, and barren thornbush burning but not being consumed. This was not God producing an apparition, a magic trick to attract Moses's attention. Had God wished to grab hold of Moses's attention, God could have produced a volcano, struck him with a bolt of lightning, or simply tapped him gently on the shoulder, and said to him: "Moses, Moses, come, let's talk. We have something important to discuss together." God chose a burning bush that was not being consumed to symbolize for Moses the state of the Israelites in Egypt. Moses had a vision of his people that emerged out of the deeply buried memories of his past. He was haunted by this vision of his small, barren people aflame in slavery, aflame in subjugation and oppression, aflame in the terror of infanticide and, yet, somehow, by some miracle, not being consumed. His memories evoked his long-suppressed but still deeply held caring and empathy for his people. That was Moses's first vision.

Moses had a second vision, too. He had a vision of a land flowing with milk and honey—a lush, richly sensuous land, a land in which his beaten and barren people could flower and flourish again, a land in which they could become virile and vital again. In other words, Moses has a vision not only of the suffering past and painful present but also of a hopeful and promising future. His memory of the past, refracted in his vision for the future, stirred his passionate courage and sense of responsibility for his people.

This double vision is a paradigm of what makes a great leader. A leader must have a clear picture of the present—with all its problems and challenges—and a second vision of a brighter, more hopeful, more promising future.

Why is this so important? A person may find himself or herself in a very urgent situation, may care deeply about the situation, and may have the necessary courage to step forth and lead. But without this double vision, he or she is unlikely to succeed in leading the group to a better place. A clear and deep understanding of the present is required for being able to chart a direction for the future. If leaders do not know where they are and how they got here, it is nearly impossible to know where they want to go and how to get there. At the same time, they must be able to imagine the future destination in some of its essential features in order to lead the group. Not all of the details of their destination need to be worked out in advance. But at least an impressionistic picture of their "Promised Land" needs to be formed to give themselves and others a sense of direction and to inspire them to reach that destination.

A person who lacks the clear vision of the present and sees only the future is not a leader but a dreamer. A person who sees only the intractability of the present and fails to envision a brighter, more hopeful future will also fail to develop into a leader and will remain a passive follower, a prisoner of the status quo. The failure to envision a better future will paralyze the visionless leader and all his or her followers. Both types of vision at the same time are necessary for effective leadership.

God chose Moses because Moses possessed not only the requisite caring and courage but also the vision to understand the present and project a more hopeful portrait of the future.

How a Leader Develops Double Vision

For a leader to develop this kind of double vision, he or she must begin by paying careful attention to the present. It is not enough to have a sense of the past or even a vision of the future. It is only by focusing on what is happening—or not—in the present, by being a keen observer of the changes that are taking place around and within, that a leader can feel the sense of urgency for change.

In the most experientially intense and dramatic episode in all of Genesis, Abraham's near sacrifice of his son on Mount Moriah, we have a foreshadowing of this leadership principle. There, Abraham's sustained "vision," his noticing a ram in the underbrush just as he was about to offer up his son Isaac, is what changes the course of his family's and his descendants' history. Abraham names the mountain on which this transformative event takes place "the mount of the EverPresent God where there is vision" to stress the importance of "seeing" what is transpiring.

The Bible uses repeated visual imagery to stress the point that Moses first had to pay careful and sustained attention to what he saw in order to have a transformative revelatory encounter with God:

> And the angel of the Lord appeared to him in a flame of fire out of the midst of a bush; and he **looked**, and, behold, the bush burned with fire, and the bush was not consumed. And Moses said, "I will now turn aside, and **see** this great sight, why the bush is not burnt." And when the Lord saw that he turned aside to **see**, God called to him out of the midst of the bush.... [emphasis added] (Exod. 3:2–4)

So it is with leadership as well. To develop a leadership strategy for the future, we first have to be watchful of all the data that is informing the present. As author and leadership consultant Jim Collins points out in his best-selling book *Good to Great*, leaders must face the present in all of its brutality.[13] This sounds so simple that it may seem like a banal point not worth mentioning, but it is actually a crucial and often overlooked aspect of leadership. Getting lost in our own headstrong conception of reality by denying, ignoring, or belittling the data of the present means that we do not have an accurate assessment from which to start the leadership journey. It is like trying to read a map without knowing where we currently are on the map. Actually, it is worse, because not only will we not know where we are starting from, but we may also not know where we are going to— our direction and even our destination may differ depending on where we actually find ourselves in the present. It is only by knowing precisely where we are in the present that the possibility exists for receiving the inspiration—divine or otherwise—as to where to head toward the future.

But confronting the present is only the first stage in developing vision. In discussing the need to create a sense of urgency, the subject of chapter 1 of Exodus, I pointed out how the Bible in both Genesis and Exodus establishes an idyllic benchmark of goodness that is then contrasted with the degeneration toward evil. In Genesis, the goodness of creation and the Garden of Eden deteriorates into the corrupt and violent generation of the Flood; in Exodus, the goodness of the initial, bountiful experience of the Israelites in Egypt deteriorates into the experience of slavery and infanticide. Benchmarking an idyllic past is crucial in understanding the source of "visioning," the process by which leaders develop a vision for the future and guide their constituencies toward change.

In *The Leadership Challenge,* Kouzes and Posner report on a study done in the early 1980s that substantiates the importance of leaders' benchmarking their past to develop a vision for the future. The study was done by Omar El-Sawy, a researcher at Stanford University. El-Sawy was trying to figure out how to develop long-term vision in corporate executives. So he conducted an experiment in which he took two groups of corporate executives who were otherwise similar and gave them the following assignments.

To the first group he said, "I would like you to write a vision of your company for the next five years, and for your own leadership role within that company in that period of time. And if you can go beyond five years, all the better." To the second group he said, "I want you to write a vision of leadership for your company and for yourself, but, before you do that, I want you to write down significant events that have happened in your company's past and in your own personal past, especially in relationship to the company. Then, I want you to construct your vision for the next five years, and again, if you can go beyond five years, all the better."

Both groups carried out their assignments. They came back, and lo and behold, the first group, the control group, which was asked to build an abstract vision of leadership, without reference to past events, had a time horizon, a time span of vision of 5.11 years, and they didn't go much beyond that. Their vision was adequate, but sort of vague, not too richly detailed, and just a blueprint outline. The second group, the group that went back to its company's past, to their own pasts, and then constructed a vision, had an average time horizon of 9.18 years, almost double that of the control group. Moreover, the vision had more texture and more detail than that of the first group.

El-Sawy concluded that what we have operating here is something he calls the "Janus Precedence Effect." Janus was a strange-looking Roman god who had two faces, one facing forward and one facing backward. What El-Sawy was saying was that if we want to develop vision, if we want to be leaders, then we have to look forward into the future and backward into the past at virtually the same time. The past becomes a refracting mirror from which we construct our vision of the future. El-Sawy concluded that if we want to create better leaders for our companies, our society, and our communities, then we should have them study and recollect their own histories, their companies' histories, and their nation's history. From their history they will be able to fashion a long-term, big-picture vision for their future.[14]

El-Sawy's point resonates with what author and Nobel Peace Prize winner Elie Wiesel has been saying for many years—that our personal and collective salvation as human beings ultimately comes from our memory. It derives from our ability to journey back into our own pasts and retrieve whatever can help us navigate the shoals of the future. The patterns of the past, when reflected upon and viewed through a wide-angle lens, help us anticipate the direction of the future.

This truth was at the core of a leadership education program that I led in the Jewish community, founded and funded by Leslie H. Wexner, the visionary founder and CEO of Limited Brands Inc. The Wexner Heritage program was based on the premise that benchmarking and reflecting on the knowledge of our past is crucial to our ability to interpret the significance of the present and develop a vision for the future. The members of the program met every two weeks in groups of twenty, and we studied the story, traditions, and values that the Israelites developed during the major epochs of Jewish history. By studying and reflecting on these stories, they learned from their successes and their failures how to be better, more informed, more articulate, and more visionary leaders of their communities. For example, by learning how central education was in Moses's vision for sustaining the life of the Israelites, many of the Foundation's members altered their philanthropic priorities to support nascent educational efforts in their respective communities. Similarly, during the late 1980s, when studying the importance of rescuing those whose physical and spiritual lives are in danger, many of the members became institutional leaders of the effort to rescue Soviet Jews and Soviet dissidents. Their institutional leadership played no small role in bringing down the Soviet regime.

In some sense, what we did together was akin to going through a process of communal therapy. Just as therapists may take their clients on a journey back into their pasts to help them understand who they are, what their values are, and what their future can potentially become, so studying the Israelites' history and heritage was a form of communal therapy. It helped our members retrieve their people's past. It uncovered for them both the painful and the joyous moments of their collective history so that they could gain much greater perspective and clarity about who they were, what they might want to accomplish as leaders, and what might be the best process for getting there. It taught them not only the leadership skills but also the leadership values necessary for them to be successful and conscientious leaders in their communities.

This kind of vision is crucial to political leadership as well. Winston Churchill, prime minister of England during World War II, once said, "The farther back we look, the farther ahead we are able to see." Churchill was an eminent English historian who was able to frame World War II in the context of the much larger historical struggle of the Western world and English-speaking peoples. It was Churchill's backbone and eloquence in articulating that glorious past that inspired the British people to resist Hitler's onslaught while the rest of Europe folded before the Nazi war machine like a deck of cards.[15] His powerful vision and oratory also played a part in stiffening American president Franklin Delano Roosevelt's resolve, despite Congressional and popular American resistance, to come to the aid of the British even prior to the Japanese attack on Pearl Harbor, which catapulted the United States into World War II. Had it not been for Churchill's foresight and powers of persuasion, history might have turned out quite differently than it did.

For business and communal leaders like Leslie Wexner and political leaders like Winston Churchill, delving back into and reflecting on the lessons of the past is the most powerful vehicle for creating a sense of urgency in the present and a powerful, compelling vision for the future. So it is for all of us across the leadership spectrum who feel an urgent need to respond to external circumstances and aspire to be visionary leaders of our constituents. For us to generate change, we need to study the history and values of our group and use them as benchmarks with which to compare the current reality. The gap between the two fosters the sense of urgency in ourselves and others to engender visionary change for the future. And change is what leadership is all about.

Tweaking the Vision

As leaders begin the process of actualizing their future vision, it is crucial that they keep a constant check on the evolving reality. No matter how on target the original vision was, changes in circumstances in the current reality may necessitate modifying the vision for the future. Leaders can easily become imprisoned in their own fixed ideas and fail to notice that their dreams, if actualized under changed circumstances, could become a nightmare for their constituencies if not modified.

Although the original vision presented to Moses emphasized bringing the people out of Egypt into the Promised Land, there was an important part to that vision that is only hinted at during the negotiations between God and Moses at the burning bush:

> *And Moses said to God, "Who am I, that I should go to Pharaoh, and that I should bring forth the people of Israel out of Egypt?" And He said, "Certainly I will be with you; and this shall be a sign to you, that I have sent you; When you have brought forth the people out of Egypt, you shall serve God upon this mountain." (Exod. 3:11–12)*

In the context of encouraging Moses to confront Pharaoh with the request to allow the Israelites to leave Egypt, God gives Moses a pretext ("a sign") for why the Israelites need to leave. That pretext is the worshipping of God at "the mountain of God," Mount Sinai. Rather than ask Pharaoh for permanent political freedom to establish Israelite sovereignty in Canaan, Moses is to ask for a spiritual pilgrimage, only a three-day journey from Egypt, to engage in religious sacrifice and celebration. Although this particular ruse does not, and is not even expected to, work ("And I am sure that the king of Egypt will not let you go, if not by a mighty hand" [Exod. 3:19]), nevertheless it is meant to give some sense of reasonableness and legitimacy to Moses's request and highlight Pharaoh's rigidity and callousness in refusing to grant that request.

This supposed pretext to Pharaoh, however, turns out not to be an afterthought but a pivotal event in the Israelites' future. For it is at Mount Sinai that God takes the Israelites to be God's "kingdom of priests and a holy nation ... a treasured people from amongst all the peoples" and that the Israelites accept God's sovereignty, come to believe in Moses as God's messenger, and commit in public to follow God and God's commands: "Everything that God says we will do" (Exod. 19:8).

This covenant of mutual acceptance and obligation between God and the Israelites becomes central to their future identity. Had the Israelites, when they exited Egypt, been a disciplined, civilized nation with a moral system of justice, they could have made a beeline to the Promised Land. But this rabble of former slaves proved themselves to be anything but disciplined and civilized. As to justice, what did they know of justice except for the "justice" of Egypt, where the mighty ruled and the weak were oppressed? The vision of taking the Israelites out of Egypt therefore took on a crucial, additional dimension: taking Egypt out of the Israelites. To do that, they had to accept and commit themselves unequivocally to a new Sovereign (God); a new human leader to carry out the Sovereign's vision (Moses); and a new system of values, culture, and justice embodied in law (the Ten Commandments). Thus, what seemed like a throwaway line in the original vision, "they will serve God on this mountain," was amplified along the way to become the crucial bridging moment for actualizing the vision of bringing them to the Promised Land.

Their abject dependence and lack of discipline during the early journey out of Egypt (see the sections on credibility and trust and on achieving small victories) made it necessary for God and Moses to "modify," "tweak," or "fill in" the original vision presented to the Israelites from being merely a geographic one (Egypt to the Promised Land) to being a transformative, nation-building one (from frightened, dependent slaves to a disciplined, holy nation). For the people to be truly free from the house of bondage (cultural bondage and all) and to reach the proverbial Promised Land, they had to change not merely their residence but also themselves.[16] Their inability to do so in a single generation made it necessary for them to wander for forty years in the desert, die a natural death, and give birth to a new generation born in freedom, who internalized the discipline and values necessary to enter the Promised Land.

Leaders in business and public-sector organizations often face a similar challenge. They may be prepared to enter a bold new endeavor, and they can take themselves out of the old milieu, but they often feel challenged removing the old milieu from their way of thinking. The story of Exodus teaches us that adding the bridging piece of the vision, the Mount Sinai "mission statement," can enable the leader and the organization to transition from the old milieu to their bold new "promised land," and it may be the missing link that ultimately enables the venture to succeed.

Principle 4: Recruit a Guiding Coalition (Exod. 3–4)

No leader can lead alone. Leaders must recognize their strengths and weaknesses and recruit qualified people who share their values and vision and complement their skills. Leaders must solicit the support of others so that they arrive at a similar diagnosis of the present and buy into the leader's general prescription for the future. This core group needs to be able to talk openly among themselves and communicate to others the coming change, the reasons for it, and the value it will bring to the organization. Based on his thirty years of research in the field of leadership, John Kotter argues that any serious change project needs a core group of between three and five such individuals to guide the change process during the first year.[17]

This core team should include at least one individual who has the power and resources to fuel the effort, at least one strategic thinker who has the vision of the present and the future as well as the courage to lead the project, and at least one front person who will support the visionary and help communicate the message enthusiastically to the outside world. As the project develops, two other recruits will often become necessary: a person who has access to and the trust of a significant constituency that is necessary for the success of the mission but that is not within the sphere of influence of the original three, and an effective manager with particular tactical skills to implement the project. A leadership team, a "guiding coalition," of five such powerful and talented individuals has what it takes to initiate and lead transformative change.[18]

In the book of Exodus, God heard the cries of the Israelites and saw their dire predicament. God "knew" (Exod. 2:25) that while God possessed the raw power to face down Pharaoh and Egypt and free the Israelites from slavery, God needed a man like Moses, a human "interpreter," to explain to Pharaoh and the Israelites the meaning and purpose of God's power. Without a human interpreter, the plagues would have been understood by Pharaoh, the Egyptian nation, and even the Israelites as a string of unrelated catastrophes or perhaps the demonic work of one or several scorned Egyptian deities. God needed Moses to translate the plagues as a firm moral message to Pharaoh to free the Israelites from bondage, thereby establishing God's credentials and credibility with Pharaoh and the Israelites.

God chose Moses to be God's emissary to both Pharaoh and the Israelites because Moses had previously demonstrated the caring and courage to stand up and speak truth to power. God apparently hoped that he would have the temerity to do so again. Hence, despite hearing every imaginable objection from Moses, God remained steadfast in recruiting Moses.

*And Moses said to the Lord, "O my Lord, I am not eloquent, nei-
ther yesterday nor the day before, nor since you have spoken to your
servant; but I am slow of speech, and of a slow tongue ... O my Lord,
send, I beseech you, by the hand of him whom you will send ..."
(Exod. 4:10, 13)*

Moses knew that while he possessed certain qualities of leadership (e.g.,
caring, courage, and vision), he was not much of a communicator. One
imagines that after decades of living as an exile in Midian, his facility
with the Egyptian language may have been a bit rusty. Nor was he an
"insider" with the Israelites or with the Egyptian court. He had been out of
Egypt for so long that he did not have a good grasp of the politics there.
Shepherding his father-in-law's flocks in Midian did nothing to sharpen
his political skills or gain him political standing. He was concerned that
he lacked the authority to stand before Pharaoh and to command the
respect of the Israelites.

Then, too, despite Moses's displays of courage in his youth, he was
older now, had a wife and children to look out for, and was understandably unnerved by the thought of attempting to do it alone. Moses may
have even anticipated that his wife, Tziporah, would be unhappy with
his sudden, inexplicable decision to return to Egypt. She knew he had fled
Egypt as a fugitive of justice and that Pharaoh had ordered his execution.
She must have felt anxious about Moses's returning to Egypt as a wanted
man. In fact, on the way down to Egypt, in one of the strangest and enigmatic tales of the entire Bible, Tziporah's premonition of the danger
entailed in returning to Egypt was nightmarishly realized:

*At a night encampment on the way, the Lord encountered him and
sought to kill him. So Tziporah took a flint and cut off her son's fore-
skin, and touched his legs with it, saying, "You are truly a bridegroom
of blood to me!" And when He let him alone, she added, "A bridegroom of blood because of the circumcision!" (Exod. 4:24–26)*

While commentators throughout history have struggled to explain this
passage, one plausible reading is that it expresses the anxiety that Moses
and his family experienced on the way down to Egypt. Tziporah's utter-
ance about Moses being a bloody bridegroom should be read as an
expression of her anger and exasperation that he was leaving their safe and

secure home in Midian—endangering himself and perhaps his children—
to rejoin his endangered, circumcised people.[19] Tziporah and the children
apparently returned back home to Midian shortly after that incident.[20]
Moses may have intuited that he would be left alone, without the moral
support of his family, as he engaged in his mission. He needed someone
from inside the Israelites' own leadership ranks who would "hold him"
(see Exod. 17:12), who would accompany and support him while he
attempted to take hold of Pharaoh (see Exod. 4:4) and gain the confidence of the Israelites.

Hence, while Moses is prepared to be the second member of God's
leadership team, he negotiates in a shrewd and wily manner until God
agrees to send Moses's elder brother, Aaron, to support him and to function as his spokesperson. God recruits Moses for his courage, caring, and
vision, and Moses recruits Aaron for his political positioning, communication skills, and to have a family member whom he knew and trusted
stand by his side. Aaron's standing with the Israelites was so strong that,
upon his death forty years later, the Bible tells us all the Israelites mourned
his loss for thirty days, a testament to his leadership not even accorded to
Moses (see Num. 20:29 and Deut. 34:8).

Although Moses and Aaron may have had some sway over the men,
later on in the story they needed their sister Miriam to motivate, inspire,
and lead the women (Exod. 15:20–21). Miriam became the fourth member of the nascent guiding coalition. Just how important Miriam was to
their leadership enterprise becomes apparent a little over a year after the
Israelites leave Egypt. After Miriam criticizes her brother, Moses, for his
relationship with a black woman, she is stricken with leprosy, forcing her
to stay outside the camp for seven days. In response to her malady, the
entire people halt their long-awaited journey to the Promised Land until
Miriam returns into the Israelite encampment (Num. 12). Clearly, Miriam
established herself as a revered and pivotal member of the people's
leadership.

Later, when the Israelites began their journey in the desert and faced
an unexpected military threat from the Amalekites (Exod. 17:8–13),
Moses, knowing that he, Aaron, and Miriam were not military leaders,
brings Joshua, a general, as the fifth member into the guiding coalition.
Joshua, in turn, hews so close to the center of power that the Bible later
describes him as Moses's personal aide-de-camp "who did not budge from

the tent of meeting" (Exod. 33:11). When a threat to Moses's authority arose, Joshua was often Moses's point man (e.g., Num. 11:28, 32:28). In the end, Joshua was designated as Moses's successor (Num. 27; Deut. 34).

Together, those five—God, Moses, Aaron, Miriam, and Joshua—constitute the core group of leadership for the Israelites during the first year of the change enterprise. In the early going, they proved sufficient to accomplish the first objective of the Exodus—getting the Israelites out of Egypt and on the road to the Promised Land.

Principle 5: Establish Positioning to Secure Legitimacy and Authority to Lead. Build Credibility and Trust by Promising and Delivering (Exod. 5–14)

To lead any group of people, leaders need to establish positioning. To get their foot in the door of the people they are trying to persuade or influence, leaders need to empower themselves with the credentials and authority that will prompt others to give them a fair hearing. Then they must hold themselves in front of the people with the confidence and stature befitting someone with their credentials and title. Further, as leaders recruit the members of the leadership team, the leader needs to bear in mind whether the new members of the team will bolster their positioning with the people they represent and with their adversaries. A contemporary example of this positioning consideration is the way presidential candidates in the United States often select their vice-presidential running mates.

When God comes to Moses at the burning bush and solicits him as God's partner in leading the Israelites out of Egypt, Moses is not only concerned with his own, personal inadequacies as a leader—his poor language and communication skills—but also with his lack of legitimacy with Pharaoh and the Israelites. How will the Israelites know that he is God's legitimate emissary and not a manipulative charlatan? How will Pharaoh know that he is the legitimate representative of both his enslaved people and the Sovereign of the universe? Moses understands that he will not get a hearing from the Israelites and certainly not from the king of Egypt unless he establishes his credentials first. This is the real import of Moses's comeback to God: "Who am I that I should go to Pharaoh and free the Israelites from Egypt?" (Exod. 3:11).

Neither God's promise to be with him nor God's promise to bring the people to the mountain adequately addresses Moses's concerns. God may indeed always be with him, but God is invisible. Moses may hear God's voice, but neither Pharaoh nor the Israelites do. And God's prediction that Moses will free the people and bring them to the mountain constituted mere words that were not yet reflected in physical reality. Therefore Moses tries again and this time receives a somewhat more substantive response:

> *Moses said to God, "When I come to the Israelites and say to them,*
> *'The God of your fathers has sent me to you,' and they ask me, 'What*
> *is God's name?' what shall I say to them?" And God said to Moses,*
> *"Ehyeh-Asher-Ehyeh." "I Will Be What I Will Be." God contin-*
> *ued … "Now go and assemble the elders of Israel and say to them:*
> *'The Lord, the God of your fathers, the God of Abraham, Isaac, and*
> *Jacob, has appeared to me and said, "I have taken note of you and*
> *of what is being done to you in Egypt, and I have declared: I will take*
> *you out of the misery of Egypt to the land of the Canaanites, the*
> *Hittites, the Amorites, the Perizzites, the Hivites, and the Jebusites, to*
> *a land flowing with milk and honey."' They will listen to you; then*
> *you shall go with the elders of Israel to the king of Egypt and you shall*
> *say to him, 'The Lord, the God of the Hebrews, manifested Himself*
> *to us. Now therefore, let us go a distance of three days into the wilder-*
> *ness to sacrifice to the Lord our God.'" (Exod. 3:13–18)*

Although God reveals God's identity and assures Moses that the elders of Israel will listen to him and accompany him to Pharaoh, Moses is not so sure. Putting himself in the shoes of the Israelite elders, Moses feels that God is still begging the question. Moses's verbal claim that God has sent him doesn't prove anything: they are still being asked to rely on his testimony without good cause or corroborative evidence.[21] Nor was Moses confident that the Israelite elders would have the courage to stand with him shoulder to shoulder before Pharaoh and demand the freedom of their people. He remembered well that when an Israelite was being beaten by an Egyptian none of his brethren had the courage to save the Israelite's life. Why should things have changed now? In fact, later on Moses was proven correct on both counts: the elders do not believe Moses's words (uttered by Aaron) until after the miraculous signs are performed

(Exod. 4:30–31) and the elders do not, in the end, possess the courage to accompany Moses and Aaron to Pharaoh's palace (Exod. 5:1 and *Rashi*, op. cit.).

Moses is not yet convinced and seeks yet more proof:

> *But Moses spoke up and said, "What if they do not believe me and do not listen to me, but say: 'The Lord did not appear to you'?" The Lord said to him, "What is that in your hand?" And he replied, "A rod." He said, "Cast it on the ground." He cast it on the ground and it became a snake; and Moses recoiled from it. Then the Lord said to Moses, "Put out your hand and grasp it by the tail"—he put out his hand and seized it, and it became a rod in his hand—"that they may believe that the Lord, the God of their fathers, the God of Abraham, the God of Isaac, and the God of Jacob, did appear to you." (Exod. 4:1–5)*

These signs may prove persuasive to the Israelite elders (they are) and perhaps even to Pharaoh (they are not). But Pharaoh knows good and well—and if not, will find out soon enough—that Moses has not lived among his people for some forty years; hence he lacks positioning to be taken seriously as their legitimate representative. This is perhaps the reasoning behind Moses's final retort to God before acquiescing: "Please send someone else" (Exod. 4:13).

God responds:

> *There is your brother Aaron the Levite. He, I know, is an able speaker. Even now he is setting out to meet you, and he will be happy to see you. You shall speak to him and tell him what to say and I will be with you and with him as you speak, and tell both of you what to do—and he shall speak for you to the people. Thus he shall serve as your spokesman, with you playing the role of God to him; and take with you this rod, with which you shall perform the signs. (Exod. 4:14–17)*

Moses is pleased with this solution. With Aaron, a resident Israelite, accompanying him and doing the actual speaking, Moses and Aaron as a team will together possess the legitimacy to represent the people; and Moses, carrying the staff that will perform the miracles, will carry the authority of God as well. The rod will be God's scepter, as it were, which will give him and Aaron standing as divine representatives before the people and before Pharaoh.

The back-and-forth dialogue between God and Moses at the burning bush points to the importance of leaders acquiring positioning and legitimacy before they can even begin the process of building trust with their constituents and credibility with their adversaries. The credentials and authority that leaders and their partners possess and acquire are indispensable for moving forward and beginning the process of persuasion and change.

Building Credibility and Trust

Once leaders have acquired legitimacy, the formula for establishing future credibility and trust is deceptively simple: promise and deliver. Leaders must have the courage to share their vision with the people, and then have access to the resources to make that vision become a reality. Without communicating a promising vision for the future, leaders are unlikely to draw the attention of their followers; unless they deliver on that hopeful vision by accessing those who have the requisite power, the followers are likely to desert rather than stand by their elected leaders. Similarly, in challenging their adversaries, leaders must have the ability to follow up on their demands with compelling actions if they hope to establish their own credibility and earn their opponents' grudging respect.

In the book of Genesis, Joseph established his trustworthiness and credibility, first with Pharaoh's personal butler, whose imminent promotion he correctly foresaw, and then with Pharaoh's personal baker, whose imminent execution he also correctly predicted. Earning the trust of the former, a person with direct access to the king, led in turn to Joseph's being introduced to Pharaoh before whom Joseph correctly forecast seven years of abundant prosperity followed by seven years of drought and famine. By establishing his legitimacy as a prescient interpreter of dreams and building up his credibility and trust, Joseph succeeded in having Pharaoh appoint him to the second most powerful position in all of Egypt.

Likewise, chapters 5 through 14 of the book of Exodus deal with the challenges that the Israelite leadership team of God, Moses, and Aaron faced in establishing and sustaining credibility and trust. When Moses first returns to Egypt after his encounter with God at the burning bush, he and Aaron share the promise of redemption with the Israelite elders:

Moses and Aaron went and gathered all the elders of the Israelite people. Aaron related to them all the things which God had told Moses and performed the miraculous signs before the people. The people heard and believed that God had remembered the Israelite people and had seen their suffering, and the people knelt and bowed down. (Exod. 4:29–31)

In their initial attempt, Aaron and Moses succeed in gaining the attention and working trust of the Israelites' existing leadership. Soon, however, the reversals begin. They approach Pharaoh, who brushes them, and their message of redemption, aside.

And after that Moses and Aaron came and said to Pharaoh, "Thus said Adonai, the God of Israel: 'Send out my people that they may celebrate with me in the desert.'" So Pharaoh said, "Who is Adonai that I should listen to his voice? I never knew of Adonai, and I will not send out the Israelites!" (Exod. 5:1–2)

What Moses was afraid of when he conversed with God at the burning bush—that he would have no standing before Pharaoh ("Who am I to go before Pharaoh?"[Exod. 3:11])—has proven not to be the problem after all. It is God, not Moses, who lacks standing before Pharaoh!

Worse yet, the repercussion of Moses's visit to the Egyptian king is an intensification of the people's workload:

The same day Pharaoh commanded the taskmasters of the people, and their officers, saying: "You shall not give the people any more straw to make bricks, as till now. Let them go and gather straw for themselves. And you shall hold them accountable for the count of the bricks, which they made till now; you shall not diminish the count one iota. For they are idle; therefore they cry, saying: 'Let us go and sacrifice to our God.'" (Exod. 5:6–8)

The people will not only have to forge the bricks to erect the buildings, to build Pharaoh's fortified cities, but they will also have to scavenge the area to find and gather the straw necessary to form those bricks in the first place.

When the Israelite overseers learn of the added workload that Pharaoh has imposed on the people as a result of Moses and Aaron's visit to the palace, and are beaten mercilessly for the inability of their charges to meet their daily work quotas, their previous reliance on Moses and Aaron's promise of redemption turns to righteous indignation. "And the overseers said to Moses and Aaron: 'God should look upon you and judge you because you have depleted our spirits in the eyes of Pharaoh and his servants, putting a sword in their hands to kill us'" (Exod. 5:21). Nor is it only the Israelite overseers who have lost trust in Moses and Aaron. When Moses and Aaron repeat God's promises of liberation and redemption directly to the enslaved Israelites, "the Israelite people did not listen to Moses because of their shortness of breath/spirit and their hard labor" (Exod. 6:9). Moses and Aaron's early attempts at communicating God's message have degenerated into incredulity and mistrust.

Having suffered this initial setback, even Moses begins to lose trust in his divine partner and mission as he witnesses the plight of his people going from bad to worse:

> Then Moses returned to the Lord and said, "O Lord, why did You bring harm upon this people? Why did You send me? Ever since I came to Pharaoh to speak in Your name, he has dealt worse with this people; and still You have not delivered Your people." (Exod. 5:22–23)

At this moment, God and Moses's credibility are zero. Fortunately, God knows a thing or two about leadership after God's experiences in the book of Genesis and understands that the first step is to paint an inspiring picture of the coming redemption and thus reassure Moses:

> Then the Lord said to Moses, "You shall soon see what I will do to Pharaoh: he shall let them go because of a greater might; indeed, because of a greater might he shall drive them from his land … Say, therefore, to the Israelite people: I am the Lord. I will free you from the labors of the Egyptians and deliver you from their bondage. I will redeem you with an outstretched arm and through extraordinary chastisements. And I will take you to be My people, and I will be your God. And you shall know that I, the Lord, am your God who freed you from the labors of the Egyptians. I will bring you into the land which I swore to give to Abraham, Isaac, and Jacob, and I will give it to you for a possession, I the Lord." (Exod. 6:1, 6–8)

Having reinflated Moses's flagging conviction, God then works together with Moses, through the process of the plagues, to cultivate the respect of both Pharaoh and the Egyptian people, and they succeed in doing so by the night of the Exodus from Egypt.

Pharaoh's magicians are the first to acknowledge God's awesome power. After the plague of lice, the third of the ten plagues and the first one that the magicians are unable to replicate, they say to Pharaoh, with a combination of fear and awe, "It is the finger of God!" Still, "Pharaoh's heart was hardened and he would not listen to them" (Exod. 8:15).

By the end of the plague of hail, the seventh plague, even Pharaoh has come around, at least on the surface. The man who initially would not even acknowledge Adonai's existence, much less bow to God's demand to send the Israelites out of Egypt, assures Moses and Aaron (albeit, as it turns out, disingenuously): "I have sinned this time, Adonai is righteous and I and my people are the wicked ones. Pray to Adonai to stop the thunder and the hail, then I will send them [the Israelite people] out, and you will not have to stand before me" (Exod. 9:27–28). Of course, once the hail and the thunder subside, Pharaoh reneges on his promise and refuses to send out the people. Nevertheless, inroads are clearly being made. When Moses comes to Pharaoh announcing the imminent arrival of the eighth plague of locusts, Pharaoh's servants beg their king to reconsider his previous backtracking and capitulate to Moses (Exod. 10:7).

And Pharaoh's servants said to him, how long shall this man be a snare to us? Let the men go, that they may serve the Lord their God! Do you not know yet that Egypt is destroyed? (Exod. 10:7)

Pharaoh's stubborn incorrigibility continues. Nevertheless, by the time the ninth plague is over, when the Israelites seek to "borrow" silver and gold from their Egyptian neighbors for their upcoming "religious festival" in the desert, the Bible tells us that Pharaoh's servants and even the Egyptian people are graciously accommodating to the Israelites "because the man Moses was very great in the land of Egypt, in the eyes of Pharaoh's servants and in the eyes of the [Egyptian] people" (Exod. 11:3). Not only God but also Moses has achieved a position of power and respect that comes from consistently keeping one's word.

Finally, after the tenth plague, Pharaoh, under unbearable pressure, comes running to Moses and Aaron and says, "Arise and leave my people, you and the children of Israel, and go worship Adonai as you spoke ... and bless me too!" (Exod. 12:31–32). It takes ten plagues for God and Moses to build their credibility with Pharaoh and his people, but at the conclusion of that devastating tenth plague, Pharaoh finally relents and allows the Israelites to leave.[22]

While the leadership team of God and Moses is able to build credibility with the Egyptian nation through the ten plagues, it takes the Israelites a bit longer to trust the dynamic duo. Having been put through hundreds of years of slavery, the Israelites are less trusting of authority, and understandably so. It is not until they witness with their own eyes that their tormentors, Pharaoh and the Egyptian legions, who pursued them after they exited Egypt, have drowned in the Sea of Reeds, that they begin to trust the saving power of God and Moses: "And the Israelites saw the great hand which God used against Egypt, and they saw God, and they trusted in God and in Moses, His servant" (Exod. 14:31).

One of the central purposes of the ten plagues and the miracles at the Sea of Reeds was to build the credibility of the early leadership team.[23] By foretelling the plagues in advance and executing them as promised, God and Moses, who came to Egypt as "outsiders," built up their credibility with the Egyptian nation. Pharaoh and his people learned from the plagues, and through the drowning of the Egyptian army at the Sea of Reeds, that there was a moral power in the universe that would no longer tolerate their cruel and unjust behavior. The Egyptians came to understand the enormous pain and suffering they had inflicted on their former slaves. At the same time, the Israelites learned through the plagues and by witnessing the stunning events at the Sea of Reeds that there was a benevolent force in the universe who was willing to reverse nature to free them from the agony of slavery and infanticide. And they learned that Moses was God's emissary.

Nor is it only with the Israelites and Egyptians that credibility was built. The impact of the ten plagues and the splitting of the sea was felt by other nations of the region. Acting according to the leadership dictum of "act locally, think globally," God and Moses, through the medium of the ten plagues and the wondrous events at the Sea of Reeds, catapulted the Israelites into a force to be reckoned with in the ancient Near East. As the Song at the Sea exclaims:

> *The Peoples hear, they tremble; agony grips the dwellers in Philistia*
> *... All the dwellers of Canaan are aghast. Terror and dread ascend*
> *upon them; through the might of Your arm they are still as stone—till*
> *Your people cross over, O Lord, till Your people cross, whom You have*
> *ransomed ... For the horses of Pharaoh with his chariots and horse-*
> *men entered the sea and the Lord turned back on them the waters*
> *of the sea but the Israelites marched on dry ground in the midst of the*
> *sea. (Exod. 15:14–19)*

The Bible echoes the larger impact that the miracles of the Exodus had on the other peoples of the Near East when later on in the narrative it tells us about the arrival of Jethro, Moses's father-in-law, the priest of Midian:

> *Jethro ... heard about all that God had done for Moses and for the*
> *Israelites, his people, that God had brought the Israelites out of the*
> *land of Egypt ... Jethro said, "Blessed is God who saved you from*
> *the hands of the Egyptians and from the hands of Pharaoh, who*
> *saved the people from under the hands of Egypt. Now I know that*
> *God is greater than all the deities, for the very thing that they plot-*
> *ted [to drown the Israelite males] was done to them [their male sol-*
> *diers were drowned in the Sea]." (Exod. 18:1, 10–11)*

So powerful were the repercussions from the events at the sea that forty years later they are recalled by a lowly resident of the city of Jericho as Joshua prepares to conquer the Promised Land:

> *Joshua, son of Nun, secretly sent two spies from Shittim, saying, "Go,*
> *reconnoiter the region of Jericho." So they set out, and they came to*
> *the house of a woman ... named Rahab and lodged there. The spies*
> *had not yet gone to sleep when she came up to them on the roof.*
> *She said to the men, "I know that the Lord has given the country to*
> *you, because the dread of you has fallen upon us, and all the inhab-*
> *itants of the land are quaking before you. For we have heard how*
> *the Lord dried up the waters of the Sea of Reeds for you when you*
> *left Egypt, and what you did to Sihon and Og, the two Amorite kings*
> *across the Jordan, whom you doomed. When we heard about it, we*
> *lost heart, and no man had any more spirit left because of you; for the*
> *Lord your God is the only God in heaven above and on earth below."*
> *(Josh. 2:1–11)*

Yet we learn repeatedly from the Bible's narrative that even after leaders establish credibility and trust, those commodities must be constantly renewed. As we just read, while Pharaoh sent the Israelites out of Egypt, several days later he changed his mind and led the Egyptian army in hot pursuit of the former slaves. God and Moses, even after bringing the ten plagues and extracting the people from Egypt, had to engineer the splitting of the sea, rush the Israelites through the dry riverbed in an all-night voyage, and then drown the entire Egyptian legion at the break of dawn to keep intact their credibility with the Egyptians and the trust of their own people.

Similarly, although the Israelites trust and "believe in God and Moses" immediately following the splitting of the sea (Exod. 14:31), God and Moses seem to lose their credibility three days later as the peoples' throats become parched with thirst. Moses and God must then provide potable water, and later a daily supply of heavenly food (manna), to sustain their credibility with the people (Exod. 15:16, 22–25). And not all of the surrounding nations seem to be impressed by the miracles of the Exodus. Several weeks after leaving Egypt, the Israelites are attacked by the marauding tribe of Amalek, who threaten the morale and survival of the nascent Israelite nation. Moses calls on the military skills of his disciple, Joshua, and the moral support of his brother, Aaron, and his brother-in-law, Hur, to weather that crisis (Exod. 17:8–13).

Even after all of these confidence-building victories, God still feels the need to shore up Moses's credibility as God's emissary through the revelation of the Ten Commandments at Mount Sinai. On the day prior to the revelation, God reassures Moses, "And the Lord said to Moses, 'Behold, I come to you in a thick cloud, that the people may hear when I speak with you, and believe in you forever'" (Exod. 19:9).

Apparently, the people, for one reason or another, had begun to doubt Moses's divine connection. Perhaps the losses suffered at the hands of the Amalekites began to erode their confidence in Moses's leadership. Perhaps the arrival and counsel of Moses's father-in-law, Jethro, from whom Moses adopted the judicial system for the Israelites, led the people to speculate that the content as well as the system of justice was of human rather than divine origin. Whatever the cause of the Israelites' doubt, the revelation at Mount Sinai apparently did the trick of restoring the people's faith in Moses's divine connection:

And all the people saw the thunderings, and the lightnings, and the sound of the shofar, and the mountain smoking; and when the people saw it, they were shaken, and stood far away. And they said to Moses, "You speak with us, and we will listen; but let not God speak with us, lest we die." And Moses said to the people: "Fear not; for God has come to test you, and that His fear may be upon you so that you will not sin." Still, the people stood far away, and Moses drew near to the thick darkness where God was. (Exod. 20:15–18)

These episodes after the people's miraculous departure from Egypt point to the fact that even after establishing credibility with their adversaries and trust with their followers, leaders must continue to deal with the intervening crises and lapses of faith that can easily undermine their credibility and derail the leadership journey. The Bible teaches us that trust is the most precious commodity of leadership and the most difficult to earn and sustain consistently. By handling those "small" crises and unsubstantiated lapses successfully, leaders earn that trust, strengthen their credibility, and maintain the group's forward momentum. I will expand on this point later.

Principle 6: Communicate, Communicate, Communicate! (Exod. 15, 19, 24)

To develop and maintain loyalty, the leader must communicate the vision for the group and the values necessary to achieve that vision in a way that the people can internalize and remember. Because different people use different senses to learn and remember, leaders must use different sensory modalities—every available media—to transmit the message.

In leading Abraham first to the Promised Land and then to ever deeper levels of relationship and responsibility, God, in the book of Genesis, used multiple modalities to communicate: the verbal to describe the rewards of his journeying to the land; the kinesthetic when commanding Abraham to circumcise himself and the male members of his household; and the visual when establishing the fiery covenant of the pieces and sending the three angels to tell him of Sarah's impending motherhood. Cumulatively, God's leadership communications transform Abraham.

Although Abraham responds to all three modalities most people have only one primary modality, upon which they rely and find persuasive.

Some people are primarily auditory learners: they learn and are most inspired by hearing. For such individuals, the use of music as the vehicle to convey the vision is an especially powerful way for them to listen to and internalize the message. Therefore, as soon as the military threat of the Egyptian army has been dispelled, Moses leads the people in the Song at the Sea, which captures the emotional catharsis of the people's newfound liberation, the vision of God's loving relationship with the saved people, and the final destination of the people's journey:

> *Who is like You, O Lord among the celestials, who is like You, majestic in holiness, awesome in splendor, working wonders! ... In Your love You lead the people You redeemed; In your strength You guide them to Your holy abode. You will bring them and plant them in Your own mountain, the place You made to dwell in, O Lord ... The Lord will reign for ever and ever! (Exod. 15:11, 13, 17–18)*

In a more contemporary example, following the events of September 11, Americans at nearly every public gathering began singing "God Bless America" as a way of expressing their solidarity with each other and their determination to defend their way of life. Music is a powerful pathway to communication.

For others who are more visual learners, it is the use of visual metaphors describing God's special, protective relationship with the Israelites that excites their imagination and motivates them to want to connect to the leader and his or her vision. In the days leading up to God's dramatic revelation of the Ten Commandments at Mount Sinai, Moses used poetic, visual metaphors to represent the new relationship between God and the Israelites:

> *Thus shall you say to the house of Jacob and declare to the children of Israel: "You have seen what I did to the Egyptians, how I bore you on eagles' wings and brought you to Me. Now then, if you will obey Me faithfully and keep My covenant, you shall be My treasure among all the peoples. Indeed, all the earth is Mine, but you shall be to Me a kingdom of priests and a holy nation." These are the words that you shall speak to the children of Israel. (Exod. 19:3–6)*

These passionate visual metaphors created indelible images in the minds of the listeners and became motivating slogans for the people on their journey. Indeed, the use of metaphors is one of the central ways that leaders are able to powerfully communicate difficult and abstract ideas to their followers.

In the hours leading up to the revelation, God and Moses put on a stunning sound and light show to dazzle the Israelites:

> On the morning of the third day, there was thunder and lightning, and a thick cloud over the mountain and the sounds of the shofar were very loud, and all the people trembled in the camp ... and the mountain of Sinai was filled with smoke because God had descended upon it in fire, and the smoke rose like the smoke of a furnace and the whole mountain trembled. And the sound of the shofar continued very loudly, Moses would speak and God would respond in a thunderous voice. (Exod. 19:16–19)

This spectacular, three-dimensional experience captured the attention and the imagination of the Israelites. For those present it truly was an unforgettable spectacle: "And all the people saw the thunderings, and the lightnings, and the sound of the shofar, and the mountain smoking; and when the people saw it, they were shaken ..." (Exod. 20:15).

For others, who were kinesthetic learners, it was the blood and guts of the climactic covenantal ceremony at the end of chapter 24 that sealed their "buy in" to the covenantal vision:

> Moses took half the blood and poured it into bowls [for the people], and half the blood he sprayed on the altar [for God]. And he took the book of the covenant and read it aloud to the people and they said: "Everything that God said we will do and obey." And Moses took the blood [of the bowls], sprayed it on the people, and said: "Behold this is the blood of the covenant ..." (Exod. 24:6–8)

Although our own aesthetic sensibilities may be repulsed by the bloodiness of this ceremony, for those who participated in it whose learning style was of the kinesthetic variety, it was an emotionally powerful, visceral, bonding experience between the Israelites and God. By Moses spraying the sacrificial blood on the altar, God's receptacle, and on the collective people, a "blood bond" was established between the two, not unlike the blood bond of circumcision that brought Abraham, and later Moses's son, into God's covenantal relationship. In short, God and Moses used a variety of communication vehicles—some auditory, some visual, and some kinesthetic—to convey their leadership vision.

God and Moses also used the principle of continuous repetition to drive home their vision and values. To the casual reader, the Bible's admonitions often seem redundant, conveying the same information over and over again with small variations in a number of different places. However, God and Moses seemed to grasp that the danger of leadership is not in *over*communicating the message but in *under*communicating the message. According to Kotter, leaders tend to undercommunicate their message by a factor of ten.[24]

Moses precociously knew what twenty-first-century leadership experts have only recently concluded: that leaders must communicate the vision over and over, in every possible medium, if they are to succeed in leading change.

In counseling both corporate and communal leaders across North America, I have often heard them lament about how they delivered an important address or sent out a high-priority written memo about a significant change in their organization only to find that their message seemed to fall on deaf ears or was otherwise ignored. When I asked them how often they communicated the message and in which media, more often than not they said that they had attempted to communicate their message only once or twice and usually in the medium in which they, the leaders, felt most comfortable. I would point out to them that *expressing* a message is not the same thing as *communicating* a message. Communication comes from the word *commune*, "to intimately share or come together." The fact that the leader transmitted the message doesn't mean that the follower received and internalized the message. For communication to take place, repetition is necessary and the media used need to be ones with which the followers are most comfortable, not necessarily those with which the leader is most comfortable. Because different followers have different ways of decoding and internalizing information, multiple media need to be used many times over to have the best chance of achieving true communication and effective change. When these leaders went back and did a more thorough job of communicating their message in their corporate or communal settings, their communication success improved commensurately, a predictable result and one consistent with God and Moses's teaching and example.

Confirming Receipt of the Message

One way of assuring that genuine communication has taken place is to have our constituents explicitly and publicly commit to the terms of that communication. At Mount Sinai, this seems to have been what was intended by the thrice repeated shuttling of Moses up and down the mountain to verify that the people explicitly assented to the terms of the covenant and to the rules governing the revelation.

Toward the end of these protracted negotiations, God insists that Moses go down a third time to make sure that the people understand God's instructions clearly. Moses initially thinks this is an unnecessary trip down the mountainside. God, however, seems to understand what Moses does not: that charging the people does not mean they have internalized the charge.

In fact, despite all the shuttling and the Israelites' public commitment to keep the covenant both before and after the revelation of the Ten Commandments, they abandon that commitment only forty days later, when they worship the golden calf. Even public pronouncements and dramatic declarations do not necessarily add up to an internalized commitment. As God teaches Moses, even after being verbally acknowledged, new values and behaviors take time and multiple repetitions to become internalized, to become part and parcel of an individual's or a group's permanent character. Corporate and nonprofit leaders today would do well to internalize the importance of overcommunicating rather than risk under-communicating their message to their constituents.

Principle 7: Implement the Vision

Although leaders require vision before they can lead, once they formulate and communicate their vision, they need to begin implementing that vision on a day-in/day-out basis. Two crucial steps in the process of implementation involve generating a series of small wins and broadening governance to strengthen the leadership.

Generate Small Victories (Pick Low-hanging Fruit/Achieve Short-Term Wins) (Exod. 15–17)

Communication is talk. Ultimately, leaders must not only talk the talk, but they must also walk the walk—they must go through the arduous task of implementing the vision so real change can occur. To do so, they must be prepared to generate short-term wins to overcome the foreseeable as well as the unexpected obstacles that inevitably pop up along the way.

A long-term vision, by its very definition, takes a protracted period to actualize. Therefore, leaders must act to generate small victories along the way that enable people to reach the longer-term goal. The necessity of achieving small victories is for objective and subjective reasons. Objectively, certain smaller goals have to be achieved in order to realize the single larger vision. To get to the Promised Land, the people must make their way across the desert and physically survive the journey. Subjectively, the people need to feel a sense of momentum; they need to feel that forward progress is being made in order to bolster their confidence and belief in the worthiness of the journey. The more successful they are, the more invested the people will feel in their mission.[25]

Perhaps God learned this principle in leading Abraham. In Genesis, Abraham, whom the nineteenth-century Danish theologian Søren Kierkegaard, in his landmark essay, "In Fear and Trembling," referred to as God's "knight of faith," seemed to waver in that faith after being in the Promised Land for ten years without God's promises of progeny or land being granted to him. Although God had blessed Abraham with great wealth, God needed short-term wins to keep up Abraham's faith and belief in God's making good on God's other promises. God then entered into a symbolic treaty with Abraham to assure him of God's intentions regarding the land, the "Covenant of the Pieces" (Gen. 15), and shortly thereafter enabled Abraham to father his first son, Ishmael (Gen. 16). Later on, to secure a foothold in the land, Abraham purchases the cave of *"machpela"* a burial site for his wife, Sarah, and for the matriarchs and patriarchs that followed. Abraham's grandson Jacob, to gain his own foothold in the land, purchases a field outside of the biblical city of Shechem that later becomes the burial site for his beloved son Joseph. These small winnings of land gave some reality to God's promise to the patriarchs that all the land would be bestowed upon their descendants.

Now in Exodus, the psychologically fragile former slaves, recently freed from Egypt, need to be assured that their leaders can consistently provide the basic necessities of surviving the desert trek, lest they lose heart in their leaders and their mission and return, defeated, to their former Egyptian masters. Therefore, even prior to reaching Mount Sinai, where the covenantal mission will be formalized, Moses and God have to confront a number of mini-crises, any of which might have been enough to halt the journey and send the people scurrying back to Egyptian bondage.

Toward the end of chapter 15, only three days after the splitting of the sea, the Israelites travel inland through the desert and find themselves without a source of potable drinking water:

> So Moses brought Israel from the Sea of Reeds, and they went out into the wilderness of Shur; and they went three days in the wilderness, and found no water. And when they came to Marah, they could not drink of the waters of Marah, for they were bitter; and the people murmured against Moses, saying, "What shall we drink?" And he cried to the Lord; and the Lord showed him a tree, which he then threw into the waters and made the waters sweet ... (Exod. 15:22–25)

The people complain to Moses, who in turn cries out to God. God shows Moses how to sweeten the water and thus temporarily alleviates the crisis. Shortly thereafter, God and Moses preempt a second water shortage in the arid wilderness by leading the people to an oasis, where there is plenty of water (twelve wells, one for each tribe) and ample shade (seventy date palm trees, one for the descendants of each of the seventy Israelites who first came down to Egypt [Exod. 15:27]). Later on, as the people continue their journey in the hot and dry desert and are faced with a scarcity of water for yet a third time, God shows Moses how to extract water from a desert rock, a metaphor for the challenge Moses faces in bringing forth spirit from this hardened people.

> And the people thirsted there for water; and the people murmured against Moses, and said, "Why have you brought us up out of Egypt, to kill us and our children and our cattle with thirst?" And Moses cried to the Lord, saying, "What shall I do to this people? They are almost ready to stone me!" And the Lord said to Moses, "Go before the people, and take with you some of the leaders of Israel; and your rod, with which you struck the Sea, take in your hand, and go. Behold, I will stand before you there upon the rock in Horeb; and you shall strike the rock, and water shall come out of it, that the people may drink." And Moses did so in the sight of the elders of Israel. And

> he called the name of the place Massah ["testing"] and Meribah
> ["quarreling"], because of the quarreling of the people of Israel, and
> because they tested the Lord, saying, "Is the Lord among us, or
> not?"(Exod. 17:3–7)

Apparently, the people were not only lacking in water, they were also lacking in spiritual faith that God was really with them, which in turn undermined their faith in themselves and in the viability of their journey to the Promised Land. This third provision of water had to slake the people's physical thirst and satiate their spiritual qualms. Therefore, God instructed Moses to lead a delegation of leaders to the mountain of Horeb. On that mountain would be the rock from which the water would come gushing forth, and on which the Divine Presence and the Ten Commandments would be revealed several days later. The water rolling down the mountain trickled all the way back to where the people were encamped and drew them to the mountain of God. There, the Divine Presence would become manifest to them, as it previously became manifest to Moses at the burning bush on the same mountain. Thus, the people's physical and spiritual thirst would be quenched—they would be reassured that the "force" was indeed with them and their confidence in their mission and in their leaders would be strengthened.

The Israelites' journey shows us that people have certain basic survival needs that have to be satisfied before they can go on to higher aspirations. The great twentieth-century humanist-psychologist Abraham Maslow, in his book *Motivation and Personality*,[26] described a hierarchy of needs to explain human behavior. Maslow argued that people's needs for sustenance, security, and love (the "lower" half of the hierarchy) have to be satisfied before their aspirations for self-actualization, spiritual growth, and self-transcendence (the "upper" half of the needs pyramid) can be addressed. Three million people trekking through the arid, sweltering wilderness required a reliable source of water so that they could have the presence of mind to dream, rather than hallucinate, about being God's treasured people living in the Promised Land. Moses and God's ability to meet these fundamental human needs time after time was a necessary underpinning for their continued leadership. By showing that they could consistently produce what was necessary for the people to survive, they continuously made deposits in the people's "trust" account, upon which they could draw when the going got rough in the future.[27] "Nothing succeeds like success," the old adage goes. The leadership team's success in procuring water began to build the momentum of success for the people and instill the confidence in them that their leadership genuinely cared for them and had what it took to bring them to their ultimate destination.

In a similar vein, as they journeyed further into the desert toward Mount Sinai in Exodus 16, it was not water but food that was lacking. Having trekked for thirty days, the people had exhausted the dry, flat matzah bread that they baked on their backs as they left Egypt (Exod. 12:39). Again the people came complaining to Moses but this time with even more of a bitter edge:

> And the Israelite People said to them [Moses and Aaron], "If only you had allowed us to die in the land of Egypt where we sat around the pot of meat and ate enough bread to satiate us, rather than take us out to this desert to kill the entire community through starvation!" (Exod. 16: 3)

Faced with this accusation by the people of malignant neglect, Moses and God were able once again to provide for the people's needs:

> And God said to Moses, "I have heard the complaints of the Israelite People, speak to them saying, in the evening you will eat meat and in the morning you will be sated with bread, and you will know that I am Adonai your God." And it was in the evening that the quail rose and covered the camp, and in the morning there was a layer of dew, around the camp ... and behold on the surface of the desert there was a thin layer of white substance, thin like the frost on the ground. And the Israelite People saw it and said to each other, "What is this?" because they didn't know what it was, and Moses said to them, "This is the bread which God has given you to eat" ... and its taste was like a honeycomb. (Exod. 16:11–15)

The provision of the quail and especially the manna bread reassured the Israelites that God would not neglect their fundamental human need for sustenance as they journeyed through the desert to the Promised Land. God provided the newborn people with a sweet, white substance to suckle them in their infancy. The manna's pearly white color and its honey-like taste was also meant to hint at the ultimate destination of the Promised Land, "a land flowing with milk and honey."[28]

The prophet Jeremiah, who lived several hundred years after the Exodus, pointed to the willingness of the Israelites to follow God and Moses into the desert without preparing provisions for the journey as the source of God's affection, centuries later, for the people: "I remember your loving-kindness, the days of your youth as a bride, when you followed me into the desert, in a land unsown" (Jer. 2:2).

Having been provided with water and food in the desert, the Israelites continued their journey and suddenly confronted human enemies, who matched the natural enemies of hunger and thirst they had confronted previously. The people found themselves under attack by a marauding tribe of Amalekites, who picked off the old, weak and infirmed stragglers in the rear and sent panic throughout the camp.[29] The Israelites were now confronted with exactly what God had sought to prevent—a premature engagement in battle:

> When Pharaoh sent out the people, God did not lead them through
> Philistine territory even though it was the shorter route, because
> God said if the people encounter war they may lose heart and return
> to Egypt. Rather, God made them take a roundabout path by way of
> the desert to the Sea of Reeds, even though the Israelite People were
> armed when they left Egypt. (Exod. 13:17–18)

The challenge posed by the tribe of Amalek was particularly acute because the ultimate vision of settling the nation in the Promised Land would require a lengthy period of military conquest. If the people felt helpless dealing with the guerrilla attack of a desert tribe, how would they be able to overcome the military might of the seven established nations in the land of Canaan? God's concern that they would lose heart in their mission and run back to Egypt if they encountered a military threat before they were prepared to do battle seemed right on the mark.

Then, too, a military defeat at the hands of the Amalekites would quickly erode among the Canaanite nations the aura of invincibility and the psychological edge that the Israelite people had radiated after the ten plagues and the splitting of the sea. The Israelites depended on this aura of invincibility to get them safely through the desert and into the land of Canaan. Moses realized what was at stake and also acknowledged that he was unable to handle this challenge alone. Thus he recruited into the guiding coalition a fifth member, Joshua, who apparently had the military prowess to lead the people in battle. Moses also summoned two other strong supporters to bolster his leadership efforts, his brother Aaron and his brother-in-law Hur:

> *Amalek came and attacked Israel in Rephidim. Moses said to Joshua, "Choose men for us and prepare for battle against Amalek. Tomorrow, I will stand on top of the hill with the staff of God in my hand." Joshua did as Moses had told him, engaging Amalek in battle. Moses, Aaron, and Hur went up to the top of the hill. As long as Moses held his hands up, Israel would be winning, but as soon as he let his hands down, the battle would go in Amalek's favor. When Moses's hands became weary, they took a stone and placed it under him, so that he would be able to sit on it. Aaron and Hur then held his hands, one on each side, and his hands remained steady until sunset. Joshua was thus able to weaken the Amalekites with the sword. (Exod. 17:8–13)*

Joshua's military success foreshadowed his ultimate succession of Moses as the people's leader who would direct the conquest of the Promised Land. More immediately, however, the successful battle against Amalek, along with the provision of water and food in the arid wilderness, constituted the important small victories that enabled and encouraged the people to continue their journey to the Promised Land.

So it is for every leader with long-term goals—along the way, small wins need to be constantly generated to maintain confidence and keep momentum going in the desired direction. By consistently handling those "small" crises with success, the leader's credibility is strengthened and forward progress is maintained. The leader's success enables him or her to leverage the added credibility and tackle even larger issues necessary for generating transformational change. These larger issues may include appointing more appropriate people into the leadership ranks and codifying the new values of the organization. This is precisely what Moses and God did after their string of small victories in the desert.

Broaden Governance and Create Management Hierarchies (Exod. 18)

As the movement toward change begins to gain momentum through a succession of small victories, the core leadership group will, over time, require additional personnel to govern and manage the people as they transition from the old to the new. The need to broaden governance is not a sign of the failure of current leadership but rather of their burgeoning success. Yet bringing on additional management means that the leadership structure which has been governing until now, in which each person has a differentiated yet relatively egalitarian role, will have to turn into a leadership pyramid, with people on the top, in the middle, and on the bottom—a managerial hierarchy. It is possible that Moses initially resisted adding personnel to govern the people precisely because he did not want to create such a management pyramid reminiscent of the hierarchal leadership structure in Egypt.[30] Perhaps Moses did not trust the people from whom he would have to draw additional managers with the responsibility of governing themselves (the incident of the golden calf, which occurred only several weeks later, proved this lack of trust to have substantial basis). Or perhaps, as is often the case in rapidly growing institutions, Moses and the core leadership team were simply so overwhelmed with managing the burgeoning conflicts of the people that they did not realize they could no longer handle the responsibility of governance alone.

Finally, it is plausible that (as in the case of many chief executives who try to do everything themselves and who define themselves by their work) Moses was in a type of denial. Deep down, Moses may have intuited that he could not lead all the people by himself but he was unwilling to admit this to himself or others. He may have thought admitting he needed help would somehow evince vulnerability or weakness; in fact, the opposite is the case. It is the inability of a leader to ask for help that leads to organizational weakness. Leaders who are secure and lead balanced lives have the maturity to recognize their own limitations and are able to bring on people to share the burden of governance.

Often, in such circumstances, an outsider, such as a consultant, who can view the big picture objectively, will be called in to identify problems, suggest possible solutions, and then depart once the recommendations are implemented. If the consultant provides especially effective advice, he or she may be asked to stay on and help implement the recommendations. In the book of Genesis, Joseph, an outsider unsullied by the internal politics of the Egyptian court, played this consultant-turned-staff-member role when he was called upon by Pharaoh to interpret his disturbing dreams. Pharaoh was so impressed by Joseph's keen insight and his proposed solution that he subsequently appointed him to oversee the project that Joseph recommended to rescue Egypt from famine.

In the book of Exodus, Moses's father-in-law, Jethro, an experienced tribal leader in his home country of Midian, played this important consultant role for Moses and the Israelites:

> *And it came to pass ... that Moses sat to judge the people, and the people stood by Moses from the morning to the evening. And when Moses's father-in-law saw all that he did to the people, he said, "What is this thing that you do to the people? Why do you sit by yourself alone, and all the people stand by you from morning to evening?" (Exod. 18:13–14)*

Moses is trying to govern the people by himself. Jethro immediately grasps that this venture of bringing the people through the desert to the Promised Land can no longer be managed like the mom-and-pop store that has been providing for all of the needs of the people until now. Management by the seat of the pants is no way to shepherd God's growing flock. Moses, perhaps taken aback by his father-in-law's criticism, tries to parry Jethro's thrust, but the content of his response shows that he is too overwhelmed or too far steeped in denial to appreciate Jethro's salient point: "And Moses said to his father-in-law, 'Because the people come to me to inquire of God; When they have a matter, they come to me; and I judge between one and another, and I make them know the statutes of God, and His laws'" (Exod. 18:15–16).

Moses is explaining that the people are coming before him to adjudicate their conflicts and the important judicial role that he, Moses, is trying to perform. But that is not Jethro's point at all. Having spent the day observing the people approaching Moses, he knows exactly why the people are there and what Moses is trying to do. Either his son-in-law is being disingenuous with his reply because of his aversion to hierarchy, his distrust of the people, and his denial of his limitations or, as seems to be the case, he is too deeply enmeshed in the day-to-day job to see the larger picture. Therefore, Jethro explains that Moses cannot, and should not, try to govern the people alone.

> *And Moses' father-in-law said to him, "The thing that you do is not good. You will certainly wear away, both you, and this people who are with you; for this thing is too heavy for you; you are not able to perform it yourself alone." (Exod. 18:17–18)*

Like Joseph, Jethro does not simply diagnose the problem; he also proposes a potential solution:

> *"Listen now to my voice, I will give you counsel, and God shall be with you; Represent the people before God, that you may bring the causes to God; And you shall teach them ordinances and laws, and shall show them the way where they must walk, and the work that they must do."* *(Exod. 18:17–20)*

Jethro, an experienced senior official in his home country of Midian, and a God-fearing man in his own right, responds first to Moses's stated intention—teaching the people what it is that God wants from them—and then to Moses's human limitations and the people's need for a more expeditious system of justice. It is Jethro who first suggests that Moses assume the role for which he is later best known in the Jewish spiritual tradition: to be *Moshe Rabbeinu*—Moses, the master teacher of the Israelites. His primary role should be to educate and thereby lead the people, not to adjudicate and thereby manage their petty disputes. Who, then, will attend to the judicial needs of the people?

Jethro suggests:

> *"And you shall choose out of all the people able men, such as fear God, men of truth, hating unjust gain; and place such over them, to be rulers of thousands, and rulers of hundreds, rulers of fifties, and rulers of tens; And let them judge the people at all seasons; and it shall be, that every great matter they shall bring to you, but every small matter they shall judge; so it shall be easier for yourself, and they shall bear the burden with you. If you shall do this thing, and God commands you so, then you shall be able to endure, and all this people shall also come to their place in peace."* *(Exod. 18:21–23)*

Additional qualified people must be brought on board to help maintain order and dispense justice as they journey to the Promised Land. Moreover, these persons must be aligned in a managerial pyramid where only the most difficult cases will come before Moses. Appointing four ascending levels of judges to deal with the nation's legal and spiritual issues will free Moses to adjudicate only those issues for which his previous teachings and counsel did not provide guidance. This will lighten Moses's workload so that he does not burn out as their leader, and it will prevent people from getting frustrated and angry waiting for their turn at the bar of justice.

In addition, the expansion of the governing authority, despite creating new hierarchal strata, may generate greater "buy in" and support from the new appointees and perhaps from the people as a whole. In Jethro's vision, Moses's mission is to become a leader of leaders rather than the lone leader of his people.[31] By addressing all the issues that Moses raised and the issues that he was previously unable to articulate, Jethro convinces his son-in-law to follow his advice:

> *So Moses listened to the voice of his father-in-law, and did all that he said. And Moses chose able men from all Israel, and made them chiefs over the people, rulers of thousands, rulers of hundreds, rulers of fifties, and rulers of tens. And they judged the people at all seasons; the difficult cases they brought to Moses, but every small matter they judged themselves. And Moses let his father-in-law depart; and he went his way to his own land. (Exod. 18:24–27)*

Although Jethro departs at this point in the biblical narrative, less than a year later Moses asks him to stay as a sort of in-house consultant to keep an eye on the people as they journey toward the Promised Land. Moses so appreciated Jethro's valuable advice that he wanted him to come on board as permanent staff. As with Joseph, this scenario of a consultant being invited to become a valuable staff member is not an infrequent occurrence and helps bring fresh blood and an experienced outsider's perspective to a leadership team.

It is instructive to note the difference between Jethro's description of the prescribed appointees and the people that Moses actually chooses. Although Jethro advised Moses to choose "able men, such as fear God, men of truth, hating unjust gain," Moses chose "able men from all Israel." Perhaps the term "able men" is merely shorthand for the four attributes that Jethro had delineated and that Moses's appointees possessed those three additional qualities.[32] It is more likely, however, that Moses was unable to find people who met all these qualifications, or at least people who lived up to Moses's high expectations. Instead, he had to settle for the best available appointees on the market, "able men."[33] Given the historical and geographical context in which this story takes place, this interpretation is more plausible. After all, where were the Israelites of Egypt supposed to learn to be God-fearing men of truth who hated unjust gain? From the idolatrous society and travesty of justice that was ancient Egypt? God had not yet revealed the Ten Commandments or the series of just laws that were to govern the Israelites. Therefore, Moses, like many of us who have to fill positions of responsibility rapidly in our organizations, had to make do with what he found, at least for the time being. Later on, in the book of Numbers, these initial appointees will prove to be inadequate. Then, Moses will have to transfer some of his own spiritual vision to seventy additional appointees to help him manage the burden of leading the people.

These stories in Exodus and Numbers teach us that broadening governance and creating necessary hierarchies are important stages in growing a successful enterprise. Although three to five talented, strong-willed individuals may be enough to lead a change project in its first year(s), sooner or later the original guiding coalition will find itself overwhelmed by the success of its efforts, yet may fail or stubbornly refuse to recognize the need to add capable personnel. If not addressed early on, this failure to recognize our own limitations can stall and even derail the leadership effort. As the journey of the Israelites so vividly portrays, once one begins to build momentum through a series of small victories, the need to bring more people on board to manage the project is a necessary and logical step in implementing the vision.

It is crucial, however, to recognize which hierarchies are necessary and rationally justifiable. As we will see, a countervailing truth will be embodied in Moses's fellow tribesman Korach's revolt in chapter 16 of the book of Numbers. The creation of apparently unnecessary hierarchies— divisions of status that do not seem to the outside observer to be warranted or justified, especially ones tainted by apparent nepotism—is likely to generate problems and lead to failure.

Principle 8: Establish the Vision by Codifying the Values, Policies, and Laws Necessary for Actualizing the Vision (Exod. 20–23)

When leaders bring new personnel on board, they need to excite and inspire them with the promising potential of the organization and the organizational vision. Leaders should paint colorful pictures in words and images of the desired destination to fuel their new recruits' imaginations. This is what God did with Moses when he first communicated with him at the burning bush and later in Egypt, when God reassured Moses of the people's great future when Moses's confidence began to waver. But describing the final destination in sweeping, even romantic terms is not sufficient: leaders must also give their new recruits a viable strategy and at least some specific, detailed plans for reaching the envisioned destination. They must teach the new recruits the values, principles, and policies necessary for actualizing and sustaining the vision.

For the Israelites to merit settling the Promised Land and displace the native populations residing there, they needed to fulfill God's purpose in selecting them in the first place: to constitute a nation that could fulfill God's dream for humanity at creation and the Israelites' role in the community of nations. They needed to develop the character to be, in effect, God's partner, God's agent in history. They needed to embody a set of values and behavioral norms that would be a vast improvement over the indigenous and morally corrupt nations of Canaan that they were to displace (see Deut. 9:5).

God's dream at creation had been to create beings in God's own image who would act with sensitivity and responsibility toward God and other human beings. God's dream for the Israelites was for them to be the vanguard in fulfilling humanity's potential. They were to constitute a people who would serve as God's "kingdom of priests and holy nation." They would function as an exemplary nation to humanity, serving, teaching, and modeling how to live in passionate relationship with God and how to interact in responsible relationship with each other.

Now that Moses has recruited the newly appointed judges to work toward this vision, those judges have to be taught what justice means within that framework. It is not sufficient to appoint people as judges and tell them to go out and dispense justice. Different societies have different definitions of what is just and what is not. Egyptian society, where despots ruled cruelly and arbitrarily and their slaves were treated as dispensable chattel, was not the type of society God and Moses envisioned for the Promised Land. Canaanite society, in which children were offered as human sacrifices to pagan gods and in which incest, bestiality, and adultery were rampant, was not the type of civilization that God and Moses had in mind either.[34] The purpose of the Exodus was to create a new civilization with radically different ethical values and social norms than those that existed in ancient Egypt and Canaan. It was that innovative, humane society, what has been since called "ethical monotheism," that God and Moses envision taking root in the Promised Land.

Therefore, after appointing a hierarchical judicial authority in chapter 18 of Exodus, and describing the vision of covenantal responsibility in chapter 19, the Bible begins to spell out in chapter 20 the fundamental strategic values necessary for achieving that vision:

1. I am the Lord your God, who has brought you out of the land of Egypt ...
2. You shall have no other gods before Me ...
3. You shall not take the name of the Lord your God in vain ...
4. Remember the Sabbath day, to keep it holy ...
5. Honor your father and your mother ...
6. You shall not kill.
7. You shall not commit adultery.
8. You shall not steal.
9. You shall not bear false witness against your neighbor.
10. You shall not covet ... (Exod. 20:2–14)

These Ten Commandments were not merely ten specific laws governing human behavior. Rather, they conveyed the large, axiomatic, strategic values that were to guide the Israelites on their historic mission.

The first commandment identifies God as the freer of slaves. God chooses to preface God's laws as the one who rescued the Israelites from Egyptian bondage. Serving such a God and not serving another (the second commandment) means making the ideal of freeing human beings from captivity, enabling them to experience liberty and redemption, the core aspiration of God's people. The first two commandments might be thought of in contemporary terms as the oaths of loyalty to our country.

Not taking God's name in vain (the third commandment) protects this core value from being cheapened or belittled; it must remain central, sacred, and unique. The third commandment might be thought as the biblical equivalent of today's law against defacing the American flag.

The establishment of the Sabbath (the fourth commandment) does not merely establish the seventh day as a day of rest; it creates the institution of the "week." Unlike the twenty-four-hour day, the (lunar) month, and the (solar) year, the seven-day week is not a natural passage of time. The concept of a unit of seven days regulating people's rhythm of work and rest was not an accepted norm in the ancient world before God and Moses brought this concept to the Israelites, and the Israelites, in turn, brought it to the world. The six-day workweek capped by the Sabbath on the seventh day was a revolution in the ancient Near East.

The divine stamp of authority is given to the Sabbath in its first iteration in the book of Exodus, where it is established because, as Genesis describes, God created the world in six days. The logic of the fourth commandment is that if God can create a universe in six days and rest on the seventh so can and should human beings, who are created in God's image. Moreover, the purpose of God ceasing work on the seventh day and commanding people to do the same is to allow human beings and God to have the quality time to relate to each other that would otherwise not be available.

A second iteration of the Sabbath, in the listing of the Ten Commandments in the book of Deuteronomy, humanizes and democratizes the workweek, giving a day of rest not only to all the members of one's family, but also to one's servants, to the strangers in one's midst, and even to one's animals:

> Observe the Sabbath day and keep it holy, as the Lord your God has commanded you. Six days you shall labor and do all your work, but the seventh day is a Sabbath of the Lord your God; you shall not do any work—you, your son or your daughter, your male or female slave, your ox or your ass, or any of your cattle, or the stranger in your settlements, so that your male and female slave may rest as you do. Remember that you were a slave in the land of Egypt and the Lord your God freed you from there with a mighty hand and an outstretched arm; therefore the Lord your God has commanded you to observe the Sabbath day. (Deut. 5:12–15)

God self-identified as the liberator of the slaves in the first commandment, and the Sabbath continued the trajectory of the Exodus by God's freeing every human being from toil and labor, including the slave and the maid, one day every week throughout the year, throughout one's lifetime.

The commandment of honoring one's father and mother (the fifth commandment) codifies and sanctifies the institution of the family. In the master-slave world of Egypt, the integrity of the family was regularly violated. Masters had their way with a slave's wife, mistresses had their way with their male slaves, and the children of a slave belonged to the slave's owners. In a slave society, it was the master and mistress that a slave had to honor, not the slave's father and mother. The fifth commandment, one of several protecting both mother and father (Exod. 21:15, 17; Lev. 19:3; Deut. 21:18–21), restores the respect due to parents and the primacy and sanctity of the family as the fundamental building block of civilized society.

There is another point in the fifth commandment. Because the parents were the primary ones entrusted with educating their children about how to live in relationship with God and with each other (Deut. 6:7, 20–25), to respect them was to respect God and God's teachings. This continuum between parents and God will be further strengthened in Deuteronomy, where God is referred to as father (Deut. 32:6), God is implicitly depicted as mother (Deut. 32:13), and the people of Israel are repeatedly referred to as God's children (Deut. 14:1; 32:5, 19–20). Even the reward for following the divine "parent" is identical to the reward for respecting one's father and mother in the Ten Commandments (Exod. 20:12): "In order to extend your life on the land ... " (Deut. 32:47). This equating of honoring one's parents with honoring God accounts for the placement of the fifth commandment on the first tablet of the Ten Commandments in the list that otherwise enumerates one's responsibility to God. The command to respect one's father and mother includes the command to respect God and reinforces the previous four commandments that delineate *how* to respect God.

On the second tablet, the commandments not to murder, commit adultery, steal, and bear false witness (commandments 6–9) are designed to teach people how to act responsibly toward other human beings: to respect others' lives, bodily integrity, property, and right to justice. The Israelites' prior history in the book of Genesis was full of violations of these very values. Cain's murder of Abel, Ham's violation of his father's bodily integrity, Eve's stealing of God's fruit, and the false reports offered to Jacob by Joseph and his brothers are just some examples of the violations of the commandments codified in the book of Exodus. The tenth commandment, not to covet, the fifth commandment listed on the second tablet, like the fifth commandment on the first tablet, is meant to reinforce the preceding four commandments. The urge to murder, cheat, steal, or offer false testimony is usually motivated by greed and lust—the two elements that comprise coveting or desire. Coveting of others—

whether their property or their person—eats away at one's relationship with them and undercuts the social fabric. In the cases mentioned above that took place in Genesis, each of the violations of the four preceding values on the second tablet was precipitated by some form of coveting. Conversely, respect for, and responsibility toward, others and their property builds trust among people and reinforces social harmony.

The Ten Commandments address the fundamental spiritual and ethical values that the nation as a whole needed to internalize and inculcate in their children to become the kinds of people and the type of nation that God and Moses envisioned in the Promised Land. The commandments are the medium by which to teach the people how to be responsible to God and responsible to each other. The necessity of the Israelites' experiencing Egyptian slavery for hundreds of years in the first place only makes sense when understood in retrospect. It was a gruesome, experiential laboratory for educating the people as to what they should *not* become in their own land (Deut. 29:3). Egypt's idolatrous polytheism, sexual licentiousness (Lev. 18:3), and state-sponsored slavery (Exod. 1:8–22) shows the corruption and devolution of human society that the Bible depicted as the unfortunate natural state of humankind (Gen. 6:5,11–12; 8:21). The values embodied in the Ten Commandments are the corrective to that chaotic and corrupt natural human state. They establish the nonnegotiable laws of what constitutes a just society and a holy nation.

As we saw at the burning bush, God's vision was not merely for Moses to physically lead the people out of Egypt and bring them to the land flowing with milk and honey. The vision was to bring them to the Promised Land only after they underwent a national transformation on God's mountain and became God's special emissaries to the world (Exod. 3:12, 19:5–6). Egypt was not merely a geographical location but an all-pervasive cultural reality: Moses's task was to lead the people out of Egypt geographically, culturally, and morally. The geographical exodus took approximately one year; the cultural and moral exodus took nearly forty years and even then was not totally successful in rooting out the corrupting influences of ancient Egypt (see, for example, Num. 25:1–6, 31:9, 32:5–8). Still, whatever success was achieved can be attributed to God and Moses's teaching of the Ten Commandments and the laws of the covenant.

So, too, leaders need to set out in writing the nonnegotiable values and principles that are the bedrock of their organizations. Whether those principles are contained in a mission statement, a "covenant," or a simple list of "what we stand for," such a body of values is the key for anchoring the organizational culture on firm ground. The values must be clear, reiterated, and explained at every opportunity. Most important, they must be consistently implemented by the organization's leadership.

The Ten Commandments in chapter 20 were only the beginning; what followed in chapters 21–23 was an extensive set of detailed laws that expanded on the underlying values embodied by the Ten Commandments for the newly constituted Israelite nation. Collectively, these laws constituted the Book of the Covenant that Moses read to the people and to which they voiced their enthusiastic consent in Exodus 24:7.

If the Ten Commandments were the overall strategy, then the Book of the Covenant was the more detailed game plan for how a "kingdom of priests" was to evolve. As biblical scholars have previously noted, many of these covenantal laws were intended to reverse the perverse injustice that governed Egypt and much of the ancient world at that time.[35] For example, although the formal institution of slavery remained, it was thoroughly humanized in the Bible to protect the life, bodily integrity, property rights, right to rest, and eventual freedom of the slave. The sanctity of human life, whether that of prince or slave, was equally protected under biblical law—not the case in the ancient Near East, which was then under the jurisdiction and influence of the reigning Hammurabi Code. In that world, the powerful and wealthy were protected by the law, while the weak, and enslaved were not.

In the Book of the Covenant, laws regarding injury to others committed with criminal intent because of lack of vigilance or outright neglect conveyed the principles of both criminal law and the laws of torts and agency to the newly appointed judges and their subjects. Teaching the Israelites through these laws that they were legally responsible for their actions and the consequences of their actions was the way the Bible instilled in the people the lessons about responsibility embedded in the book of Genesis.

The delineation of an entire corpus of law to educate the newly appointed judges and internalize its values in the population at large was an essential step toward institutionalizing God and Moses's vision of forming a "holy people." Yet, as I mentioned previously in discussing leaders' need to overcommunicate, delineating a series of laws only once is not enough. Whenever an organization is expanding governance, its leaders must repeatedly communicate and educate the new managers/leaders as well as the people at large in the distinct values and culture of the institution. This is especially true in a case where the values and culture represent a significant departure from the prevalent norm of that time and place. If the new managers are not educated in the values and culture of the core leadership team using every possible opportunity and using all means of communication, then the values and cultural expectations of the society at large will overwhelm the group, and the innovative vision of the guiding coalition will erode and ultimately disappear. If, however, the new values and culture are consistently and repeatedly communicated to the managers and the people by word, by visual display, and by deed, then real change is more likely to be achieved.

Leadership is therefore rooted in learning. If the Bible portrays the character of God as learning how to be an effective and just leader in the book of Genesis, then, certainly, human leaders, and the people who were "chosen" to be God's servant-leaders in the world, need to learn the art and values of leadership. The detailed laws in chapters 20 through 23 set out to do just that.

Another crucial point in setting out new values, norms, and rules of governance is achieving "buy in" for those laws from your constituency. Both immediately prior to and subsequent to spelling out the detailed laws and rules that would henceforth govern the society, God and Moses made sure that the people gave their public, verbal consent to what was proposed. Before hearing the commandments and the laws:

> Moses went up to God, and the Lord called to him from the mountain, saying, "Thus shall you say to the house of Jacob, and tell the people of Israel" … And Moses came and called for the elders of the people, and laid before them all these words which the Lord commanded him. And all the people answered together, and said, "All that the Lord has spoken we will do." And Moses returned the words of the people to the Lord. (Exod. 19:3–8)

After hearing the commandments and the laws:

> Moses came and told the people all the words of the Lord, and all the laws; and all the people answered with one voice, and said, "All the words which the Lord has said will we do." And Moses wrote

all the words of the Lord, and rose up early in the morning, and
built an altar under the hill, and twelve pillars, according to the
twelve tribes of Israel. And he took the Book of the Covenant, and
read it in the hearing of the people; and they said, "All that the Lord
has said will we do, and obey." (Exod. 24:3–8)

The decision to accept God's covenant was both an act of freedom and
an assumption of responsibility by the Israelites. Both God and Moses
understood this, which accounts for the importance they attached to this
covenantal agreement.

To God's credit, both before and after stating the Ten Commandments and the laws of justice, God supports the people's buy in by communicating (via Moses) the rewards for adhering to the covenant. First,
Moses tells the people of God's promise that, in keeping the covenant,
they will be God's treasured nation:

"You have seen what I did to the Egyptians, and how I carried you
on eagles' wings, and brought you to Myself. Now therefore, if you
will obey My voice indeed, and keep My covenant, then you shall be
My own treasure among all peoples." (Exod. 19:4–5)

Then, Moses tells them that God will send an angel, who will assist them
in successfully conquering the Promised Land. Moreover, he assures them
of God's special providence that will protect them from the maladies
with which God will afflict their future enemies (Exod. 23:22–30).

God has learned something since first commanding Adam and Eve
not to eat of the Tree of the Knowledge of Good and Evil, lest they die:
threats alone are no way to get buy in from people. Only a soaring, positive vision like the one God gave to Abraham is likely to elicit an enthusiastic, positive response. Just as this juncture of broadened leadership
demanded greater delineation of the law, so, too, it required reiteration
of the promising vision to motivate the people to keep the law.

Principle 9: Institutionalize the Vision by Building Sacred Space and Carving Out Sacred Times
(Exod. 25–31, 35–40; Lev. 23)

It is not enough for leaders to state the group's values and vision in words
and promises or even codify them in mission statements and laws. Ulti-

mately, those words need to be institutionalized in reality to keep the focus of the group and constantly remind members of their values and vision.

In religious cultures, institutionalization takes place through the designation of the holy or the sacred. To mark something as holy, whether object, space, or time, is to build a figurative (in some cases, an actual) protective fence around it. It is to provide it with protective boundaries that set it apart from other like objects, areas, or times. Those boundaries give the object, place, or time a sacrosanct distinct identity. God describes God's self as *kadosh*, "holy" or "sacred." Out of God's sacredness, all other forms of sacredness are derived: "The Lord spoke to Moses, saying: 'Speak to the whole Israelite community and say to them: "You shall be holy, for I, the Lord your God, am holy"'" (Lev. 19:1–2).

The behavior taught in the Ten Commandments and the Book of the Covenant was one type of sacredness. Those laws institutionalized how people were to act in sacred relationship to God and to each other. They were designed to transform a group of former Egyptian slaves into a "sacred people." But there were two other forms of sacredness communicated to the Israelites and institutionalized by the Bible: sacred space and sacred time, each of which was meant to reinforce the people's collective story and communicate the underlying values of that story throughout the generations. Wherever and whenever God's presence became manifest, those places and times were designated as sacred.

Establishing Sacred Space

In the book of Genesis, the first sacred space and time is the Garden of Eden on the Sabbath day. Because God's presence was manifest to Adam and Eve in the circumscribed Garden and the Sabbath day was set aside from the task of working and preserving the Garden, making it possible to relate instead to each other and to God, that place and that time were sacred. After the expulsion of Adam and Eve, the Garden's sacred space was protected by an angel who sealed off its boundaries with a twirling, flaming sword, while the sacred time of the Sabbath was to be protected by the Israelites (Deut. 5:12).

In the book of Exodus, the first designation of sacred space and time takes place on the night of the tenth plague. Moses instructs the Israelites to mark the doorposts and lintels of their houses with the blood of the Passover sacrifice to differentiate them from the homes of their Egyptian neighbors.

The blood will be a signpost on your houses and I will see the blood and will hover over your houses and there will be no destructive plague among you when I strike in the land of Egypt. And this day will be a day of remembrance for you, you will celebrate it as a holiday to God for generations, you are to observe it as holiday for eternity. (Exod. 12:22–24)

Marking their doorposts and lintels separated the Israelites' homes from those of the Egyptians. It transformed those homes into makeshift altars, and the blood of the Passover sacrifice acted as a substitute for the blood of the lives of the people inside the homes. Thus, while the lives of the Egyptians' firstborns were taken by God, the lives of the Israelites' firstborn were spared, saved by the substituting Paschal Lamb. Like the sacrificial altar in the Temple, the houses, too, were dedicated to God (God's presence hovered over the houses) and were thus sacred. The events that transpired that night in the sacred spaces of the Israelites' homes created the basis for the sacred time of the first night of Passover—a night set aside each year to remember the redemptive events of that fateful night in Egypt recorded in the Bible.

In the book of Exodus, the second instance of creating sacred space is recorded in the events surrounding the divine revelation of the Ten Commandments at Mount Sinai. There, too, Moses had twelve pillars built to mark off the circumference of the mountain and an altar built on which to offer animal sacrifices. Both ensured that the people would not ascend the mountain and become unwitting human sacrifices by violating the mountain's designated sacred precincts. The events that occurred in that sacred space are also commemorated with a sacred day.[36] As with the Garden of Eden and the Israelites' homes in Egypt, the temporary creation of sacred space is followed by a permanent designation of sacred time.

The third instance of the designation of sacred space in Exodus is the lengthy description of the construction, dedication, and operations of the biblical sanctuary. The purpose of the sanctuary was to institutionalize and embody the vision and values of the Israelites' first year of existence as a free people.

This journey from Egyptian homes in the book of Exodus to desert mountain to golden temple is analogous, if sacrilegiously so, to a company that begins its life as a start-up in someone's garage or home office, then moves up to renting designated space in someone else's proper building, then finally builds permanent corporate headquarters to reflect the company's successful vision, values, and culture.

Institutionalizing our values and vision through the construction of our company's permanent, national headquarters requires advance planning. We must plan what the institution should look like, how it will function and reflect our group's values and vision, and what effort will be required to get it off the ground. There are four steps in building such a physical structure:

1. Planning the institution from bricks and mortar (including architectural blueprints) to furnishings and interior design.
2. Planning the campaign to raise the resources necessary to build the institution.
3. Motivating and overseeing the team that raises the resources and constructs the institution.
4. Celebrating the institution's completion in an emotionally charged and memorable ceremony (Exod. 40:34–38; Lev. 9; Num. 7).

In the Bible, these steps are largely accomplished in chapters 25 through 31 and 35 through 40 of the book of Exodus. Chapters 25 through 31 set out a detailed description of the biblical sanctuary. The sanctuary is to be built at the very center of the camp and be the focal point for the Israelite nation camped around it. The architectural blueprints and interior design are set out in incredible specificity. The materials necessary for construction and consecration are delineated. The individuals who are to manage the project are selected. And, in general terms, the fund-raising plan is set out.

Then, in Exodus 35:1–36:7, the Bible describes the actual fund-raising campaign. So successful is this campaign that the campaign must be cut off prematurely because the builders are inundated with materials and resources. Finally, the book of Exodus concludes with the building and assembly of the sanctuary in 36:8–40:33 and with the resting of the Divine Presence in the sanctuary in 40:34–38. In the books of Leviticus and Numbers, the inauguration ceremony is spelled out in great detail.

Metaphorically, the people's creation of a home for God reciprocates and brings full circle God's creation of a home for human beings in the opening chapters of the book of Genesis. It also prospectively provides for

God what God has promised to provide for the people: a home of their own in which to dwell among their loved ones. So important an event in the life of the people is the completion of the sanctuary that the Bible records—and celebrates—that event in three different books from the perspectives of God, the priesthood, and the tribal heads, who represent the people en masse.

In nearly all serious leadership undertakings, the raising of financial and material resources and the building and maintenance of a physical structure are necessary for addressing the needs of an expanding group and a successful enterprise. In part, this is so because a larger governance structure needs commensurately larger and more permanent resources in order to function. This is not only a "size" issue—a larger group requires larger governance, which requires larger resources and organizing structures. It is also a matter of communicating and reinforcing the group's values and vision to ever-expanding circles of people who do not yet "get" what the group's mission is about. Most people, most of the time are more concrete than cerebral; words and ideas go in one ear and out the other. What grabs and holds people's attention are concrete structures that embody what the group stands for and proudly communicate that identity outward.

Case in point: A group of people get together and want to worship as a community. They decide to meet on a rotating basis in each other's homes. The initial group is motivated and begins to worship, but as the group expands, and in order for the group to really take off, it will require a more permanent physical structure. Once the group has an address with walls and a roof and a sign outside, more people will be likely to try it out. If they feel comfortable with their experience, they will return again and again. At the beginning, a rented physical structure may do, but in order to sustain membership over the long run, a building will have to be purchased and designed to reflect the members' aesthetic tastes and underlying values.

So it was with the Israelites in the desert. Immediately following the revelation of the Ten Commandments, God said to the people that they could worship God in a very modest way:

> *And the Lord said to Moses, "Thus you shall say to the people of Israel, 'You have seen that I have talked with you from heaven. You shall not make with Me gods of silver, nor shall you make for yourselves gods of gold. An altar of earth you shall make to Me, and shall sacrifice on it your burnt offerings, and your peace offerings, your sheep,*

and your oxen; in all places where I cause My name to be pronounced
I will come to you, and I will bless you." (Exod. 20:19–21)

Moses and the people follow suit by simply building an altar and offering up sacrifices at the foot of Mount Sinai. Nevertheless, in the very next
chapter, God and Moses set about planning a far more elaborate and ele-
gant place of worship that will henceforth anchor and focus the relationship between the Israelites and God:

> *And the Lord spoke to Moses, saying, "Speak to the people of Israel,*
> *that they bring Me an offering; from every man that gives it willingly*
> *with his heart you shall take My offering. And this is the offering*
> *which you shall take from them; gold, and silver, and bronze, and*
> *blue, and purple, and scarlet, and fine linen, and goats' hair, and*
> *rams' skins dyed red, and goats' skins, and* shittim *wood, oil for the*
> *light, spices for the anointing oil, and for sweet incense, onyx stones,*
> *and stones to be set on the* ephod, *and on the breastplate. And let*
> *them make Me a sanctuary; that I may dwell among them."* (Exod.
> 25:1–8)

That the people needed such an institutional connection to reassure them
of God's abiding presence and concern became evident in their first seven
weeks of journeying in the wilderness. The people grumbled about the
lack of water and food, wondering whether God was really with them or
whether they had been abandoned to perish in the desert (Exod. 17:1–8).
True, God subsequently revealed God's presence in an impressive display
at Mount Sinai, but now that the people were supposed to travel away
from the mountain toward the Promised Land, God and Moses were concerned that they might again feel anxious and insecure, doubting whether
God was with them or not. After all, this is what happened forty days
earlier when they traveled inland away from the shores of the Sea of Reeds.
Although the people had witnessed God's saving presence there, within
three days they were doubting God and Moses's leadership. Now Moses
and God correctly anticipate a rerun unless they act proactively and give
the people some concrete assurance that God is present among the people
wherever they journey. Hence, after communicating the values and the
laws that comprise the covenant, they set about immediately planning the
construction of an elaborate Tabernacle to house God's presence and

direct the people's worship. That Tabernacle will become the tangible symbol of God's abiding presence among the people while they journey.

Paradoxically, as we will see, Moses's absence from the encamped Israelites as he and God are planning the Tabernacle acts as a catalyst for the people's insecurities and precipitate their creation of a surrogate god—the golden calf. But that is getting ahead of ourselves. The intention to build a physical institution to house God's presence in their midst was a good one, even if the absence of their leader during the planning process left much to be desired.

Raising Resources

Aside from preparing a detailed business plan, the best way to motivate people to raise resources for a capital campaign is to hire an architect, draw up blueprints, and, if possible, build a model of the planned structure. Once people have a clear picture of what the project will look like when completed, they are much more likely to be generous and forthcoming in the appeal for resources. In addition to using inspiring verbal language, communicating through the visual and the concrete is the best way to motivate people. Seeing is believing, and believing leads to action.

In the book of Exodus, before Moses goes to the Israelites with his fund-raising appeal, God plans with Moses, in intricate detail, every aspect of the Tabernacle. The text makes the point several times that God "showed" Moses what the Tabernacle and its furnishings were supposed to look like (Exod. 25:9, 40).

Although the Bible never says so specifically, it would be fair to assume that Moses sketched out what God was showing him just as he wrote down what God was telling him. This is especially likely to have been the case because Moses did not oversee the construction of the Tabernacle but rather commissioned two general contractors/interior designers, Bezalel and Oholiav, to execute the project. Without an architect's blueprint in hand based on what God showed Moses up on the mountain, it would have been impossible for these two talented individuals to direct the work. These blueprints may account for the Israelites' remarkable enthusiasm to the appeal for resources to build the Tabernacle:

> And Moses spoke to all the congregation of the people of Israel, saying, "This is the thing which the Lord commanded, saying: 'Take you from among you an offering to the Lord; whoever is of a willing

heart, let him bring it, an offering of the Lord ...'" The people of Israel brought a willing offering to the Lord, every man and woman, whose heart made them willing to bring for every kind of work, which the Lord had commanded to be made by the hand of Moses ... And they received of Moses all the offerings, which the people of Israel had brought for doing the work on the sanctuary, and they still brought to him free offerings every morning. And all the wise men, that did all the work of the sanctuary, came every man from his work which they made; And they spoke to Moses, saying, "The people bring much more than enough for the service of the work, which the Lord commanded to make." And Moses commanded, and they proclaimed throughout the camp, saying, "Let neither man nor woman do any more work for the offering of the sanctuary." So the people were restrained from bringing. For the stuff they had was sufficient for all the work to make it, and more. (Exod. 35:4–5, 29; 36:3–7)

When a project is marketed correctly with creative blueprints in hand, people view the opportunity to contribute material resources a privilege, rather than a burden. The people understood that this sanctuary would give expression to the pride they felt in being God's treasured people. Consequently, the people voluntarily contributed not just enough resources to complete the work but also more than was needed. This prompted Moses and Bezalel to halt the capital campaign even as the people continued to donate.

In building institutions, leaders must not merely create a functional space; it must be an aesthetically pleasing one that communicates the key ideas and values that their enterprise embodies. The Tabernacle was not only aesthetically impressive, built with silver, gold, copper, precious gems, fine woven fabrics, etc., but it also symbolically told the story and communicated the values of the Israelites. Each major object in the sanctuary was sacred and reminded the people of a key event in the first year of their collective journey:

- The altar upon which the sacrificial animals were offered reminded the people of their first communal altar and sacrifice: their homes-turned-altars and the Passover offering in Egypt on the night of the Exodus.

- The pitcher and washbasin reminded the people of how God and Moses had miraculously split the Sea of Reeds and then poured the walls of water into the sea basin over the pursuing Egyptian legions. (When King Solomon built the Temple in Jerusalem, the washbasin was appropriately named *yam*, "the sea").
- The table and shewbreads reminded the people of the heavenly bread, the manna, that rained down on the Israelite camp each morning to feed the people in the desert. Twelve breads were offered each week, a loaf of thanks from each of the twelve tribes for the manna that sustained them.
- The seven-branched menorah reminded the people of the gift of the seven-day week capped by the Sabbath day. The falling of a double portion of manna every Friday and lasting through the Sabbath was the way that Moses ingrained in the people the rhythm of the seven-day week and the freedom from work on the seventh day after centuries of uninterrupted slavery. Hence, the menorah was placed exactly opposite and cast a glow upon the shewbreads, the symbol of the heavenly manna bread.
- The incense altar, which emitted a cloud of sweet-smelling incense, reminded the people of the sweet cloud of forgiveness in which God hovered over the tent of meeting after the people's sin of worshipping the golden calf.
- The Ark containing the Ten Commandments reminded the people of God's revelation at Mount Sinai.

When the people gazed upon the completed sanctuary, with the cloud of the Divine Presence filling its precincts, they not only witnessed God's abiding presence but also remembered the many ways that God demonstrated divine love for the people: by gracing them with political and religious freedom, military victory over their oppressors, physical sustenance, spiritual respite, just laws, and compassionate forgiveness. These, in turn, reinforced the same values that were to become the body politic of the Israelites: freeing the slave, intervening against a person who pursues another with intent to harm, providing sustenance to the poor and the stranger, giving servants and animals days for rest and regeneration, upholding the law, and behaving with compassion toward one another.

Every organization, profit or nonprofit, that wants to institutionalize their own distinctive cultural values and instill a sense of pride in their employees or members, will pay as careful attention to the design and arrangement of their "sacred" space as God and Moses did with theirs.

Establishing Sacred Times

Edgar Schein, in his leadership classic, *Organizational Culture and Leadership,* formulates the primary role of a leader, especially a founding leader, as the creator of group culture. Building physical structures is one way that leaders demarcate their vision and values in the concrete, physical world. But time, not only space, is the stuff of which human life is made and is an equally important component in shaping culture.[37]

God and Moses did not merely lead the effort to establish a sacred physical sanctuary, but they also set aside special times in which the people would reenact the peak moments of their collective, historical experience. Although the biblical sanctuary and even the sanctuary's successors, the Temples in Jerusalem, are long gone, the sacred times established by the Bible are still part of the cultural tradition observed by millions of people around the globe. For the nearly two thousand years that the Israelites lived in exile without a sanctuary or temple and far from their homeland, it was their sacred times that held and brought them together as a distinctive spiritual community and that reinforced their common cultural and spiritual identity.

Regulating time and setting aside special (sacred) time to commemorate or celebrate key events in a group's history is an exceptionally effective way of institutionalizing the common purposes and experiences that keep people alive and bonded together. To cite just two examples, in the United States, the celebration of Thanksgiving marks the Pilgrims' arrival to the shores of the New World and reinforces the American value of freedom from religious persecution; July Fourth celebrates American independence and reminds us of the value of political freedom. America's sacred times, the national holidays of the United States, record the American journey from religious, political, and human persecution to freedom, independence, and human dignity.

Three millennia before America came into existence, the Bible set aside what it refers to as "meetings," which marked the journey of the Israelites during the first year of their existence as a free people. Each one of those moments was marked by a perceptible revelation of God's presence—in fact, the events that the holidays commemorate were the only times during the people's first year of existence that God's presence was manifested. Reliving those key moments of meeting God reinforced the memory and the lasting significance of those pivotal moments in the change process:

Sacred Days

- The first night of Passover relives the Israelites' newfound religious freedom. The seven remaining days of the holiday symbolize their collective political and cultural freedom from Egyptian slavery, culminating on the seventh day with the splitting of the Sea of Reeds and their military victory over the Egyptian army.

- The bringing and counting of the Omer and the offering of the two omers of wheat bread on the holiday of Shavuot (the "feast of weeks," also known as Pentecost) recall the miraculous falling of one omer of manna from heaven every weekday during the Israelites' forty-year trek through the desert and two omers of manna on Friday to prepare for the Sabbath.[38]

- The annual sounding of the ram's horn on the holiday of Rosh Hashanah recalls the inauguration and acceptance of God as sovereign at Mount Sinai, which was accompanied by blasts of the ram's horn.

- Yom Kippur, the day of forgiveness, recalls God's forgiveness of the Israelites after they violated the first two, perhaps three, of the Ten Commandments through the sin of the golden calf.

- Sukkot, the seven-day holiday of "Tabernacles," recalls the building and the weeklong dedication of the biblical Tabernacle. The eighth day, known as *Shmini Atzeret*, the "eighth day of assembly," celebrates the consecration of the Tabernacle's altar on the eighth day amid the assembly of the entire people. Because prayer was not yet established as a legitimate form of religious worship, the sacrificial service on the altar was the primary means by which the people could communicate and commune with God. God's fire, which dramatically appeared and consumed the people's sacrifices offered on the altar, signaled God's loving acceptance of the people's gifts. The altar's consecration ceremony took place on the first anniversary of the day God instructed Moses to begin the Israelite calendar and tell the people to prepare for the Exodus (Exod. 12:2ff.).

Reliving these peak experiences in the Israelites' "honeymoon year" with God established a culture in which the realities of the present were connected to and made meaningful by the sacred memories of the past. By focusing the people's attention back to these "sacred moments of meeting" throughout the year, the people were reminded of what was important to them collectively: freedom from idolatry and freedom from tyranny (Passover), caring for the hungry and those afflicted by poverty (counting the Omer and celebrating the feast of weeks), acceptance of God's sovereignty and God's rules for civilized behavior (Rosh Hashanah), repentance and forgiveness (Yom Kippur), and living a life in which God could dwell in their midst and in which they could live in communion with God (Sukkot and *Shmini Atzeret*).

Sacred Years
Aside from the yearly calendar, the Bible instituted two other sacred times, the Sabbatical and Jubilee years, to institutionalize the values of freedom and equality, the antithesis to the institutions of slavery and hierarchy that marked the culture of Egypt. The Sabbatical year prohibited working the land and collecting personal debts every seventh year. This gave the poor an opportunity to "catch up" to their wealthier brethren and get a breather from their economic misery. In the Jubilee year, all slaves were freed, and they and the landless poor returned to the ancestral homes they had sold to others in the preceding forty-nine years due to economic need. This enabled the poor to regain the dignity of living on their own land and gave them the opportunity to become once more economically self-sufficient through agricultural production. Just as God redeemed the Israelite slaves from Egypt with economic means so that they could begin their new lives with assets (see Exod. 11:3), so, too, did the Bible establish laws that enabled each generation to begin from a freshly restored economic base.

By setting aside these sacred years in addition to the yearly sacred days, Moses was able to reinforce his and God's values and vision of a society ruled by God and marked by freedom and equity.

In developing the institutional culture of an organization, leaders would be especially wise to use time and space creatively to convey the key moments and values of their institutions. The birthday of the organization, the achievement of significant milestones, and the inauguration of new headquarters are examples of three moments that could be annually marked and celebrated in order to teach and instill organizational history and pride in the participants. In addition, the nation's sacred times are other occasions when an organization's mission can be celebrated by tying in the organization's mission to the nation's values. Finally, the architecture and interior design of an institution's physical structure should express the distinctiveness of the organizational vision in a way that members of the organization will understand and value.

In sum, the implementation and institutionalization of the vision that would bring the people to the Promised Land required several key intermediate steps along the way: generating a series of small victories; bringing more qualified people into the governance structure; delineating the values and laws that would shape the new culture and behavior of the people; and creating sacred space and sacred times that would anchor and unify the people by institutionalizing their memories, vision, and values. Every large-scale leadership project requires similar mediating steps to achieve the final goal. The order and time frame in which these steps occur is less important than that these steps take place to move the vision from conception to reality to permanence.

Principle 10: Protect the Vision by Dealing Decisively with Detractors (Exod. 32–33)

One of the great dangers of any change effort occurs when leaders declare victory too soon. Just when it seems that everything is going smoothly and proceeding according to plan, there is usually an undercurrent of potential trouble brewing to which the leader needs to be attentive. It cannot be otherwise. If real change is taking place, then real resistance should be fermenting and brewing just beneath the surface as well. Only if the change is cosmetic and merely structural will resistance be minimal or easily dealt with. If people's positions, lifestyles, and vested interests are being affected, then chances are they will not accept change without putting up a fight and picking the right moment to do so.

Often, the "right moment to do so" is when the leaders of the change effort are busy celebrating an early victory. Celebration, while being an important reinforcement for group identity, brings vulnerability. Leaders may become distracted by the festivities of the celebration, let down their guard, and fail to focus on the challenges that still remain. They may feel on some unconscious or conscious level that, having achieved an early victory, they can sit back and rest on their laurels.

This is apparently what happened with Moses and the Israelites after the mass covenant ceremony at Mount Sinai. God's presence and the Ten Commandments had been revealed. A huge communal feast was held. On the heels of this celebratory feast, feeling bolstered and perhaps overconfident by the entire people's twice-repeated verbal acceptance of God's sovereignty and the covenant, Moses climbed to the top of the mountain for forty days and nights to receive from God the stone tablets containing the Ten Commandments and instructions for building the Tabernacle.

In the interim, resistors to the new order, who had been lying low, cowered by the intimidating presence of Moses and the revelation of God, seized upon the feeling of victory and Moses's lengthy absence. Drawing on the people's lack of confidence and emotional vulnerability, they sought a visible and palpable surrogate for the invisible God of Israel and the absent Moses. In the process, these counterrevolutionaries almost destroyed the entire enterprise of the Exodus from Egypt:

And when the people saw that Moses delayed to come down from the mount, the people gathered themselves together to Aaron, and said to him, "Arise, make us a god, that shall go before us; and as for this Moses, the man who brought us out of the land of Egypt, we do not know what became of him." And Aaron said to them, "Take off the golden earrings which are in the ears of your wives, of your sons, and of your daughters, and bring them to me." And all the people took off the golden earrings which were in their ears, and brought them to Aaron. And he received them from their hand, and fashioned them with a graving tool into a molten calf; and they said: "These are your gods, O Israel, which brought you up out of the land of Egypt!" And when Aaron saw it, he built an altar before it; and Aaron made a proclamation, and said, "Tomorrow is a feast to the Lord!" And they rose up early on the next day, and offered burnt offerings, and brought peace offerings; and the people sat down to eat and to drink, and rose up to play.

> *And the Lord said to Moses, "Go down! For your people, whom you brought out of the land of Egypt, have corrupted themselves; They have turned aside quickly from the way which I commanded them; they have made them a molten calf, and have worshipped it, and have sacrificed to it, and said, 'These are your gods, O Israel, which have brought you out of the land of Egypt.'" And the Lord said to Moses, "I have seen this people, and, behold, it is a stiff-necked people; Now therefore let me alone, that my anger may burn hot against them, and that I may consume them; and I will make of you a great nation." (Exod. 32:1–10)*

The resistance to Moses's leadership, and to the civilizing values that he attempted to teach the people, should have come as no surprise either to him or to God. In fact, one contemporary political scientist, Michael Walzer, author of *Exodus and Revolution,* suggests that God (and Moses?) purposely create a vacuum of leadership to instigate the resistors to come out of the woodwork and show their true colors. By doing so, the detractors are exposed as the philo-Egyptian fifth columnists that they really are, which allows Moses to execute them in a pique of summary justice without due process of law:

> *And Moses turned, and went down from the mount, and the two tablets of the Testimony were in his hand … And it came to pass, as soon as he came near to the camp, that he saw the calf, and the dancing; and Moses's anger burned hot, and he threw the tablets from his hands, and broke them beneath the mount. And he took the calf which they had made, and burned it in the fire, and ground it to powder, and scattered it upon the water, and made the people of Israel drink of it … And when Moses saw that the people were wild [literally, "Pharaohitic"] … Then Moses stood in the gate of the camp, and said, "Who is on the Lord's side? Let him come to me." And all the Levites gathered themselves together to him. And he said to them, "Thus said the Lord, God of Israel, 'Put every man his sword by his side, and go in and out from gate to gate throughout the camp, and slay every man his brother, and every man his companion, and every man his neighbor.'" And the Levites did according to the word of Moses; and there fell of the people that day about three thousand men. (Exod. 32:14, 19–20, 25–28)*

Walzer's contemporary reading of the golden calf episode as a sort of Leninist purge of the counterrevolutionaries has ancient echoes in a passage found in the later book of Ezekiel:

> *"As I remonstrated with your fathers in the wilderness of the land of Egypt, so will I remonstrate with you," says the Lord God. "And I will make you pass under the rod, and I will bring you into the bond of the covenant; and I will purge out from among you the rebels, and those who transgress against me; I will bring them out from the country where they sojourn, and they shall not enter into the Land of Israel; and you shall know that I am the Lord." (Ezek. 20:36–38)*

Both Ezekiel and the astute contemporary reader assume that the rise of resistance to Moses was so obviously expected that the entire episode can only be seen as God and Moses's way of removing the leaders of that resistance before commencing the next step of the journey to the Promised Land. They assume that smart leaders would know and expect there to be dangerous detractors to the vision and would have concocted a Machiavellian type of plan to purge them from their midst and thus preempt them from succeeding.

Even a more benign, straightforward reading of the text, which assumes no such cynical forethought or devious divine intent, still ends up teaching us the same lesson: radical change will generate radical opposition. A people enslaved by and steeped in Egyptian culture for hundreds of years cannot and will not delete that experience from their consciousness by witnessing miracles, sound and light shows, and other such episodic spectacles—however impressive—over a three-month period. Only a multiyear (multidecade?) process of education and disciplined practice as free persons, to counterbalance the centuries-long "education" and indoctrination they received as Egyptian slaves, can transform these Egyptian Israelites into the "kingdom of priests and holy people" about whom God rhapsodized at Mount Sinai. Fundamental change is almost always more difficult and far more time-consuming than leaders anticipate.

Leaders of serious change projects must anticipate serious resistance from those steeped in the old ways and must develop several strategies for dealing with that resistance. In Exodus, Moses deals with the instigators of the golden calf episode by executing the three thousand people who incited the worship of the golden idol. Why such a furious and lethal response in this case? Because of the dire threat that the golden calf represented. The Israelites, forty days prior, had celebrated their covenant with God and publicly proclaimed their fealty to their new sovereign: "All that God has spoken [in the Ten Commandments] we will do and obey" (Exod. 24:7). Now, only forty days later, they "corrupted themselves," to use God's words, by violating the first two, and possibly three, commandments.

The term *corrupting* is used advisedly by God. The last generation to have corrupted themselves was the generation of Noah in the book of Genesis; that generation was entirely wiped out. Moreover, Moses's generation does not violate the first two or three of the Ten Commandments in any old way: they do so by throwing their Egyptian jewelry at Aaron to mold an Egyptian idol (the bull-god of Egypt), and then engaging in festive orgiastic worship of their newly formed "god" (" … and they ate and drank and got up to play … "). This represents a symbolic repudiation of God, the commandments, and the entire purpose of their 210-year enslavement and subsequent Exodus: to teach the people what they should not become. As John Lightfoot, a Puritan preacher, put it in 1643: "Out of Egyptian jewels, they made an Egyptian idol … they intended to return to Egypt."[39] It is not only the physical return to Egypt that Lightfoot is reading into the people's actions but also the metaphoric return to Egyptian values. Moses had little choice, if he wanted to continue his mission, other than to take drastic measures and nip this counterrevolution in the bud.

Fortunately, leaders don't have to deal with detractors by killing or otherwise permanently removing them from the organization. Sometimes opponents can be co-opted into joining the guiding coalition. This is especially true when the opposition is motivated by self-interest—that is, regaining their privileged positions in the old order—rather than by deep-seated conflicts of values or principles with the leader of the new order. Under those circumstances, the offer of commensurate positions of leadership within the coalition and inclusion in the leadership planning process may not only quell their opposition but also win them over as leaders for the new vision. Similarly, some opponents can be bought off or persuaded to join the coalition by being offered specific things of value that matter to them.

Later on, in the book of Numbers, Moses will try each of these approaches. On at least two occasions he will try unsuccessfully to co-opt opposition interest groups. First, in the incident of the spies, which we will examine more extensively in Book III, he will appoint leaders of each of the tribes to embark on a "fact-finding mission" to the land of Canaan in the hope of winning their tribes' support for the coming conquest of the land. This plan, however well intentioned, backfires when the tribal leaders return from their mission. Rather than offering encouraging support to Moses's quest to lead the people to the Promised Land, they demoralize the people by concluding that they are incapable of conquering the land's mighty inhabitants. Their negative assessment will result in a forty-year postponement of the conquest and a life sentence in the desert for the generation that left Egypt (Num. 13–14).

Similarly, in the second case, Moses will try to co-opt the Levites, who have aligned themselves with the rebellion of Moses's fellow tribesman, Korach, by pointing out the prestigious position that they hold in the new order (Num. 16:9–10). This attempt will also fail to stem their revolutionary impulses. Thirty-nine years later, Moses will be more successful in buying off the two tribes that will threaten to secede from the remaining ten tribes at the conclusion of the book of Numbers. Moses offers them what they want—the verdant territories of the eastern bank of the Jordan River—in return for their leading the conquest of the land of Israel alongside their brethren.

The lessons of these attempts seems to be that, although co-opting and buying off the opposition may work when merely issues of power and material resources are concerned, if the resistance is motivated by an irreconcilable clash of principles and values, then attempts at co-option and neutrality are likely to fail. In those instances, leaders must be prepared, in one way or another, to remove the opposition from the organization in a rapid, decisive, and permanent way.

A third alternative is for leaders to muster the persistence to wear down the opposition over time, while maintaining the loyalty of their own troops. That wearing-down strategy, however, runs the danger of exactly the opposite occurring: one's supporters wearing down while the opposition gains strength and ultimately prevails. In a sense, that is what happens with the people who may have been responsible but were not executed by Moses over the golden calf. Their continued complaints and pining for their Egyptian lifestyle reaches its apogee after the spies return when they rally the people to go back to Egypt. This leads God to terminate the entire generation in the desert and permit only the next generation to enter the Promised Land. Perhaps if God had done away with a larger number of insubordinates immediately after the golden calf episode, as God initially thought of doing, the rest of that generation may have been salvaged.

There is also, of course, a fourth option, and that is to surrender to the opposition and retreat from actualizing the vision. This in turn can take two forms—one is total surrender; the other is a temporary or partial surrender. In total surrender, one closes up shop and admits defeat; in partial or temporary surrender, one retreats from the original vision in order to regroup, come back, and wage successful battle another day.

The latter strategy may be thought of as another form of "tweaking the vision." In discussing the attribute of vision in chapter 3 of Exodus, I spoke of the necessity of tweaking the vision as circumstances necessitate. As leaders progress along the journey to their "promised land," they may have to modify the process by which they get there to accommodate the limitations of the people. But to modify the process by which we achieve our vision is not to change the ultimate destination; it must be only a modification, not a fundamental alteration. The danger is that leaders may be seduced into abandoning the essential vision and surrender because of the difficulties and resistances they encounter along the way.

Such a "tweaking" took place in the Bible on the way to the Promised Land. The change in process came as a result of the people's inability to adapt and live up to the standards and expectations that God and Moses set out for them. The event that triggered the modification was the episode of the golden calf; the event that sealed the modification was the second of the Israelites' two great deviations: the incident of the spies in the book of Numbers, which we will examine in depth in Book III. After the debilitating report of the spies, the pace of the journey has to be slowed from several months to forty years to allow the Israelites time to develop courage in themselves, internalize trust in God, and become self-reliant. Although the same destination, the land dripping with milk and honey, was reached, it required an entirely different generation of Israelites to actualize Moses's original vision. Moses retreated from his original vision of bringing the first generation to the Promised Land, regrouped with the next generation, and lived to witness the beginning of the process of successful conquest (Num. 21).

The bottom-line lesson for leadership is that leaders of serious change efforts must anticipate not only "push backs" from their constituencies but also "counterrevolutions," and they must have multiple strategies at their disposal to deal with them. Leadership and contingency planning go hand in hand. Leaders must also recognize that only sustained communication, using every available medium and opportunity over long periods of time, will consolidate their efforts at serious, "adaptive" change. Assuming anything less is naïve, and not what it takes to live and lead in the real world. It is the harsh, challenging, real world that the Israelites and their leaders enter in the book of Numbers.

Book III

THE CHALLENGES OF LEADERSHIP

Why Leaders Are Responsible for Their Followers' Decline

Knowing the principles of leadership does not, by itself, assure leadership success. We have to follow through and act on that knowledge. "Just do the right thing," like "just say no," is not nearly as easy as it sounds. As a leader, there are so many mistakes that one can make, especially under challenging circumstances. There are nearly as many actions that leaders need to avoid as there are actions in which leaders must engage. Even previously successful leaders, such as God and Moses, who, in the book of Exodus, exemplify the Ten Guiding Principles of Leadership (see page 83), commit in the book of Numbers eight egregious errors when faced with challenges to their leadership. The very values and principles that Genesis and Exodus teach us that leaders must practice—taking responsibility, demonstrating courage, communicating constantly, and sustaining trust and credibility—are also the values and principles that leaders tend to violate repeatedly when their leadership is challenged. To be forewarned is to be prepared.

What makes or breaks any group of people, including entire generations, are the values, skills, and actual leadership in real time of their appointed leaders. Groups succeed or fail based on their leader's skill in guiding and sustaining change in the face of adversity: in communicating and maintaining the urgency of the situation, in clearly and forcefully communicating why changes are necessary, in the trust that they are able to sustain with their followers by promising and delivering, in the credibility they are able to retain by demonstrating genuine caring and respect for their constituents, and generally, by going through the process described in the ten leadership principles embedded in the book of Exodus. Leaders who breach their followers' trust by abandonment or abuse, who unexpectedly change direction yet fail to communicate persuasively why change is necessary, who focus on managing processes rather than motivating people, and who overextend their authority and power, doom their organization and their followers to failure. As we will see in the book of Numbers, the leadership team of God, Moses, and Aaron makes precisely these mistakes and consequently dooms the first generation of their followers. At the same time, they learn from their errors and develop into truer and more successful leaders of the second generation after their failed experiences.

To appreciate the leadership narrative in the book of Numbers, we must recall the leadership narrative in the book of Exodus. The story of leadership in the book of Exodus is one of remarkable movement and progress. In tandem, God and Moses succeed in freeing the Israelites from hundreds of years of slavery. The people achieve political freedom, gain confidence and momentum on their journey, learn the basics of what will constitute their civilization, and are graced with God's intimate presence. These accomplishments accrue despite several challenges and one significant setback along the way—the people's worship of the golden calf—which, as we saw at the conclusion of Book II, the leadership and the people appear to have overcome.

The apparent success of the leadership team in the book of Exodus, makes the apparent failure of the leadership team in the book of Numbers all the more unexpected. If a leader's job is to generate and sustain change, then much of the book of Numbers is a story of leadership failure. Throughout much of it, the people psychologically and spiritually regress back to Egypt rather than progress toward the Promised Land. But why? What causes the people's reversal?

Indeed, it is difficult to understand why the entire enterprise of bringing the people out of Egypt and into the Promised Land implodes in the course of only several calendar months and several biblical chapters: Numbers 11 through 17. Although the traditional reading of the biblical text seems to put the onus of this implosion on the incorrigibility of the people, it seems upon closer reading that the people's leadership fails concurrently and, quite likely, precipitates the people's decline and disintegration.

In fact, we would have to hold the leadership accountable for the dismal devolution of their followers even if the leaders' failures had not been so apparent. Ultimately, when all is said and done, leaders are responsible for the welfare of their followers. The book of Genesis in its entirety teaches us that assuming responsibility, not only for the actions but also for the welfare of others, is the absolute essence of life and of leadership. It would make little sense, having hammered home that lesson over and over again in the book of Genesis, for the Bible to reverse course 180 degrees in the book of Numbers. As Rabbi Adin Steinsaltz, the brilliant contemporary scholar and translator of the Talmud, once shared with me in a personal conversation some twenty years ago, this is ultimately why Moses perishes in the wilderness. He must share the fate of his generation, whom he failed to ferry across to the Promised Land.

Where, then, is the leadership failure and responsibility to be found? Not merely in chapters 11 through 17 of the book of Numbers. Although the book of Exodus ended on a high note, there is unfinished business latent in Exodus that carries over to the book of Numbers.

This is similar to the latent link that we looked at briefly between the books of Genesis and Exodus. One cannot understand the story of the enslavement of the Israelites in the book of Exodus without tracing back their history to Joseph's enslaving of the Egyptian people in chapter 47 of the book of Genesis. In the Bible's narrative, Joseph is responsible for creating an all-powerful centralized government in Egypt that is then turned, upon his demise, against his own people.

Similarly, if the entire generation that witnessed the Exodus from Egypt is doomed in the book of Numbers to perish in the sweltering, barren wilderness without ever laying eyes on the Promised Land, then one has to trace their catastrophic decline back to the people's leadership in the closing chapters of the book of Exodus and the early chapters of Numbers. Catastrophes don't just occur to a nation, or a corporation, for that matter, out of the blue; they are precipitated most often by the earlier decisions of their leaders. This was true in biblical times, and it is true today.

Nor can one successfully pin all the blame on the Israelites' for their sudden turning toward evil, as most traditional commentators have done. First, the human condition is a constant. As I pointed out in Genesis, from the Bible's point of view, people have never been and, barring some fundamental genetic alteration, probably will never be good or civilized by nature. Civilization is a thin veneer that shatters into a thousand pieces when put under extreme stress. Almost any group, organization, or nation that is not educated and inspired from within and motivated and given incentives from without to behave appropriately, will, when put under anxiety and increasing pressure, act out its innate tendencies in aggressive, violent, and destructive ways. This is at least part of what the Bible means when it says in Genesis that God realizes "the nature of man is evil from its youth" (Gen. 8:21). Civilization and civility are possible only when people are educated and trained to be civilized.

Second, not only is the Bible's expectation of human evil a constant, but also, as we have seen, people, by their nature, will resist others' attempts to change them for the better. They will feel anxious at the thought of the unknown and will be afraid of the losses that accompany significant change, even when the change is for their own benefit. Change is disorienting. Change can take place, but only at the pace at which the slowest of the people can handle. This is a variation of what professor Eli Goldratt calls the "Theory of Constraints."[1] Change can be accelerated through positive incentives, persistent positive communication, encouraging actions, and sustained trust. Take away any of the above and change will take place at a snail's pace, if at all.

Third, it is not as if God and Moses did not know what to expect of this particular generation that they had to lead. Already in the book of Exodus they experienced the whining and complaints of the people, their insecurities, selective memory, and backsliding toward Egypt in the first year following their freedom from bondage. Neither God nor Moses should have been surprised by more of the same in the book of Numbers, the second year of their journey out of Egypt.

Nor could they—or an impartial observer, for that matter—really hold this people fully accountable for their ignoble behavior. Despite having witnessed a series of amazing miracles over a short period of time, a people that has been brutally oppressed and enslaved for successive generations could hardly be blamed for expressing insecurity and yearning for the known and predictable—even if oppressive—conditions in Egypt. Yet the responses of the leadership, both God's and Moses's, are wholly different in the books of Leviticus and Numbers than in the book of Exodus. Instead of being understanding, patient, and supportive of the people—a leadership strategy that kept the people on course toward the Promised Land during challenging times in the book of Exodus—both God and Moses in Numbers seem to behave in ways that could doom any generation of followers, not only the generation that was rescued from Egypt.

The failure of the generation that left Egypt to enter the Promised Land did not occur only because the people were evil and incorrigible—

they were, but they were also evil and incorrigible in Exodus—but also because, as paradoxical as it may sound and as difficult as it may initially be to accept, the core leadership team of God and Moses had not yet fully internalized the ten principles of successful leadership that they exercised in Exodus. Inadvertently, they doomed their followers in the process. Perhaps stated more correctly, the principles of leadership, like the Bible in which they are embedded, had not yet been written down and enshrined. Thus, God and Moses had to learn the "bible of leadership" together, through trial and error (as with the case of most learning, through more error than trial), to be able to crystallize and record it in the written form that we have today and teach it to future generations.

Unfortunately, instead of the downtrodden Israelites that left Egypt living to behold their children and grandchildren frolicking in the towns of Judah and the outskirts of Jerusalem, they were doomed, because of their leaders' failures, to a life sentence of wandering in the wilderness of Sinai and ultimately perished of old age in the desert. True, their descendants did make it to the Promised Land. Nevertheless, the generation that experienced the Exodus did not live to witness and behold their descendants' joyous arrival.

Although it is impossible to know for certain, based on what we learned about leadership in the book of Genesis and the first three-quarters of the book of Exodus, it is plausible that it could have been otherwise. The generation that left Egypt could very likely have been salvaged had the leadership team not made the fateful decisions that they did. The failure of the generation that left Egypt to reach the Promised Land in the book of Numbers is biblical testimony not only to that generation's stiff-necked resistance but also to the failure of their leaders, God, Moses, and Aaron, to overcome their leadership challenges and bring them there. Our advantage is that we now have their experience to learn from so that we do not do likewise.

The Eight Recurring Challenges of Leadership

1. To not abandon the people "like a flock without a shepherd"
2. To halt losing streaks ASAP
3. To "hold" the people and not to falter or otherwise communicate indecisiveness in their presence
4. To fulfill our promises and explain sudden strategic changes

5. To maintain the sense of urgency
6. To not overmanage and underlead
7. To avoid unnecessary hierarchies, nepotism, and even the appearance of impropriety
8. To compromise, be flexible, and not become Pharaoh

Challenge 1: To Not Abandon the People Like "a Flock without a Shepherd"

After Moses fled Egypt and settled down in Midian, the Bible tells us: "Moses was shepherding the flock of his father-in-law Jethro, the priest of Midian, and he drove the flock into the desert, and came to Horeb, the mountain of God" (Exod. 3:1).

In a sense, Moses never changed professions. He made a lateral move from being the shepherd of his father-in-law's sheep to being the shepherd of his "Father's" (i.e., God's) flock, the Israelites. He even shepherds them to the same spot, God's mountain, Horeb, also known as Mount Sinai. Once there, he communes with God and is told twice to return to his people—at the burning bush, to take them out of Egypt and after the revelation of the Ten Commandments, to, in effect, take Egypt out of them. Toward the end of his life, when Moses asked God to appoint a successor to his leadership, he resorted to the same shepherding theme:

"Moses spoke to the Lord, saying, 'Let the Lord, Source of the breath of all flesh, appoint someone over the community who shall go out before them and come in before them, and who shall take them out and bring them in, so that the Lord's community may not be like sheep without a shepherd'"(Num. 27:15–17).

Groups, whether comprised of sheep or human beings, require firm leadership. They need someone who will be a formidable presence in their lives to guide them toward greener pastures, toward a figurative "promised land flowing with milk and honey." Without the leader out front to guide them, individual members of the group, and the group collectivity, who depend on the leader for direction and assurance, will find themselves feeling lost, disoriented, and anxious.

As we saw in Books I and II, leaders must constantly renew their trust and credibility with their constituents. Trust is the glue that bonds the leader-follower relationship. It is therefore nearly axiomatic that leaders cannot disappear for long periods of time without undermining that trust and ripping the relationship asunder. As Bruce Soll, chief of staff for corporate and philanthropic leader Leslie H. Wexner, often said to me, "Showing up and being present for our followers is a prerequisite of leadership." This is especially true when a group is in its infancy and the connecting glue between leader and followers has not yet fully congealed.

When leaders, because of circumstances beyond their control, must absent themselves, especially during the early stages of their leadership tenure, they need to leave capable surrogates in charge and be precise as to when they intend to return. In addition, before they depart, leaders must assign the people a challenging but doable task to keep them productive, positive, and constructive in their absence. Finally, leaders must provide their surrogates and their followers with a foolproof way of getting in touch with them in case of an unexpected, dire emergency. The worst possible scenario is to leave a young group for an extended period of time, without a challenging mission to keep them occupied, without a sure date of return, and without a way for them to access their leader in case of emergency. Doing so creates a vacuum that will inevitably be driven by anxiety and filled with regressive and destructive behaviors (just ask any substitute teacher).

At the end of Book II, we examined the episode of the golden calf from the perspective of the leader's need to deal with detractors. However, to understand the narrative in Numbers, we have to examine the same episode from the perspective of the followers' need for the presence of their leader. When we do so, we realize that prior to the debacle of the golden calf, Moses did what he himself asked God not to do, forty years later, as he approached his last days: he left his constituents like "a flock without its shepherd." Moses should have known better. Moses, the faithful shepherd of his father-in-law's flocks in Midian, who drove them to the mountain of God where he experienced God's first revelation at the burning bush, should have known that he could not abandon God's flock after God's revelation of the Ten Commandments at Mount Sinai. Yet abandon them he did when God summoned Moses up to Mount Sinai to commune with God, study God's plans for the Tabernacle, and receive the stone tablets inscribed with the Ten Commandments.

> The Lord said to Moses, "Come up to me on the mountain and wait there, and I will give you the stone tablets with the teachings and commandments which I have inscribed to instruct them." So Moses and his

attendant Joshua arose, and Moses ascended the mountain of God. To the elders he said, "Wait here for us until we return to you. You have Aaron and Hur with you; let anyone who has matters to settle, approach them." When Moses ascended the mountain, the cloud covered the mountain. The Presence of the Lord abode on Mount Sinai, and ... appeared in the sight of the Israelites as a consuming fire on the top of the mountain. Moses went inside the cloud and ... remained on the mountain forty days and forty nights. (Exod. 24:12–18)

To his credit, before going up the mountain, Moses put two of his supporters in charge, Aaron and his brother-in-law, Hur, so that at least there would be competent and familiar people available to deal with the people's issues during Moses's absence (see also Exod. 17:12). What Moses did not apparently do, perhaps because he did not know, was to tell his leadership surrogates and the people precisely how long he would be away.[2] Nor did Moses leave the people with an important, challenging task on which to focus their energies while he was gone.

In addition, the people who encamped around Mount Sinai had no way of reaching Moses in case of an emergency. Why? Because as we saw in Book II, God had Moses repeatedly and absolutely forbid the people from ascending and even touching the mountain, lest they die (Exod. 19:12–13, 21–22, 24). In fact, even Joshua, Moses's faithful disciple, who was apparently an exception to this rule and was waiting for Moses's return halfway up the mountain, was wholly out of touch with the reality transpiring below because no one had the courage, in the face of Moses's multiple warnings, to ascend the mountain, report on what was going on, and ask Joshua for help.[3] Nor was Moses visible to the people—he had entered into the fiery inferno and terrifying cloud of smoke at the top of the mountain and disappeared from the people's sight (Exod. 24:16–18).

To understand the deeper psychological significance of Moses's absence at this point in the biblical story, it is useful here to return to a leadership metaphor cited by professor Ronald Heifetz, a psychiatrist by training, in his books on leadership, which I briefly mentioned in the Ten Guiding Principles of Leadership: that of the "holding environment." This metaphor emerges from the work of social scientists in studying infant and adolescent behavior vis-à-vis their parents. The theory of holding environments, like that of much of psychology, explains adult behavior in the context of human experience in the formative years of life, experiences that program our basic needs and instincts even as mature adults.

The child as an infant is held close to and nurtured by her mother and therefore feels safe in her arms (the primal, human "holding" environment). As the infant begins to crawl and soon turns into a toddler, the child's curiosity to explore begins to act in tension with the child's desire to stay close to the mother, the source of the child's warmth, safety, and nurturance. The child balances that tension by keeping the mother within sight, looking back frequently to make sure that the mother is still there as the child explores her world. As long as the child can see the mother, she remains within the now expanded holding environment. If the child looks for but cannot see or find the mother—that is, if the mother becomes invisible, then the anxiety of the child rises and results in the child's ceasing her exploratory behavior, crying out for her mother to return and hold her again. A parallel process takes place in adolescence, with the teenager exploring not merely her physical environment but her identity and the boundaries of her competencies. There, too, the knowledge that the parent is accessible and present for support, a far wider and more abstract "holding environment," to be sure, is crucial for the healthy and secure development of the adolescent.

A similar dynamic takes place with adults and in leadership situations, even of the most prosaic sort. For instance, should a leader of a seminar of adults excuse herself after 15 minutes of a two-hour session and walk out without indicating when she will return, without providing a way of being reached, without giving the seminar participants a meaningful, challenging, time-consuming task to complete in her absence, then the anxiety of the seminar participants will grow. Eventually, the group's anxiety will almost certainly lead to the participants getting up and leaving the seminar room after fifteen or thirty minutes of apprehensive bewilderment. For the seminar students to remain in class, they must feel "held" by the seminar leader—by the leader's physical presence, by a task that the leader has left the students to complete in her absence, or by the sure knowledge of when the leader intends to return.

In the book of Exodus, the people were only out of Egypt for fifty days when Moses left them and disappeared up the fiery, smoky mountainside. Moses himself describes the people as a nation akin to a suckling, infant child that needs constant attention and nurturing:

"Did I conceive all these people, did I bear them, that you should say to me 'Carry them in your bosom as a nurse carries an infant,' to the land that you have promised to their fathers? Where am I to get meat to give all these people when they whine before me: 'Give us meat to eat?'" (Num. 11:12–13)

A responsible mother would not leave her seven-week-old infant to a nurse's care for such a lengthy period of time to spend an extended honeymoon with her spouse. Nor should a responsible father expect that of the mother. Yet, paradoxically, this metaphor of Moses as the nursing mother, and God as the father whose role is to "bring home the meat," is exactly the one that Moses uses to lament his impotence in nursing the people.

Nor is Moses's ascent up Mount Sinai to receive the stone tablets containing the Ten Commandments the first time that Moses has physically abandoned the people. At Mount Sinai, Moses was away for a mere forty days, but decades earlier, when Pharaoh put a price on his head for killing an abusive Egyptian taskmaster, Moses abandoned his people in Egypt for forty years. Perhaps, on the occasion of his first fleeing Egypt and abandoning the people, they were not yet ready to be redeemed. But this time, ready or not, God and Moses have raised the people's expectations by taking them out of Egypt and promising them that they would proceed to the Promised Land (Exod. 6:6–8). It is likely that the people who had seen their nascent leader disappear earlier imagined that he might do so again. Under the circumstances, to leave the young nation with only surrogate caretakers for such a long period of time was not smart—and bordered, even, on negligence.

In fact, just a week or so prior to God's revelation at Mount Sinai, when the Israelites had run out of water while camping at Rephidim, Moses took along an entourage of leaders and left the people for perhaps less than a day's journey to Mount Horeb to find water. Even this short departure precipitated a crisis—an attack by the Amalekites on the leaderless nation. This primal need of the people to be "held" by Moses, especially when they felt unsure of God's invisible presence, explains why, during the battle against the tribe of Amalek on the following day, Moses went up to the top of Mount Horeb, where he could be seen by the people, and kept his arms raised during the course of the battle, thus reassuring them of his leadership presence and strength. As long as the people could see Moses's arms raised, staff in hand, pointing toward the sky, in the exact pose that Moses struck when he split the Sea of Reeds and drowned the Egyptian army, their own confidence and fighting spirit were lifted, and they emerged victorious.

This picture of Moses being held by two of his trusted confidantes (Aaron and Hur) while Moses "held" and gave his support to the people is a perfect metaphor for the leadership experience. According to Heifetz, the leader must hold the people with his presence, but to do so, the leader needs to be held by those close to him. Otherwise the weight of "holding" the people becomes too great to bear.[4]

When Moses ascended Mount Sinai again to receive the stone tablets, left the people in the care of his two supporters, Aaron and Hur, and disappeared from the people's visual field for forty days, the people's anxiety began to rise. One can easily imagine that this anxiety did not take forty days to manifest. Probably after only a few days, several days at most, the people began to feel uneasy, wondering what had happened to their leader. The frightening spectacle of the fire and smoke at the top of the mountain and of Moses entering into the fiery conflagration must have terrified the people. Nor had Moses taken with him any provisions of food or drink. Under those conditions, without being allowed to check in on Moses, with no idea as to when Moses might return, with nowhere to go and nothing to do but get more and more anxious and worked up, it is little wonder that during those forty days the people began to seek a physical symbol to comfort and reassure them, to "hold" them and replace the missing Moses: thus, the golden calf. In effect, the Israelites created a projection, a golden image of their own infantile state: that of a dependent, milk-suckling child (i.e., a calf). The analogy becomes even more pronounced because the food that God provided and Moses procured for them in the desert, the manna, is variously described as being white with a honeylike taste of rich cream, an obvious allusion, as the sages of early Judaism pointed out, to mother's milk.[5]

What was the leadership team of God and Moses thinking when God summoned Moses for what turned out to be not a short visit but a forty-day summit meeting on Mount Sinai? Perhaps God planned to test the people and the leadership of Moses and Aaron, to see whether this generation was worthy of entering the Promised Land (see Exod. 20:17). God was, in effect, gauging both the people's character and the limits of Moses and Aaron's leadership ability. If this is the case, then both failed the test, at least initially. The people regressed toward orgiastic idol worship, Aaron was a compliant accomplice to their infidelity, and Moses effectively abandoned them without a word of protest, at a time when he should not have done so. It is not an overstatement to say that Moses's physical abandonment of his people was the precipitating event that prompted the people to create the golden calf:

> And when the people saw that Moses delayed to come down from the mount, the people gathered themselves together around Aaron, and said to him, "Arise, make us a god, that shall go before us for this man, Moses, the one who brought us out of the land of Egypt, we do not know what became of him." And Aaron said to them, "Remove the golden earrings which are in the ears of your wives, of your sons, and of your daughters, and bring them to me." And all the people took off the golden earrings that were in their ears, and brought them to Aaron. And he took them from their hands, and fashioned them with a graving tool into a molten calf; and they said: "These are your gods, O Israel, which brought you up out of the land of Egypt!" And when Aaron saw it, he built an altar before it; and Aaron made a proclamation, and said, "Tomorrow is a feast to the Lord!" And they rose up early on the next day, and offered burnt offerings, and brought peace offerings; and the people sat down to eat and to drink, and rose up to play. (Exod. 32:1–6)

God and Moses never again made the mistake of physically abandoning the people. In the book of Numbers, however, Moses commits variations on the abandonment theme, of the kind that might be called in contemporary divorce law "constructive abandonment" by failing to "hold" the people through periods of crisis, even though he remained physically present.

Moses's successive abandonments of the people is another example of the phenomena we first saw in Genesis—that leaders often make the same mistake multiple times. We will examine those cases more closely, after examining how God and Moses respond to the crisis of the golden calf.

God's Response

What is God's response to the episode of the golden calf? Put another way, what happens in the Bible when God becomes deeply disappointed in those in whom God has become emotionally invested and with whom God had sought to be in relationship?[6] In Genesis, we saw how God created the world in order to have a relationship with human beings and how excited God was at the thought of creating a being in God's own image. Yet human behavior from the beginning did not turn out as God wished it to be, and God, feeling frustrated, angry, and depressed, first tried exile, and then ultimately destroyed Noah's entire generation to begin again. It is not surprising that we find God responding in a similar fashion after the episode of the golden calf. Although cited previously in Book II, it is worth reciting the text here:

> *And the Lord said to Moses, "Go down; for your people, whom you brought out of the land of Egypt, have corrupted themselves; They have turned aside quickly from the way which I commanded them; they have made them a molten calf, and have worshipped it, and have sacrificed to it, and said, 'These are your gods, O Israel, which have brought you out of the land of Egypt.'" And the Lord said to Moses, "I have seen this people, and, behold, it is a stiff-necked people; Now therefore let me alone, that my anger may burn hot against them, and that I may consume them; and I will make of you a great nation." (Exod. 32:7–10)*

The term that God uses to describe the people's behavior is that they have "corrupted" themselves. As I alluded to previously, this is precisely the language used by the Bible to describe the behavior of Noah's generation. As with Noah, God is seeking to start all over again, this time with Moses. Yet in Moses's finest moment as the selfless leader of his people, he proves himself to be a far superior leader to Noah:

> *And Moses pleaded with the Lord his God, and said, "Lord, why does your anger burn hot against your people, whom you have brought out of the land of Egypt with great power, and with a mighty hand? Therefore should the Egyptians speak, they will say, 'For an evil intent did he brought them out, to slay them in the mountains, and to consume them from the face of the earth!' Turn from your fierce anger, and repent of this evil against your people. Remember Abraham, Isaac, and Israel, your servants, to whom you swore by your own self, and said to them, 'I will multiply your seed as the stars of heaven, and all this land that I have spoken of will I give to your*

seed, and they shall inherit it forever.'" And the Lord repented of the evil which he thought to do to his people....

And Moses returned to the Lord, and said, "Oh, this people have sinned a great sin, and have made gods of gold. Yet now, if you will forgive their sin, good; and if not, blot me, I beg you, from your book which you have written." And the Lord said to Moses, "Whoever has sinned against me, him will I blot from my book. Therefore now go, lead the people to the place about which I have spoken to you; behold, my Angel shall go before you; nevertheless in the day when I make an accounting I will account their sin against them." And the Lord plagued the people, because they made the calf, which Aaron made. (Exod. 32:11–14, 31–35)

Despite having initially abandoned his people, Moses, being a learning leader, succeeds in persuading God to change the course of events. God will not wipe out the Israelites as God wiped out Noah's generation in one fell swoop. However, God does not forgive them totally either. God gives them only provisional forgiveness—henceforth, the people will be on a short leash. Any infraction, God implies in the verses that follow, will bring with it an immediate, incendiary response (Exod. 33:1–6).

That being the case, God tells Moses in the next chapter to lead the people by himself to the Promised Land, without God's presence, lest God's wrath consume the people in a future moment of their indiscretion (Exod. 33:1–3):

Then the Lord said to Moses, "Set out from here, you and the people that you have brought up from the land of Egypt, to the land of which I swore to Abraham, Isaac, and Jacob, saying, 'To your offspring I will give it' ... But I will not go in your midst, since you are a stiff-necked people, lest I destroy you on the way." (Exod. 33:1, 3)

Again, Moses tries to persuade God to change course and to accompany the people as a sign of their favored status. After much back and forth, God reluctantly agrees to accompany the people, not because of them but because of his intimate relationship with Moses (Exod. 33:17).

Rather than be the exuberant leader that God was before the revelation of the Ten Commandments, God has become a grudging leader of this generation—God will not forget nor totally forgive. As God, shortly thereafter, explains to Moses, "God ... does not wipe the slate [of sin] clean but visits the iniquity of parents upon their children and their children's children, upon the third and fourth generations" (Exod. 34:7). God temporarily goes along with Moses until, as will become apparent a year later, the people prove definitively that they really are not ready or worthy of continuing on to the Promised Land.

Although the remainder of Exodus tries to make it seem as if the relationship between God and the Israelites has been fully restored, that is not really the case. God and Moses's abandonment of the people and the people's betrayal of their mission has ripped apart the bonds of trust that are necessary for any relationship, especially a leadership relationship, to endure. When leaders try to lead their constituents while harboring a grudge, it is only a matter of time before that relationship spins out of control into a downward spiral of decline and destruction. That is what will happen in the narrative of Leviticus and Numbers, until the entire generation meets its end. This leads us to challenge number two.

Challenge 2: To Halt Losing Streaks ASAP

In Book II, we looked at the importance of generating a series of small victories on the way to the "promised land." Rosabeth Moss Kanter, in her important book, *Confidence* (Crown Publishing, 2004), describes how winning and losing streaks become self-perpetuating mechanisms with a life of their own. As groups begin to succeed, the members of the group, as well as other potential stakeholders, heighten their investment of energy, time, and resources in anticipation of the group's continued success. Everybody wants to identify with a winner. In contrast, when groups begin losing streaks, members of the group as well as potential or actual stakeholders begin to divest their energy, time, and resources in anticipation of the group's continued failures. In stock market terms, they sell short. No one wants to find themselves on board a sinking ship.

From Kanter's analysis, it is obvious that winning streaks need to be stoked by the leader as they become something like self-fulfilling prophecies of the group's ultimate success; in contrast, losing streaks need to be snuffed out by the leader as soon as possible, lest they, too, become self-fulfilling prophecies of defeat and failure. Although personal understatement and modesty by a leader are generally virtues, during a losing streak, rallying our followers back from the brink of despair is a necessity.

After the nearly fatal episode of the golden calf, it was the leadership's responsibility to make strenuous efforts to begin another winning streak. One way of viewing the building of the biblical sanctuary is as an attempt by God and Moses to help the people regain traction and start a new winning streak. The resting of the Divine Presence in the sanctuary in the final verses of Exodus and the acceptance of the people's first offerings to God in the ninth chapter of Leviticus were indeed reasons for rejoicing by the people, who felt that the worst was now behind them and that a new string of successes was about to unfold.

But instead of beginning a new winning streak, the people are given a rude awakening of the tight leash they are now under in the "post–golden calf world." In the first narrative episode of the book of Leviticus, on the very day that the brand-new Tabernacle is inaugurated, Aaron's two sons offer incense that was not commanded by God. The result, as God predicted would happen if God was incensed, is that both of Aaron's sons are immediately consumed by a divine fire. Aaron is silent, literally dumbfounded by the tragedy of his sons, perhaps because he suspects that God has exacted payment for his role in forming the golden calf. Having told Moses "I hurled it [the gold] into the fire and out came this calf!" (Exod. 32:24), Aaron now sees his sons "offer a strange fire before God" and, as a result, be consumed by fire (Lev. 10:1). To his credit, Moses tries to reframe the episode in a positive light and thereby transform the beginning of the new losing streak into a continuation of the victory in establishing the Tabernacle:

> Moses said to Aaron, "This is what the Lord meant when He said: 'Through those near to Me I shall be made holy and before all the people will I be honored!'" But Aaron was silent. (Lev. 10:3)

Aaron's more honest emotional reaction neutralizes Moses's attempt. This incident, one of only two narratives in the book of Leviticus, does not portend well for the Israelites, for whom Aaron's sons are only a down payment for the costly sin of betraying God with the golden calf. A new losing streak has begun.

The second narrative in Leviticus adds fuel to God's fire. In a grisly tale found in Leviticus 24:10–23, a man curses God's name while in the midst of a physical altercation. Moses inquires from God what ought to be done to the man. God commands Moses to have the congregation stone him to death. The execution is carried out as commanded.

When the narrative in Numbers resumes at the beginning of chapter 11, the losing streak begins to take on ghastly momentum:

*And the people complained, and it was evil in God's ears; and the Lord heard it; and His anger was kindled and the fire of the Lord burnt among them, and consumed those who were on the margins of the camp. And the people cried to Moses; and when Moses prayed to the Lord, the fire was quenched. And he called the name of the place Taberah; because the fire of the Lord burnt among them. Then the riffraff in their midst expressed a gluttonous craving; and then the Israelites also wept and said, "If only we had meat to eat! We remember the fish that we used to eat free in Egypt, the cucumbers, the melons, the leeks, the onions, and the garlic. Now our gullets are shriveled. There is nothing at all! Nothing but this manna to look at."
… and God's anger was greatly kindled and … a wind from God started up, sweeping in quail from the sea and strewing them … all around the camp. The people set to gathering quail all that day and night and all the next day. But with the meat still between their teeth, the anger of the Lord blazed forth against the people and the Lord struck the people with a very severe plague. (Num. 11:1–10, 31–33)*

The people are obviously frightened. They are feeling increasingly uncertain about the volatile and vindictive nature of God's relationship with them. First the people on the edge of the camp, those farthest away from the Tabernacle and perhaps most alienated from God, complain amorphously; they are immediately consumed by a divine fire. As anxious people often do, the people then seek to comfort themselves with familiar foods, including meat, but there is only the ethereal manna to be had. God is furious with the ungrateful people for rejecting God's heaven-sent food and in a sarcastic pique, sends the people what they want—meat in the form of quails—but, with the birds comes a plague that wipes out a great, if unspecified, number of the Israelites who had lusted for it.

If God's anger against the hoi polloi is not enough, God, in another fit of rage, then strikes Moses's sister, Miriam, with leprosy for criticizing her brother behind his back:

Miriam and Aaron spoke against Moses because of the Cushite woman he had married: "He married a Cushite woman!" They said, "Has the Lord spoken only through Moses? Has He not spoken

through us as well?" The Lord heard it ... Suddenly the Lord called
out, "Aaron and Miriam!" The two of them came forward; and He
said, "Hear My words: When a prophet of the Lord arises among you,
I make Myself known to him in a vision, I speak with him in a
dream. Not so with My servant Moses; he is trusted throughout My
household. With him I speak mouth to mouth, plainly and not in rid-
dles, and he beholds the likeness of the Lord. How then did you not
shrink from speaking against My servant Moses!" Still incensed with
them, the Lord departed and ... behold, Miriam was stricken with
snow-white scales. And Aaron said to Moses, "O my lord, account not
to us the sin which we committed in our folly. Let her not be as one
dead, who emerges from his mother's womb with half his flesh eaten
away." So Moses cried out to the Lord, saying, "O God, please heal
her!" But the Lord said to Moses, "If her father spat in her face,
would she not bear her shame for seven days? Let her be shut out of
camp for seven days, and only then let her be readmitted!" So
Miriam was shut out of camp seven days; and the people did not
march on until Miriam was readmitted. (Num. 12:10–15)

It is one thing for God to vent divine fury toward the people at large, quite
another to lash out at the woman who watched over and saved Moses as
a child. Clearly something is very badly amiss in God's relationship with
the Israelite nation.

Having endured five consecutive setbacks—two in Leviticus and
three in Numbers, the people encounter a sixth, when Moses sends a
dozen spies in advance of the Israelite invasion of the Promised Land. Ten
of the twelve spies come back to report that the land is unconquerable
by the Israelites. This last setback, among other factors (see challenges 3
and 4), undermines the trust and the legitimacy of the leaders and sends
the people into a panic.

Although by the strict letter of the law, God may have been justified
in each of these cases for punishing those who trespass God's commands
and who yearn to return to the land and fleshpots of Egypt, God's successive use of punitive force in Leviticus and Numbers virtually make the
implosion of the people into a self-fulfilling prophecy. The leaders have
begun and perpetuated a losing streak that completes the disheartening of
an already faint-hearted people. Through a series of divine disciplinary
actions, the people have been bludgeoned into a sense of helplessness and

hopelessness. After hearing from ten of the twelve spies that the land is unconquerable, the best option that the desperate and frightened people can imagine is to return to their old homes and way of life in Egypt:

> *The whole community broke into loud cries, and the people wept all that night. All the Israelites railed against Moses and Aaron. "If only we had died in the land of Egypt," the whole community shouted at them, "or if only we might die in this wilderness! Why is the Lord taking us to that land to fall by the sword? Our wives and children will be carried off! It would be better for us to go back to Egypt!" And they said to one another, "Let us appoint a leader and return to Egypt!" (Num. 14:1–4)*

The people have given up on their mission of journeying with God to the Promised Land and uttered the ultimate heresy of wanting to return to their previous master, Pharaoh, and the land of their bondage, Egypt. They have finally articulated unambiguously what their actions symbolically bespoke at the golden calf—their anxiety-driven desire to dissolve their relationship with God and return to the place and the world they knew. All of God and Moses's efforts to extract them from the bondage of Egypt and to extract Egyptian bondage from their hearts are now in danger of being reversed. Perhaps the sin of the spies is exactly what God had in mind when, following the golden calf, God said to Moses with obvious prescience: "On the day of my accounting *["PaKDi"]* I shall account *["U'PaKaDiti"]* to them their sins" (Exod. 32:34). The root word, *P'K'D'*, used for holding the people "accountable," is the same root word as that used for "counting" them in the census in the book of Numbers. God makes reference to this counting when God metes out the consequences to the people for the sin of the spies:

> *Say to them: "As I live," says the Lord, "I will do to you just as you have urged Me. In this very wilderness shall your carcasses drop— all of you who were counted [PeKuDeichem] from the age of twenty years up, you who have muttered against Me." (Num. 14:28–29)*

As the text continues, God is indeed keeping count—of the people's ungrateful complaints:

> *None of the men who have seen My presence and the signs that I have performed in Egypt and in the wilderness, and who have tried*

> *Me these **ten times** and have disobeyed Me, shall see the land that I*
> *promised on oath to their fathers; none of those who spurn Me shall*
> *see it. [emphasis added] (Num. 14:22–23)[7]*

From the ten plagues, we know that God gives nations ten opportunities
to change their behavior, the tenth bringing the most severe negative consequences.[8] In this reckoning, the incident of the spies was the tenth time
that the Israelites tried God's patience, and this tenth, like the tenth generation of humanity in which Noah lived, brought with it the demise of
the generation.

In any event, the people's sins have come home to roost. As the
eleventh-century French biblical exegete Rashi comments on the punish-
ment of the spies:

> *From the time that they made the golden calf, God considered issu-*
> *ing this decree (that this entire generation would perish in the desert*
> *and not enter the Promised land), but God waited until their rebel-*
> *liousness would be filled. This is why God said at the golden calf,*
> *"On the day of my accounting I will account their sins" and here at*
> *the spies as well "for forty years they shall bear their sins"—in both*
> *cases God says "sins" in the plural, not "sin" in the singular, denot-*
> *ing multiple sins—the sin of the golden calf and the sin of the spies.*
> *(Rashi on Num. 14:34)*

The Talmud, in a somewhat similar vein, writes: "Rabbi Isaac said: 'Every
calamity which ever befalls Israel [literally, "the world"] contains within it
a bit of retribution for the golden calf" (BT, Sanhedrin 102a).

Whatever may or may not explain God's actions for the worship of
the golden calf, from a human leadership perspective, the course of action
that God undertook, which led to several consecutive losses without a
countervailing string of successes, is a sure recipe for leadership failure.

Human leaders must do all in their power to manufacture conditions that halt losing streaks in their tracks. Bearing a grudge for past mistakes or bringing past errors to bear on the current situation is destructive
in any sort of relationship, and it is magnified in situations of leadership.

Part of halting losing streaks is a matter of spin: reframing situations in the best positive light so that the proverbial silver lining can be
salvaged from the dark cloud. But before leaders can employ spin to sal-

vage a negative situation, the leadership must be committed to turning things around. Leaders must throw in their plight with that of the people, instead of seeing themselves over and against the people they are trying to lead. If the people don't see that their leaders identify with their plight—if they see their leaders physically distancing themselves and emotionally abandoning the people—then the losing streak will go on and, though it may be hard to believe, actually get worse.[9]

In the book of Numbers, both God and Moses fail to identify with the people and instead employ a strategy of distancing God, and even Moses, from the people. The arrangement of the camp so that God's presence and sanctuary is protected from the twelve Israelite tribes by a "buffer zone" consisting of Moses, Aaron, and the Levites demonstrates in structural terms the distant relationship that the leadership now has with the people. If the structure does not make this emotional distancing clear, the narrative describing the repeated venting of God's fury against the Israelite people does. From the moment of the golden calf and onward, it seems that God's attitude is one of "Me against them." God has lost faith in the people. Indeed, it appears that God is accompanying the Israelites only because of God's high regard and affection for Moses (Exod. 33:17).

For Moses, whose success in life is now tied up with the success of this people, the picture is more complex. At times he identifies with the people and tries to save them from their own mistakes and God's wrath. At other times, the people's resistance is too much for him to cope with— then he, too, sees the people as the "them" who are over and against him and from whom he seeks relief:

> *Moses heard the people weeping ... was distressed and ... said to the Lord, "Why have You dealt ill with Your servant, and why have I not enjoyed Your favor, that You have laid the burden of all this people upon me? ... I cannot carry this whole people by myself, for it is too much for me! If You would deal thus with me, kill me rather, I beg You, and let me see no more of their wretchedness!" (Num. 11:10–15)*

Moses has clearly become alienated from the people. Neither God nor Moses empathetically identify with the people and attempt to start a successful winning streak to lead them, with patience and encouragement, step by step, back on the journey to the Promised Land. They have both, in effect, given up on this generation. As a consequence, this generation will never arrive at their destination.

It is only in the next generation that military leaders will string together a series of victories in chapters 21 and 31, generating the necessary momentum and confidence to carry the Israelites over the Jordan River and into the Promised Land.

Challenge 3: To "Hold" the People and Not Falter or Otherwise Communicate Indecisiveness in Their Presence

In the book of Exodus, we saw how the two prerequisites for successful leadership are caring and courage. God chose Moses because Moses was raised by caring and courageous role models and demonstrated those same characteristics in the trilogy of stories about his youth.

The most startling difference between Moses's leadership in the books of Exodus and Numbers is that, when challenged in Exodus, he shows the courage to stand tall, both literally and figuratively, for the principles and values that he believes in. In contrast, when challenged in the first three-quarters of the book of Numbers, Moses fails to rise to the challenge and literally and figuratively falls flat on his face in the presence of both the first and the second generation of his followers. Moses will regain his courage in Numbers only very late in his life, and he will learn to do so the hard way.

The First Generation

Although Moses should have known better than to abandon the people for forty days and nights after the episode of the golden calf, he manages to take hold of the people and pull them back from the brink of chaos and self-destruction. Moses grabs the people's attention by shattering the Ten Commandments, and he demonstratively asserts control over the people by having them drink from the water containing the ground-up powder of the golden calf. He then rallies and persuades his fellow Levite tribesmen to execute the ringleaders, who continue to present a revolutionary threat. Having regained command of the people, Moses negotiates with God, offers to die with the people, and comes away with a stay of execution for them.

In contrast, in the book of Numbers, having led the people on an emotionally grueling journey through the desert for some fourteen months, Moses feels exhausted and abandoned himself. His brother Aaron, whose support Moses always considered crucial to the success of his leadership mission, failed miserably during the episode of the golden calf. His brother-in-law, Hur, another supporter, has disappeared from the biblical text completely; an ancient tradition accounts for his disappearance by postulating that the mob assassinated him when, unlike Aaron, he resisted their demands to create the golden calf.[10] Moses's sister, Miriam, on whom he has always been able to count for moral support, temporarily withdraws that support and is instead critical of her brother's leadership. As we will soon see, Moses's father-in-law, Jethro, who had provided wise counsel for him, will refuse Moses's offer to join the people permanently and will instead return to his native land of Midian.

The guiding coalition, which was indispensable in leading the people during their first year, has begun to disintegrate. Moses has no one to hold and support him, and therefore he lacks the emotional fortitude to hold and support the people. The combination of Moses's lack of support and God's short fuse following the golden calf is what distinguishes Moses's compromised and therefore faltering leadership in the book of Numbers from his powerful and successful leadership in the book of Exodus.

So helpless does Moses feel in the book of Numbers that when the people belittle the daily manna that God has given them and demand instead meat to satisfy their cravings, Moses asks God to end his life, not as a negotiating stance to save the people like the one he took after the golden calf, but simply to save himself the agony of witnessing the people's demise in the face of God's wrath.

Similarly, when he is confronted shortly thereafter with the demoralizing report of the spies he has sent to report on the land and its inhabitants, this is what the Bible tells us transpired:

> Moses and Aaron fell on their faces before all the assembled congregation of the Israelites. And Joshua, son of Nun, and Caleb son of Yefuneh, of those who had scouted the land, rent their clothes and exhorted the whole Israelite community: "The land that we traversed and scouted is an exceedingly good land. If the Lord is pleased with us, He will bring us into that land, a land that flows with milk and honey, and give it to us; only you must not rebel against the Lord.

Have no fear then of the people of the country, for they are our prey,
their protection has departed from them, and the Lord is with us.
Have no fear of them!" Then the whole community threatened to pelt
them with stones, and the presence of the Lord appeared in the Tent
of Meeting to all the Israelites. (Num. 14:5–10)

Moses and Aaron fall flat on their faces. While Moses and Aaron are lying
prostrate, it is Caleb and Joshua who are standing up to the people for
God and country. When the mob tries to stone them into silence, it is God
who must appear to save Joshua and Caleb because Moses and Aaron are
still on the ground, presumably praying to God for assistance. Moses's failure to stand up and defend God, the Promised Land, and even his own
emissaries in this moment of acute crisis is so glaring an omission that the
fifteenth-century Spanish exegete Abravanel, in his biblical commentary,
cites this episode of the spies as the real reason that Moses was unfit to
lead the people to the Promised Land. In contrast, Joshua and Caleb's
courageous stand against the people are precisely why they do merit to
lead the second generation into the Promised Land. Moses, in reflecting
on the spies incident thirty-nine years later, implies the same:

"When the Lord heard your loud complaint, God was angry. God
vowed: 'Not one of these men, this evil generation, shall see the good
land that I swore to give to your fathers—none except Caleb … shall
see it, and to him and his descendants will I give the land on which
he set foot, because he remained loyal to the Lord.' Because of you
[people], the Lord was incensed with me, too, and He said: 'You shall
not enter it either. Joshua … who attends you, he shall enter it.
Imbue him with strength, for he shall apportion the Land to Israel.'"
(Deut. 1:34–38)

The result of Moses and Aaron's inaction and constructive abandonment
of their leadership responsibilities is the forty-year sentence of the people to wander, until an entire generation of Israelites perishes in the desert.

Subsequently, as we will see in greater detail later on, when Moses's
cousin Korach leads a Levite revolt against what appears to be Moses and
Aaron's nepotistic and failed leadership, Moses again falls on his face. He
then passes the responsibility of dealing with the rebels to God, instead of
assuming the responsibility, as he did at the golden calf, of crushing the

insurrection with his own loyalists. Moses fails to summon the courage to lead and take responsibility for the generation that he led out of Egypt. They slowly die out over the next thirty-eight years until no one is left of his generation other than he and Aaron.

The Second Generation

In the book of Exodus, when the generation that left Egypt challenged Moses for not providing water for the people at Massah and Merivah, Moses countered their complaints forcefully: "The people quarreled with Moses. 'Give us water to drink!' they said; and Moses replied to them, 'Why do you quarrel with me? Why do you try the Lord?' (Exod. 17:1–2). Moses's comeback is as forceful as the people's complaint.

In contrast, in the book of Numbers, when, thirty-nine years later, the next generation of Israelites finds itself without water and complains to Moses, his response, as it was earlier in the book of Numbers, is again feeble rather than forceful:

> The people quarreled with Moses, saying, "If only we had perished when our brothers perished at the instance of the Lord! Why have you brought the Lord's congregation into this wilderness for us and our beasts to die here? Why did you make us leave Egypt to bring us to this wretched place, a place with no grain or figs or vines or pome-granates? There is not even water to drink!" Moses and Aaron came away from the congregation to the entrance of the Tent of Meeting, and fell on their faces, and the Presence of the Lord appeared to them.... (Num. 20:2–6)

Whereas in the book of Exodus the appearance of God's presence is a sign of God's imminent salvation, the appearance of God's presence in the book of Numbers is an ominous sign, indicating a failure of Moses and Aaron to contain the people. Instead of holding their own in the face of the people, Moses and Aaron, almost 120 and 123 years of age, respectively, flee from the people, shrink into themselves, and fall to the ground in response to the people's complaints. Apparently, they have learned little in the interim decades.

Perhaps they act as they do because Miriam has just passed away, and Moses and Aaron feel bereft, no longer supported by their older sister and Moses's protector and ally from infancy. In fact, as we read below, when Moses berates the people by calling them "rebels," the word he uses for rebels, *marim*, could be read in the Hebrew text as Miriam, perhaps a Freudian slip of the intense grief and unexpressed anger that he and Aaron feel. Be that as it may, this time, following Moses and Aaron's two failures to lead after the incident of the spies and during the revolt of Korach, it is not the people but Moses and Aaron who suffer the consequences of failing to hold the people: "The Lord said to Moses and Aaron, 'Because you did not trust Me enough to affirm My sanctity in the sight of the Israelite people, therefore you shall not lead this congregation into the land that I have given them'" (Num. 20:12).

Leaders who lose the courage to face their own people, who cannot listen attentively and then stand up to their follower's emotional outbursts and maintain their outward composure, lack the requisite strength to lead them all the way to their promised lands. Leaders must have thick skin and the emotional fortitude to listen compassionately to their people's complaints and then stand up for what is right and firmly speak the truth, despite the numerical power of their constituents. It is necessary but not sufficient for leaders to be physically present for their followers; they must also be emotionally present, hold their people in their leadership grasp, and not guiltily slink away when their followers express vehement resistance.

Their threefold failure of leadership—with the spies, with Korach, and at the bitter waters episode—disqualifies Moses and Aaron from leading the people into the Promised Land.

Once Moses becomes a lame-duck leader, there is a fourth incident, the most disturbing of all, that validates God's decision to relieve the aged Moses of his duties. After Aaron passes away, the new generation, camping on the cusp of the Promised Land, is seduced by the local Moabite and Midianite women to worship a Canaanite deity, Baal Peor. Unlike the episode of the golden calf, where Moses took charge of the situation on his own initiative,[11] in this second iteration of idolatrous rebellion, God has to tell Moses to execute the ringleaders: "The Lord said to Moses, 'Take all the ringleaders and have them publicly impaled before the Lord, so that the Lord's anger may turn away from Israel.' So Moses said to Israel's officials, 'Each of you slay those of his men who attached themselves to Baal Peor'" (Num. 25:1–5).

When one of those ringleaders, in open defiance of Moses, fornicates with one of the native princesses in front of Moses and the Israelite elders, Moses and the elders stand there paralyzed, reduced to helpless weeping in front of God's sanctuary.

It is Moses's great-nephew Pinchas who does what Moses had once done and should have again done in response to this mutiny. Pinchas takes charge of the situation and executes, vigilante style, both the tribal head of Shimon and his Midianite consort:

> When Pinchas, son of Elazar, son of Aaron the priest, saw this, he left the assembly and, taking a spear in his hand, he followed the Israelite into the chamber and speared both of them, the Israelite and the woman, through the belly. Then the plague against the Israelites was checked. Those who died of the plague numbered twenty-four thousand. (Num. 25:7–9)

Pinchas's vigilante actions halt a far worse tragedy from transpiring. God hints at what might have happened had Pinchas not acted as he did:

> The Lord spoke to Moses, saying: "Pinchas, son of Elazar, son of Aaron the priest, has turned back My wrath from the Israelites by displaying among them his passion for Me, so that I did not wipe out the Israelite people in My passion." (Num. 25:10–11)

Pinchas has either witnessed or heard tales of his great-uncle Moses's actions forty years earlier after the people's worship of the golden calf, how Moses stood at the gateway to the camp and called out: "Whoever is for God, come join me!" Pinchas follows the courageous example that Moses set by taking the necessary leadership initiative here.[12]

On the other hand, because Moses is still the nominal leader of the people and he fails to act promptly, the damage done is the greatest one recorded under his leadership watch: 24,000 dead. Moses's failure to take matters earlier into his own hands is certainly a contributing cause to this debacle befalling the second generation.

The result of Moses's passivity and inaction in these four situations results in the demise of the entire first generation and the near doom of the second generation—not to mention Moses's own failure to realize his own vision of leading his people into the Promised Land.

Despite these four failures to stand up and take decisive action, however, Moses did not end his leadership journey on a passive, enfeebled note. On the contrary, even as an elderly, lame-duck leader, Moses ultimately follows the examples of his disciples, Joshua and Caleb, corrects his mistakes, and toward the very end of his life displays again the confident demeanor of his youth that his people need to see from him.

When God commands him to instruct the Israelites to wage a war of annihilation against the Midianites in retribution for their seduction of the Israelites into their pagan idolatrous worship, the Israelite military fails to carry out their orders fully. Moses stands up strongly to the military leaders and persuades them to finish their jobs. Moses takes charge of the situation and puts the military leaders and their troops back in line. He does so with firm, determined resolve and without ambivalence or hesitation (Num. 31:9–17).

Similarly, when two of the twelve tribes come to Moses seeking to remain on the east bank of the Jordan River rather than cross over to conquer the Promised Land with their Israelite brethren, Moses takes a page out of Caleb and Joshua's playbook and stands up to the two tribes who threaten to undermine the esprit de corps of the nation. Moses, being a self-reflective, learning leader, compares the new situation to the incident of the spies:

> Moses replied to the Gadites and the Reubenites, "Are your brothers to go to war while you stay here? Why will you turn away the hearts of the Israelites from crossing into the land that the Lord has given them? That is what your fathers did when I sent them ... to survey the land and they turned away the hearts of the Israelites from invading the land that the Lord had given them.... The Lord was incensed at Israel, and for forty years He made them wander in the wilderness, until the whole generation that had provoked the Lord's displeasure was gone. And now you, a breed of sinful men, have replaced your fathers, to add still further to the Lord's wrath against Israel? If you turn away from Him and He abandons them once more in the wilderness, you will bring calamity upon all this people!" (Num. 32:6–9, 13–15)

Whether the underlying motive of the two tribes was to avoid fighting for the Promised Land[13] or whether they selfishly wanted to capitalize on the fertile territory that the nation had already conquered to assure the best possible feed for their cattle,[14] Moses's fighting words have given them cause to reconsider their request. Their response to Moses's rebuke is vivid testimony to the persuasive power of firm leaders to set their followers straight: "Then they stepped up to Moses and said, 'We will build here pens for our flocks and towns for our children. And we will hasten in the vanguard of the Israelites until we have established them in their home'" (Num. 32:16–17). The two tribes back down and agree to fight for the Promised Land alongside, and even in front of, their brethren.

In reading the stories of Moses's success in confronting the military command of his troops and the two seceding tribes, one might wonder from where Moses drew his newfound strength. Perhaps from his supporters in the second generation: Elazar, the high priest and Aaron's successor, who stood at his side during both incidents, and Joshua bin Nun, his successor, who flanked him and witnessed the negotiations with the two seceding tribes. Like Aaron and Hur at the battle of Amalek, this second generation of Moses's supporters metaphorically held him, so that he could in turn hold and keep the allegiance of his people.

Moses was far from being a perfect leader, but he proved himself in the final months of his life to be a learning leader. He used his and the people's experience in both the first and the second generations to learn what not to do as a leader, and did far better, at the very end of his leadership tenure, as a result.[15]

Human nature being today what it was then, there is in all generations a great temptation of leaders to seek refuge from the burdens of leadership before their job is done—to, in effect, constructively if not physically abandon their "flock." The challenges and resistances built into the leadership enterprise, the pettiness and thanklessness that followers often exhibit, the sometimes 24/7 demands of leadership, can leave leaders feeling emotionally exhausted and in need of physical respite and spiritual replenishment.

Indeed, when leadership is challenged by an external crisis, a gnawing questioning often takes place inside the heart of the leader: Is all this effort still worth it? For what do I need the continued burden of leadership? I had a happy family and professional life without these additional leadership responsibilities—why continue to lead? Everyone is so critical of my leadership and seems to have all the answers; perhaps one of them should take the reigns of leadership! Often leaders want to let go of the responsibility of holding the people, not because they don't care, but because they reach the brink of exhaustion and despair.

Given the challenges of leadership, why stay the course or, for that matter, undertake the burden of leadership in the first place? The reason is not short-term self-satisfaction, because in the short term, leadership is not always rewarding. Leadership, like parenting, is not about us; it's about the people who need us and for whom we care. Those people, our followers, are the ones who will lose, and lose badly, if the leader fails to step up and take on—or continue—the responsibility of leading the group to their promised land. Leaving the people to their own devices, when they are unable to assume leadership themselves, is to doom them to failure. This is, in fact, what happens during Joshua's leadership tenure when he sends a small expeditionary force to conquer the Canaanite city of Ai but stays back in the camp, mistakenly assuming that the troops can emerge victorious by themselves. Instead, they are routed by the native forces. Joshua then leads the next Israelite force himself and achieves a decisive victory (Josh. 7–8).[16]

People, and the organizations or communities that they form, need strong, inspiring, visionary leadership to make progress in the long term. Although during relatively quiet times, leaders deserve and require periods of short-term refuge and regeneration, when the going gets tough, leaders must get tougher and place themselves front and center, where they can hold the people's attention, not withdraw into themselves physically or figuratively. That is what the job of leadership demands.

Nevertheless, leaders who are feeling ambivalent about assuming or maintaining the burdens of leadership are in good company. No less a leader than Moses had the same qualms, ambivalent feelings, and second thoughts about leading. Moses's painful experience teaches us that to prevent burnout during critical times, leaders must make sure they have supporters who will hold them through thick and thin. Then, with their supporters holding them, they can hold the people in their proverbial arms for as long as it takes for the crisis to blow over. Once the crisis recedes and the people are strong enough to stand firmly on their own feet, then leaders and their close supporters can lower their arms, rest for a while, and cheer their people on, as they chart their journey toward the promised land.

Challenge 4: To Fulfill Our Promises and Explain Sudden Strategic Changes

In discussing how a leader builds trust and credibility, I stated the golden rule: promise and deliver. During the ten plagues and for several weeks after the Israelite nation left Egypt until they reached Mount Sinai, the leadership team of God, Moses, and Aaron did precisely that: they repeatedly told their audience what they were going to do and then followed through, exactly as foretold. This built the people's trust and reliance on the leadership team.

Therefore, when both before and after the episode of the golden calf God promises the Israelites that God will send an angel in front of them who will banish the Canaanite nations, they have good reason to feel confident that God and Moses will follow through. In the first iteration of the covenant at Mount Sinai, God says:

> *"I am sending an angel before you to guard you on the way and to bring you to the place that I have made ready … if you obey him and do all that I say, I will be an enemy to your enemies and a foe to your foes … I will send forth My terror before you, and I will throw into panic all the people among whom you come, and I will make all your enemies turn tail before you. I will send a plague ahead of you, and it shall drive out before you the Hivites, the Canaanites, and the Hittites … I will set your borders from the Sea of Reeds to the Sea of Philistia, and from the wilderness to the Euphrates; for I will deliver the inhabitants of the land into your hands, and you will drive them out before you" … And Moses came and he told the people all the words that God had spoken…."(Exod. 23:20, 22, 27–28, 31; 24:3)*

God leaves little to the Israelites' imagination in describing the ferocity with which God's angel will drive out the inhabitants of the land and enable the Israelites to enter and settle the vacated territory.

Even after the episode of the golden calf, when one might have thought this promise of angelically mediated divine intervention would be canceled because of the people's betrayal of God,[17] we find God reiterating this scenario to Moses and the Israelites:

> *Then the Lord said to Moses, "Set out from here, you and the people that you have brought up from the land of Egypt, to the land of which*

> *I swore to Abraham, Isaac, and Jacob, saying, 'To your offspring will*
> *I give it.' I will send an angel before you, and I will drive out the*
> *Canaanites, the Amorites, the Hittites, the Perizzites, the Hivites,*
> *and the Jebusites ..." (Exod. 33:1–2)*

Later on in God's dialogue with Moses, God reinforces this message:

> *"I hereby make a covenant. Before all your people I will work such*
> *wonders as have not been wrought on all the earth or in any nation;*
> *and all the people who are with you shall see how awesome are the*
> *Lord's deeds that I will perform for you. Mark well what I command*
> *you this day. I will drive out before you the Amorites, the Canaanites,*
> *the Hittites, the Perizzites, the Hivites, and the Jebusites ... I will*
> *drive out nations from your path and enlarge your territory." (Exod.*
> *33:1–2; 34:10–24)*

This promise of God's fighting angel was no mere abstract metaphor for the generation that left Egypt. At the splitting of the Sea of Reeds, the people saw God's angel at work and the Israelites therefore had an idea of what to expect when confronting the armies of Canaan. At the sea:

> *... The angel of God, who had been going ahead of the Israelite army,*
> *now moved and followed behind them; and the pillar of cloud shifted*
> *from in front of them and took up a place behind them, and it came*
> *between the army of the Egyptians and the army of Israel. Thus there*
> *was the cloud with the darkness, and it cast a spell upon the night,*
> *so that one could not come near the other all through the night ...*
> *The Egyptians came in pursuit after them into the Sea, all of*
> *Pharaoh's horses, chariots, and horsemen. At the morning watch,*
> *the Lord looked down upon the Egyptian army from a pillar of fire*
> *and cloud, and threw the Egyptian army into panic. He took off the*
> *wheels of their chariots so that they moved forward with difficulty.*
> *And the Egyptians said, "Let us flee from the Israelites, for the Lord*
> *is fighting for them against Egypt!" (Exod. 14:19–25)*

With this kind of angel doing God's bidding on their side, the Israelites must have envisioned an easy romp into the Promised Land, with God, through the medium of the angel, doing the heavy lifting and the people left with the enviable task of dividing up the spoils, as they did after the drowning of the Egyptian legions in the sea.[18] Having thus relied on being protected from direct military encounters, the Israelites must have been taken aback when suddenly, only twenty days before they were to begin the journey toward the Promised Land, Moses received enigmatic new instructions from God to, in effect, prepare the people for battle:

> On the first day of the second month, in the second year following the exodus from the land of Egypt, the Lord spoke to Moses in the wilderness of Sinai, in the Tent of Meeting, saying: "Take a census of the whole Israelite community, by family and tribe, listing the names of every male, head by head. You and Aaron shall count them by their military groups, from the age of twenty years up, all those in Israel who are able to bear arms." (Num. 1:1–3)

Moses and Aaron do as they are instructed, and record the number of people among them: "All the Israelites, aged twenty and over ... who were able to bear arms ... numbered came to 603,550" (Num. 1:45). God then proceeds to instruct Moses and Aaron on how to arrange the tribes so that they will march in military formation—three tribes on each of the four sides, with the Levites assigned the task of protecting God's sanctuary, which was to be placed in the middle (Num. 2–3).

Having expected to inherit a Promised Land conquered for them by God's angel, the people are suddenly exposed to what appears a very different strategy of conquest. Apparently, they will be expected to fight a military battle for the land. This was not what they had anticipated! In fact, God had known that the Israelites were not ready to fight their enemies. That is why God did not take them through the most direct route to the Promised Land in the first place:

> Now when Pharaoh let the people go, God did not lead them by way of the land of the Philistines, although it was nearer; for God said, "The people may have a change of heart when they see war, and return to Egypt." So God led the people roundabout, by way of the wilderness at the Sea of Reeds [even though] the Israelites went up armed out of the land of Egypt. (Exod. 13:17–18)

Aside from their brief military encounter with Amalek, an encounter whose inspiring, perhaps miraculous, victory depended on Moses's arms being held upright, the Israelites have not engaged in any sort of military training or exercise from the time they crossed the Sea of Reeds. Rather than train for battle, the people were preoccupied with the building of, and the inauguration festivities surrounding, the Tabernacle. Now, out of the blue, they receive this order to count and regiment the Israelites and to do so on very short notice—only twenty days before they are to begin moving. Even for a nomadic people accustomed to packing and moving quickly, counting 600,000 men between the ages of twenty and sixty, and rearranging the structure of the entire camp, is a substantial undertaking. It is plausible to assume that the people were in a state of flux from the moment these new orders were given until the moment they began to travel on their journey.

The significance of this apparent sudden change of strategy on subsequent events in the book of Numbers may explain why the Bible, in the only obvious instance in the Five Books of Moses, anomalously goes out of chronological order to tell the story of this census at the very beginning of the book of Numbers.[19] Rather than commence with the celebratory dedication of the Tabernacle on the first day of the *first month* of the second year, the most logical place to pick up and the place where the narrative of the book of Leviticus leaves off, the book of Numbers begins a month later, with the census on the first day of the *second month* of the second year. Several chapters later, the story doubles back to the first month with the Tabernacle dedication and the instructions regarding the celebration of Passover that chronologically preceded the census (Num. 7:1, 9:1). By going out of order, the Bible signals that the census and the rearrangement of the camp is the seminal episode that will determine the subsequent course of events in the book. Just as God's creation of the world, the first chapter of Genesis, makes sense of all that follows in the Bible's first book, and the enslavement of the Israelites, the first chapter of Exodus, makes sense of the second biblical book, the census of the Israelites, the first chapter of the Bible's fourth book, sets the stage for all that follows in the book of Numbers.

Although the people seem to have complied with the census and regimenting of the camp, it is not too difficult to imagine the perplexity and anxiety that they must have felt. Their internal questioning must have sounded something like this: If God is sending an angel, why do all the men of military age need to be counted? Why does the entire nation, including the Levites, have to be arranged in military formation around the sanctuary and the Ark? Is God's angel unable to defend God's people and God's own home? Are we going to have to engage in physical battle with the powerful, indigenous populations of Canaan to wrest control of the land from them? This was not what was promised to us! God and Moses seem to have changed the rules of the game at the last moment without any explanation!

Their perplexity and uncertainty may have grown further when Moses, just days after they begin their march toward the Promised Land, tries unsuccessfully to persuade his father-in-law to stay with the people. When his father-in-law declines, Moses promises him two positive incentives to change his mind and accompany them: an important role as the people's "eagle-eye scout" in the desert and a share of the goodness, presumably part of the Promised Land, that God had promised to bestow upon the Israelites: "He said, 'Please do not leave us, inasmuch as you know our encampment in the wilderness and can be our "eyes." So if you come with us, we will extend to you the same goodness that the Lord grants us'" (Num. 10:29–32). The Bible does not say explicitly whether Moses succeeded in persuading his father-in-law to stay. But in the verses that follow, God's Ark, rather than any human scout, seems to guide them, implying that Moses was unsuccessful in his recruitment efforts: "The Ark of the Covenant of the Lord traveled in front of them on that three days' journey to seek out a resting place for them; and the Lord's cloud kept above them by day, as they moved on from camp" (Num. 10:33–34).

Moses's request and his father-in-law's refusal are not a good thing. In fact, in contrast to the "good" that Moses five times promises his father-in-law if he would only stay, the word that is repeated four times over again in the next chapter as they journey forward is *bad*. It is bad, because, among other reasons, Moses's trying—and failing—to recruit a desert scout communicates to the people that Moses does not fully trust the Ark and the pillar of fire and cloud that are supposed to be serving those scouting functions for the journeying nation. Moses seems to be hedging his bets between relying on divine guidance and human scouting to lead them. This, too, raises the people's anxiety that things are not going as planned.[20, 21]

From the people's perspective, God and Moses seem to be changing strategies at the last minute, going from a scenario of divine conquest to a scenario requiring at least partial human conquest, without any explanatory communication that would help the people make sense of that shift.[22] If, on the other hand, this is not the case, they are doing a poor job of communicating the purpose for the counting, military formations, and human scouting.[23]

God was concerned a year earlier that the Israelites would flee back to Egypt if they found that they had to engage in military battle, and God's original concern is apparently still justified one year later. Given the choice between the unknown military forces that lie ahead of them and their very selective memory of their lives in Egypt, the people begin to hanker to return to Egypt.

Moses is perturbed and God is angered by the people's reaction, but neither seems to recognize that the change in strategy may have contributed to the heightened uneasiness of the people. Either that, or God is purposely goading the people in order to flush out their fearful feelings and justify God's "accounting of the people for their sins," which God warned Moses about after the golden calf.

Understanding the perceived change in military strategy and the widespread anxiety it engenders among the people, it is no longer a mystery why the people demand—actually, the Bible's words are "*all* the people demand"—that Moses send a group of spies to scout out the enemy ahead of the people. If they cannot rely on God's angel to scatter their enemies in advance of the Israelites, if they need someone to help act as a human scout for their journey, if they are expected to fight themselves, then they must take prudent measures to prepare for war. Here is the beginning of Moses retelling of that incident in Deuteronomy:

> *"We set out from Horeb and traveled the great and terrible wilderness that you saw, along the road to the hill country of the Amorites, as the Lord our God had commanded us ... I said to you, 'You have come to the hill country of the Amorites which the Lord our God is giving to us. See, the Lord your God has placed the land at your disposal. Go up, take possession, as the Lord, the God of your fathers, promised you. Fear not and be not dismayed.'*
>
> *"Then all of you came to me and said, 'Let us send men ahead to reconnoiter the land for us and bring back word on the route we shall follow and the cities we shall come to.' I approved of the plan, and so I selected twelve of your men, one from each tribe. They made for the hill country, came ... and spied it out." (Deut. 1:19–24)*

Despite Moses's approval and God's consent (Num. 13:2), this reconnaissance mission, one that makes perfect sense given the new strategy that God and Moses seem to have employed, proves to be the undoing of this generation's relationship with its leaders. When the mission returns, having surveyed the military landscape, and ten of the twelve spies conclude that the land and its inhabitants are unconquerable, the people panic and begin to rush for the exit—back to Egypt. This causes God to doom this generation to a life of oblivion in the desert. The sudden, unanticipated, and unexplained change of strategy proves to have been a mistake of monumental proportions.

What one learns from this deadly chain of events is precisely what *not* to do as a leader: first, setting up high expectations for the future while making low or no demands on the people, and then reversing strategy suddenly to make unprecedented demands on the people without fulfilling their expectations—all without constant, patient communication to explain the change. Such unanticipated, radical change without such explanatory and reassuring communication is a sure recipe for causing one's people to panic. If this panic is ignored or suppressed without being dealt with honestly, it will lead to even greater tension between followers and leader and ultimately will explode in revolt (see Num. 16:1ff.).

From a theological viewpoint, perhaps this really was God's intention all along. Maybe, because of the betrayal of the golden calf, God was purposefully trying to goad the people into expressing and acting upon their deepest fears and insecurities by raising the specter of war. God's consent to sending the reconnaissance mission may have derived from God's foreknowledge that the spies would likely conclude that the nation would not be able to conquer the land. The people would, in turn, demand the divorce from God that God considered giving them after their idolatrous worship.

Whatever the lessons that leaders can learn from God's leadership in the Bible, omniscience is not one of them. Human leaders must learn a more straightforward and humbling lesson here: shifting expectations without adequate communication is a terribly dangerous leadership path to follow. How do we know? From the story in Numbers that is littered with the corpses of an entire generation of Israelites, who were unable to make the adjustment demanded of them.

If a radical shift in expectations has to take place, then the job of leaders, if they want people to follow, is to introduce those changes at a pace and in a manner that the people can handle. Leaders must explain why the sudden change is absolutely necessary, why it is worthwhile, and how it is only a change of strategy, not a deviation from the ultimate destination. They must express empathy and understanding of the challenge this change means for the people and promise to, in effect, hold their hand and lead them through the process of change. Finally, leaders must assure their followers in no uncertain terms of their ultimate success. In fact, the leader's job is to communicate these points over and over again, in as many media as possible, to help the people bridge the transition from the original to the new plan.

Like the first President Bush, who made the famous campaign promise "Read my lips: No new taxes" and then, once elected, reversed course and instituted new taxes without convincing the American people of their necessity, God and Moses's change in strategy without explanation undermined the people's trust in their leadership. The generation that left Egypt was lost in the book of Numbers because of their leadership's change in strategy and their failure to communicate its cause adequately to their people. The leaders promised but did not deliver. Contemporary leaders would be well advised not to follow their example in the book of Numbers.

Challenge 5: To Maintain the Sense of Urgency

The primary task of leaders is to initiate and sustain change: to motivate their people to journey from one real or metaphoric place to another that is far more promising and hopeful. As we saw in the book of Exodus, to reach the final destination, small steps and short-term wins need to be generated to keep the people moving in the right direction and to communicate to them that forward progress is being made. The sense of urgency that prompts the leader to initiate the change process in the first place must be sustained by the leader on a continuous basis until the ultimate objective is attained.

When the journey's progress comes to a grinding halt and the people stay too long in one place—real or metaphoric—then the anxiety level of the people begins to rise. The people begin by feeling vaguely dissatisfied with the status quo. Then as more and more time passes and less and less progress is visible, the people will become more vocal and more specific in airing their grievances, until their complaints rise to a crescendo.

During the first seven weeks of the people's journey out of Egypt, the Israelites made great forward progress, both geographically and developmentally. God and Moses demonstrated that they would take care of the people's basic needs, thus reassuring the people that they would survive the journey to the Promised Land.

In contrast, after the revelation of the Ten Commandments, their movement comes to a complete halt. First, the people have to wait for forty days for Moses to descend from the mountain. Then comes the debacle of the golden calf, followed by Moses ascending Mount Sinai for two additional sets of forty days each, once to plead for the people's forgiveness and once to receive another set of engraved stone tablets. Then the people spend six months building and nearly two weeks inaugurating the Tabernacle. After that comes the week long celebration of Passover in the desert, a culmination, perhaps, of God's promise to Moses that when he would take the people out of Egypt they would worship God *at this mountain* (Exod. 3:12). All of this takes place with the people encamped in one spot—at the foot of Mount Sinai.

While celebrating the one-year anniversary of their liberation from Egyptian slavery through the holiday of Passover, the people must have thought to themselves and said to one another, "Great! Now, right after Passover, we can finally move forward toward the Promised Land!" But another hitch develops: a small group of people, who because of ritual impurity are technically unable to celebrate Passover during its appointed time, approach Moses and Aaron, who, in turn, confer with God as to how to deal with their situation:

> *And the Lord spoke to Moses, saying: "Speak to the Israelite people, saying: 'When any of you or of your posterity who are defiled by a corpse or are on a long journey wishes to offer a Passover sacrifice to the Lord, they shall offer it in the second month, on the fourteenth day of the month, at twilight....'" (Num. 9:9–11)*

Those who could not bring the Passover offering on the fourteenth day of the first month because they were spiritually impure are given a "makeup" date exactly one month later. This seems like a compassionate response to these people who wish to celebrate Passover but are unable to do so because of "technical difficulties" beyond their control. The downside of this decision, however, is that the entire people must stay at

Mount Sinai for yet another month, waiting for this small minority to offer their surrogate Passover sacrifice and worship God, as God had predicted would happen, at the foot of the mountain. Perhaps a month's delay under other circumstances would not have been particularly troubling, but after already encamping at the foot of the mountain for almost an entire year, this additional monthlong delay may have been the proverbial straw that broke the camel's back or, in this case, the people's patience.

The result of God's decision communicated through Moses put the good of the few ahead of the good of the many. Although it allowed everyone to be part of the people's central ritual and not feel disenfranchised, this may have been a serious mistake from a leadership perspective, where maintaining a sense of urgency is crucial to success.

Leaders are responsible for the welfare of the group as a whole; that is part of what distinguishes the role of leaders, who are responsible for the collective good, from that of their individual followers, who are motivated by personal interests. When torn between taking care of the great majority of the group, the public good, versus taking care of a small minority, the private good, the needs of the great majority take precedence. This is not to say that the minority's needs should be ignored; they should be ameliorated whenever and however possible. After all, leaders have responsibility to all the people. But in doing so, leaders must make sure that they are not sacrificing the needs of the many to care only for the needs of the few.

As we saw in Genesis in dealing with the issue of conflicting responsibilities, the key to successful leadership is not in addressing one responsibility at the expense of the others. Recall that when Abraham banished his concubine Hagar and his eldest son, Ishmael, from his home to the desert, responding only to Sarah's wishes and Isaac's interests, even with divine sanction, his decision nearly made him culpable of causing Hagar and Ishmael's death. In contrast, when Abraham decided to substitute the ram for Isaac's life at Mount Moriah, he found a way of demonstrating his commitment to God while maintaining his commitment to the future destiny of his younger son.

In the present case, God and Moses could have allowed the spiritually impure to offer their Passover sacrifices while the people were en route to the Promised Land rather than while staying encamped at Mount

Sinai. Instead, by waiting thirty additional days for them to become ritually pure, offer their sacrifices at God's mountain, and only seven days later begin the journey, the nation of some two million strong sees its expectation of long-awaited progress deflated yet again.

In addition, although it at first seems unlikely, it is possible that this delay, and the restlessness that the people begin to exhibit in response, may have been what prompted the leadership team to decide to use the time "productively" by counting and then rearranging the people. We saw previously that part of the leadership team's mistake when Moses went up Mount Sinai to receive the Ten Commandments was in not giving the people a challenging task to engage them during Moses's absence. Hence, with the Tabernacle and its celebrations complete, and with Passover behind them, the leadership team may have felt the need to come up with a productive activity to occupy the people while they waited for the spiritually impure to become pure. Nevertheless, as we have seen, despite their good intentions, the decision to use the time to count and transform the camp from a civilian to a military one sends a wave of anxiety through the people. The mistake of putting the good of the few ahead of the good of the many may have triggered the mistake of communicating a change of military strategies. One leadership mistake may have triggered another.[24]

Responding to the needs of multiple interests and divergent constituencies is part of what makes leadership so challenging an enterprise. We need to think out of the box in a creative manner, to find solutions that address the essential needs of each constituency, while maintaining forward progress for the organization as a whole. It's a tall order, to be sure; then again, no one ever said that leading was simple or easy.

Challenge 6: To Not Overmanage and Underlead

Keeping up the momentum of the journey brings us to another oft-committed leadership challenge: the temptation to overmanage and underlead the people.

From the moment that Moses comes down with the second tablets, God and Moses engage the people in myriad technical management details. These details enable the people and their judicial, priestly, and Levite leaders to govern and administer the people in all their social and cultural complexity: first, regarding the construction and operations of the Tabernacle, including all the laws regarding sacrifices and holiness (Exod. 25–31, 35–40, and almost all Lev.); then regarding the counting of the people, their military formation around the Levites and the Tabernacle, and the establishment of a rigid caste hierarchy in the camp (priests, Levites, and Israelites); and finally with all the preparations in anticipation of the march to the Promised land (Num. 1–10). These are management functions: dealing with complexity through quantifying data and providing proper sequencing of complex actions to maintain order and control.

There is no change of location—no geographical movement of the people from where they are, encamped around the foot of Mount Sinai. What is also almost totally lacking in these forty-three chapters spanning three biblical books are words of inspiration and encouragement by the leadership team to raise the morale of the people, sustain their focus on the hopeful vision for the future, and move them closer to the Promised Land. God and Moses are too busy managing the enterprise and not spending nearly enough time communicating, in an encouraging fashion, with the people. In other words, they are underleading.

Although one can understand the desire of God, Moses, and Aaron to keep things in order, under tight control, as it were, after the anarchy of the golden calf, one can make a plausible argument that they may be going too far in the opposite direction by micromanaging the details and attempting to control the people through coercive threats, rather than by strategically leading and inspiring them with a positive vision. Just how far God and Moses went in the attempt to manage and control by warning of negative consequences rather than by using positive reinforcement can be seen in the prelude to the "section of rebuke" in the twenty-sixth chapter of Leviticus. In this, the one section in these fifty chapters that paints a positive picture of what the people can expect by following God's commandments, the Bible allocates just ten verses. In contrast, in discussing the potential consequences for disobeying to the commandments, the Bible allocates nearly thirty verses, a 3:1 ratio. Moreover, the thirty verses are laced with anger, vindictiveness, and sarcasm, giving the reader/listener the impression of a demoralizing rather than an empowering message. Having gotten the people as far as they have, the leadership team seems much more focused on preventing deviations from the status quo than in generating and inspiring them through encouragement and vision.

The tendency to overmanage and underlead is one of the great seductions of leadership, especially when leaders feel under pressure because of past or current failures. Management, because it deals with arranging technical matters, is far easier to accomplish than leadership, which involves galvanizing, persuading, and changing human beings. The latter is what Ron Heifetz and Marty Linsky refer to as adaptive as opposed to technical work—the real, and the most difficult, task of leadership.[25] When taken too far, overmanaging is counterproductive. For leaders, it is a form of work avoidance, a way of doing things right, perhaps, but not doing the right thing.[26] For the followers, overmanaging infantilizes them, making them more likely to do the wrong thing and fail again in the next round.

The latter is true for two reasons. First, followers lose their focus on the larger goal because of the plethora of detail to which they are subjected. Instead of keeping their eyes on the ball, they are distracted by the rules of how they ought to play the game. Then, the followers' sole desire becomes how to ease the burden of complying with the myriad rules rather than how to achieve the long-term vision.

Second, overmanaging sends the subconscious message that the leader does not trust the followers to do the right thing or to do things right, and therefore finds it necessary to micromanage every one of their actions. As we saw in Genesis regarding Adam and Eve, when leaders try too hard to control their followers through rules, enforced by the use or even threat of force, they undermine the sacred trust between leader and follower.[27] Indeed, as we saw in the cases of both Eve and Adam and Cain and Abel, trying to control another person may produce exactly the opposite response—actions that purposefully defy that control. Human beings' natural penchant for freedom and innate dignity will resist attempts at overmanagement sometimes overtly, and sometimes, if the followers are intimidated by the threat of negative consequences, covertly through passive-aggressive behavior. Leaders must motivate their followers to want to follow them, not bludgeon or coerce their followers to fall in line reluctantly and resentfully. Otherwise, when the opportunity for another revolt presents itself, they will soon find themselves with no one following behind them.

If all this sounds vaguely familiar, it is: the beginning of Numbers is a repeat of the pattern found at the beginning of Genesis. In Genesis, God was dealing with individuals and family relationships, trying to lead by heavy-handed management rather than inspiring leadership. There, too, God used the techniques of separating, dividing, and grouping to create the natural world just as God and Moses do in Numbers to create the perfectly symmetrical encampment of the Israelite nation. The Garden of Eden, with four rivers flowing out of a God-residing, sacred space in whose center stood the Tree of the Knowledge of Good and Evil, is analogous to the Israelite camp, with God's presence and the Ten Commandments that distinguish between good and evil residing in the center, surrounded by four even groupings of Israelites. The repeated statement at creation that "God saw that it was good" in creating the natural world, only to be followed by God's evaluation of human behavior as incorrigibly "evil" (Gen. 6:5), foreshadows Moses's repeated stating of the "goodness" that he assures his father-in-law in the Promised Land (Num. 10:29ff.), only to be followed almost immediately by the incorrigible evil of the Israelite nation's behavior (Num. 11:1–15). Finally, as in Genesis, where God tries to lead by threatening first Adam and then Cain, God and Moses in Leviticus and Numbers attempt to lead primarily through threats and the use of force. In both cases, God's attempts are unsuccessful, proving again that even exemplary leaders, because of changing contexts (from trying to lead individuals to learning to lead a massive nation), often fall back on old patterns and make the same mistake more than once.

What the generation of people who left Egypt needed to hear in Numbers was what Abraham needed to hear in Genesis 12: a positive, uplifting message that would give them the confidence and courage to pick themselves up and journey forward to the Promised Land. It was Moses and God's job to paint in visionary terms how they would be able to defeat their enemies and how the Promised Land, with its bucolic landscape, lush bounty, and satiety for each person, would soon be theirs. Had the leadership team communicated such a vision to the generation of Israelites who left Egypt at the outset of the book of Numbers, they might have been able to overcome their fears and assuaged their whining and griping. They could have, in effect, said to the people: "We know that you feel frightened by the prospect of war and frustrated by the lack of any familiar creature comforts; but in just another two weeks, God's angel will lead us across the Jordan, help us destroy our enemies, and enable us to eat from the land of milk and honey. The rich bounty of the Promised Land will make your Egyptian fare pale by comparison. So keep the faith, hold on just a little bit longer, and together we will soon get there."

This uplifting message is more or less what Moses did communicate eventually—but only forty years later, to the second generation of Israelites as they were poised to conquer the Promised Land:

> "Hear, O Israel! You are about to cross the Jordan to go in and dis-possess nations greater and more populous than you: great cities with walls sky-high; a people great and tall, the Anakites, of whom you have knowledge; for you have heard it said, 'Who can stand up to the children of Anak?' Know then this day that none other than the Lord your God is crossing at your head, a devouring fire; it is God who will wipe them out. God will subdue them before you, that you may quickly dispossess and destroy them, as the Lord promised you ... For the Lord your God is bringing you into a good land, a land with streams and springs and fountains issuing from plain and hill; a land of wheat and barley, of vines, figs, and pomegranates, a land of olive trees and honey; a land where you may eat food without stint, where you will lack nothing; a land whose rocks are iron and from whose hills you can mine copper. When you have eaten your fill, give thanks to the Lord your God for the good land which God has given you."
> (Deut. 9:1–3; 8:7–10)

In contrast to the way he overmanaged and underled the first generation of Israelites in Numbers, Moses, in the book of Deuteronomy, learns from God's inspiring first vision to Abraham and from his own leadership over-sights. He inspires and emotionally empowers the next generation of Israelites to journey to the Promised Land. Moses learned the hard way how to do it right the second time around. Despite the temptation that we all have to take the easy way out and manage the technical details of our projects rather than motivate and transform our followers, we need to resist that enticement. By internalizing Moses's story, we can save ourselves the trouble of having to learn again the lessons that Moses learned through trial and error.

Challenge 7: To Avoid Unnecessary Hierarchies, Nepotism, and Even the Appearance of Impropriety

In the introductions to Genesis and Exodus, we examined the tension between leaders, whose job is to initiate change, and their followers, who will resist change at all costs. This tension, if allowed to fester, will lead to the followers' attempts to depose their leaders in order to halt the change process.

After the debacle of the spies and the life sentence in the desert imposed on the entire generation that left Egypt, it is hardly surprising that some of the most distinguished and preeminent members of that generation rise in revolt against Moses and Aaron. Changing the people's destination from the land of milk and honey to the barren wilderness is more than these people can bear. Korach, Dathan, and Aviram, three prominent members of the Israelite nation, seek to capitalize on the people's disappointment by deposing Moses and Aaron, whom they blame for their generation's sorry plight.[28]

> *Dathan and Aviram ... said ... "Is it not enough that you brought us from a land flowing with milk and honey to have us die in the wilderness, that you would also lord it over us? Also, you have not brought us to a land flowing with milk and honey and given us possession of fields and vineyards. Are you trying to gouge these men's eyes out?" (Num. 16:13–14)*

Dathan and Aviram, expressing the feelings of the people, are beside themselves knowing that they are destined never to enter the Promised Land. They find little comfort in God and Moses's promise that their children will enter the Promised Land. Didn't Moses and Aaron promise this, too? Why should they believe their promise now? Finally, to get under Moses's skin, they refer to Egypt, the land of their bondage, as a land flowing with milk and honey.

If, as I have repeatedly stated, trust and credibility are built on the formula of promising and delivering then distrust and incredulity are built on the formula of promising and failing to produce. The people are disappointed, and making more promises is not the way to regain their trust. Only efficacious action that would reverse God's decree and enable the first generation to conquer the Promised Land would regain the people's trust. Yet when the people defiantly set out after the incident of the spies and follow God's decree to attempt to conquer the land, Moses refuses to lead them or to send God's Ark, the people's "eagle scout," ahead of them. The people are thoroughly routed and dealt a shattering blow by the native Canaanites and Amalekites (Num. 14:39–45). Placing their sorry plight and military debacle at the feet of Moses, the leaders of the revolt say that is time for new political leadership.

Nor is it helpful that Moses has rewarded his brother, Aaron, and Aaron's children with the plum spiritual leadership positions, while sentencing the rest of the people to a life of hopelessness in the desert. Korach, Moses's first cousin, intuits the resentment that many feel at Moses and Aaron's privileged political and spiritual status:

> Korach ... took himself ... along with Dathan and Aviram ... to revolt against Moses, together with two hundred and fifty Israelites, chiefs of the community, chosen in assembly, men of repute. They ganged up against Moses and Aaron and said to them, "You have gone too far! All of the community is holy, all of them, and God is in their midst, so why do you raise yourself above the Lord's congregation?" (Num. 16:1–3)

As was the case with Joseph's draconian decrees in Egypt, in which Joseph took exceptional care of his family while impoverishing and enslaving the rest of Egypt,[29] Moses has created the appearance of impropriety by taking care of his immediate family while emptying the people's existence of any immediate hope. From the perspective of Korach and his followers, the 250 leaders of their generation, Moses and Aaron have made themselves into surrogate royalty at the expense of their brethren.[30]

Sounding desperate and angry, Moses turns to God: "Do not pay heed to them! I have not taken the donkey of any of them, nor have I wronged any of them!" (Num. 16:15). Moses's plea that God pay no heed to the rebels because he had not confiscated a single material item misses the point almost entirely. The point is not that Moses has accrued personal financial gain from his leadership but that he has favored politically those who are closest to him. Moreover, Aaron was the principal agent in the shaping of the golden calf, the episode that triggered the string of national catastrophes. Aaron's sons violated God's precincts at the inauguration of the Tabernacle, thus extending the nation's losing streak and eliciting

God's wrath. Why should their family's misdeeds not disqualify them from priestly leadership?

Leaders, however well intentioned, put themselves in a most vulnerable position when they appoint family and friends to influential positions. Such appointments, even when meritorious and well deserved—indeed, even when divinely commanded—foster the appearance of impropriety even when none actually exists. They create what my own leadership mentor, Rabbi Herbert A. Friedman, used to call a *"Pitchon peh"*—an opening for calumny among the people one is trying to govern. Such actions undermine trust.

God defends Moses and Aaron by swallowing up Dathan and Aviram and their followers in the desert sands and immolating Korach and his followers, who wish to take over the nation's leadership. But God's actions do little good. The people are even more furious with Moses and Aaron the following day: "The next day the whole Israelite community railed against Moses and Aaron, saying, 'You two have brought death upon the Lord's people!'" (Num. 17:6).

Moses and Aaron have reached a dead end in their leadership. Although they don't say it, what Moses was afraid of in Massah and Meribah ("What shall I do with this people? They will soon stone me to death!" [Exod. 17:4]) is certainly about to occur here. God again comes to save Moses and Aaron, and in doing so, inspires Moses and Aaron to redeem themselves as leaders by saving the people:

> And the Lord spoke to Moses, saying, "Get away from among this congregation, that I may consume them as in a moment ... " And Moses said to Aaron, "Take a censer, and put fire in it from the altar, and put on incense, and go quickly to the congregation, and make an atonement for them, for anger has come out from the Lord; the plague has begun." And Aaron took as Moses commanded, and ran into the midst of the congregation; and, behold, the plague had begun among the people; and he put on incense, and made atonement for the people. And he stood between the dead and the living; and the plague was stopped. And those who died in the plague were fourteen thousand and seven hundred, beside those who died about the matter of Korach. And Aaron returned to Moses to the door of the Tent of Meeting; and the plague was stopped. (Num. 17:9–15)

Moses, and particularly Aaron, prove retrospectively why they were worthy of being the people's leaders. In the midst of destruction, they identify with the plight of the people, rush into their midst, and save them from being annihilated by God's plague. But the cost of this episode is high: 14,700 dead.

Sensing that the people are still in revolutionary mode, God tries a third time to shore up Aaron's status among the people by singling him out for the priesthood in a visible, public, and plainly miraculous way:

> And the Lord spoke to Moses, saying, "Speak to the people of Israel, and take from every one of them a rod according to the house of their fathers, from all their princes according to the house of their fathers, twelve rods; write every man's name upon his rod. And you shall write Aaron's name upon the rod of Levi, for one rod shall be for the chief of the house of their fathers. And you shall lay them in the Tent of Meeting before the Testimony, where I will meet with you. And it shall come to pass, that the man's rod whom I shall choose, shall blossom; and I will cause the murmurings of the people of Israel against you to cease ..." And it came to pass, that on the next day Moses went into the Tent of Testimony; and, behold, the rod of Aaron for the house of Levi had budded, and brought forth buds, and bloomed blossoms, and yielded almonds. And Moses brought out all the rods from before the Lord to all the people of Israel; and they looked, and each man took his rod. And the Lord said to Moses, "Bring Aaron's rod again before the Testimony, to be kept for a sign against the rebels; that there may be an ending of their murmurings against me that they die not." (Num. 17:16–20, 23–25)

God has consumed and swallowed up the leaders of the rebellion, smitten their followers with plague, and now miraculously singled out Aaron's rod to blossom; and yet the people are still not placated. The very fact that God had the need to put on these three separate displays of divine power to validate Moses's leadership and justify Aaron's appointment as High Priest shows what happens when leaders fail to deliver on their promises and, worse, create the appearance of impropriety by appointing those close to them to leadership positions.

After another miracle showing Aaron to be God's—not merely Moses's—chosen leader, the people are agitated. This time they are not angry but frightened of being consumed in another fit of divine retribution: "The people said to Moses: 'We are finished! We are all finished! Everyone who so much as ventures near the Lord's Tabernacle will die! Alas, we are all doomed to perish'" (Num. 17:27–28).

The people have come 180 degrees from the beginning of the revolt. At first, they all wanted to offer incense and serve in the Tabernacle as priests ("We are all holy, and God is in our midst, so why do you raise yourselves above the community of God?"). Now, they are frightened even to inhabit the same vicinity as God's Tabernacle! God has bludgeoned the people into a pathetic state where they are afraid of their own—or perhaps better put, God's—shadow.

God goes on to reaffirm the three-tiered arrangement of the camp consisting of the priests in the center, the Levites in the next circle, and the common Israelites in the outermost circle. This creates a buffer between the Israelites and God, while also affirming the special position of the Levites and their subordinate position to Aaron and the priesthood.

For the generation in the desert, all this is too little, too late. Their hopes have been extinguished, their dreams snuffed out. They will spend the rest of their lives in the desert walking on eggshells, frightened of offending God. What was supposed to be a relationship of loving communion between God and God's kingdom of priests has turned into a relationship of fearful and separate strata. No wonder, then, that God gives up, too. God effectively abandons the people and does not communicate with them or their leadership for the next thirty-eight years, until the generation of the desert passes from the scene.

Leaders today should read this story not merely as the tragedy that it is but for the reason it was recorded in the Bible: as an admonition of what not to do when they have the privilege of leading.

Challenge 8: To Compromise, Be Flexible, and Not Become Pharaoh

In the Bible, there are two characteristics that make Pharaoh the symbol par excellence of everything a leader should not be. The first, and most obvious, is his blatant disregard of human dignity and the value of human life. A leader who brutally enslaves an entire nation and orders the wholesale murder of their innocent infant children is the epitome of evil and the archenemy of the life-affirming values that the Bible is trying to teach.

The second and less obvious characteristic of Pharaoh as the archetype of what leaders should not be is his inability to be a self-reflective leader: to learn from his experience and to change. Pharaoh's hardened heart and his refusal to alter course brings upon him and his nation the cumulative destruction of the ten plagues and the decimation of his army at the Sea of Reeds. Leaders who are so rigid that they are unable to adjust and learn from the changing circumstances that come their way ultimately lead their constituents to destruction and fail as leaders over the long term.[31]

In almost all ways, Moses is the antithesis of Pharaoh. Whatever his faults, Moses dedicates his entire life to enhancing his people's dignity and to protecting their lives. He is especially concerned with the weakest members of the society—the outsider, the widowed and orphaned, the poor and downtrodden. Under Moses's leadership, the people who were likely deemed "worthless" in Egypt are among the most protected classes in Israelite society. He is also, as we have already seen, a self-reflective, learning leader, who alters strategies over time and responds, at least toward the end of his leadership term, to the changing circumstances and needs of his people.

Only once, in the last year of his life, does Moses for a fleeting moment resemble not the radiant image of God but the frightening visage of Pharaoh, the man whom the Israelites dreaded and whom Moses was sent to defeat. That tragic moment, previously mentioned only in passing, takes place in the story of *Mei Meriva*, the "Waters of Contention":

> *The Israelites arrived in a body at the wilderness of Zin on the first new moon [of the fortieth year; cf. Num. 33:36–38], and the people stayed at Kadesh. Miriam died there and was buried there. The community was without water, and they gathered together against Moses and Aaron. The people quarreled with Moses, saying, "If only we had perished when our brothers perished at the instance of the Lord! Why have you brought the Lord's congregation into this wilderness for us and our beasts to die here? Why did you make us leave Egypt to bring us to this wretched place, a place with no grain or figs or vines or pomegranates? There is not even water to drink!" (Num. 20:1–5)*

After Miriam passes away, the second generation of Israelites runs out of water and, sounding very much like their ancestors, they challenge the bereaved Moses and Aaron. God, who returns from a thirty-eight-year "time-out" to care for God's grieving and bereft flock, does not display the short temper that God bared against the first generation. Rather, God shows the type of patience and moral support that God and Moses exhibited in the book of Exodus. Instead of smiting the people, as God's presence invariably signaled whenever it manifested itself to the first generation in Numbers, God instructs Moses to provide water for the people of the second generation by speaking to the rock that, in response, will produce water in the people's presence. It is Moses, however, who slips out of character and acts in a way that resembles Pharaoh:

> Moses and Aaron assembled the congregation in front of the rock; and he said to them, "Listen, you rebels! Shall we get water for you out of this rock?" And Moses raised his hand and struck the rock twice with his rod. Out came copious water, and the community and their beasts drank. (Num. 20:10–11)

Instead of speaking gently to the rock, Moses speaks angrily to the people. Then, in a displacement of what he would perhaps prefer to do to the people, he strikes the rock twice.[32] In each case, Moses's actions are abusive.[33]

By arrogantly addressing the people, by arrogating to himself and Aaron the miraculous capacity to produce water ("shall 'we' get water for you … "), and by using anger and force to produce the results instead of patient persuasion, Moses has, if only for a moment, metamorphosed into Pharaoh. God will have none of that:

> The Lord said to Moses and Aaron, "Because you did not trust in Me enough to affirm My sanctity in the sight of the Israelite people, therefore you shall not lead this congregation into the land that I have given them." (Num. 20:12)

As if to drive home the meaning of Moses and Aaron's sin, in an enigmatic episode closely following this one, God uses the serpent, the symbol of Pharaoh and Egypt, to displace Moses as the people's savior:

> The people grew restless on the journey, and the people spoke against God and against Moses, "Why did you make us leave Egypt to die

> *in the wilderness? There is no bread and no water, and we have come*
> *to loathe this miserable bread." The Lord sent poisonous serpents*
> *against the people. They bit the people and many of the Israelites*
> *died. The people came to Moses and said, "We sinned by speaking*
> *against the Lord and against you. Intercede with the Lord to take*
> *away the serpents from us!" And Moses interceded for the people.*
> *Then the Lord said to Moses, "Make a figure of a poisonous serpent*
> *and mount it on a banner. And if anyone who is bitten looks at it,*
> *he shall recover." (Num. 21:5–8)*

It should be remembered that in the book of Exodus, when the Israelites needed to be inspired in the war against the Amalekites, Moses stood on the hill with his rod held high to empower the Israelites to achieve victory. After the victory in battle, Moses built an altar to God, which he named "God is my banner *[Neesee]*," clearly crediting God with the victory. Now, in an act of divine sarcasm, God tells Moses to fashion a poisonous snake, the symbol of Egypt and Pharaoh, and to mount it on a banner (*nes*, the long stick or banner perhaps representing both the rod with which Moses beat the rock and with which Pharaoh beat the Israelites). Instead of Moses pointing upward toward God to save the Israelites, a figure of a poisonous snake mounted on a rod serves to heal the Israelites. By acting in a Pharaoh-like manner vis-à-vis the Israelites during the previous episode of the "Waters of Contention," Moses has inadvertently displaced God with Pharaoh and God's scepter with Pharaoh's rod as the savior of the people.[34]

In a sense, Moses learns what God may have learned from the first generation of Israelites after thirty-eight years of self-reflection: the point of freeing the Israelites from bondage was not to enslave them and beat them into submission as they were in Egypt. When God earlier used Pharaoh's abusive tactics with the first generation of Israelites, what resulted was a derailment of the leadership journey and the collapse of the people.

If Moses and all future leaders are not to make the mistake that God made with the first generation, then they must learn not to act like Pharaoh with the second generation. The danger and temptation of leadership is that leaders will use their power and authority in an abusive manner against their constituents, treating them as just so much chattel, their possessions to be violated and discarded at will. All leaders have the potential to devolve into Pharaoh if they are not vigilant and self-aware.

The great irony and literary genius of the Bible is to use another biblical episode involving water, perhaps the ultimate source of power in
the arid Near East, to teach the lesson of the abuse of power. Recall that it
was the original Pharaoh who issued the draconian decree to drown all
the Israelite males in water; God sent Moses in response to Pharaoh's
behavior. It was a second Pharaoh who pursued the newly released
Israelites, threatening to drown them all in the Sea of Reeds; again, God
sent Moses to rescue the people and turned Pharaoh's intention on its
head. Now, it is Moses himself who turns into a Pharaoh-like figure, and
it is God who rescues them from Moses's wrath through an abundance
of water in the parched desert.[35]

Leadership, properly executed, is a boon to the leader's constituents;
abused, leadership is their bane. The temptation to abuse power is great;
learning to resist that temptation is, perhaps, the ultimate challenge of
leadership in all places and in all generations. As I will point out in Book
IV, Moses, in the book of Deuteronomy, demonstrates how well he has
internalized God's lesson against overstepping his limits and becoming
like Pharaoh. There, in his valedictory address, Moses, arguably the first
king of the Israelite nation, sets unprecedented limits on the future kingship of the Israelites.[36]

Although the book of Numbers is full of examples of the principle
that leaders act with conviction and decisiveness and not falter in front
of their constituents, the incident at the "Waters of Contention" teaches
the flip side of this principle. To be firm in holding our followers and in
carrying out our vision is one thing; to be rigid, abusive, and unyielding
is another.

Aside from their apparent abuse of power, Moses and Aaron err as
leaders at the "Waters of Contention" because they fail to meet the leadership challenge of the new generation of Israelites and alter the way they
had previously done things with the old generation. In Exodus 17, when
the first generation of Israelites was faced with a lack of water, Moses was
specifically instructed to strike the rock with his staff and miraculously
provide water for the nation. In Numbers, in contrast, God understands
that it is not a show of force but a demonstration of the power of persuasion that impresses the second generation of Israelites. For the first generation, former slaves who respected only the power of the rod or the
whip, Moses had to demonstrate the use of force to win the people's

respect and get results; for their children, who have grown up in the freedom of the wilderness, it is the power of words—not force—that is compelling. Moses's inability to recognize that change and alter his actions accordingly result in his demise as a leader.

When new information comes to light or a situation appears in a previously unseen light, then leaders need to pay attention and be flexible enough to modify their position. Indeed, that is one of the defining skill sets of leadership: to recognize a change in the environment and lead change among one's constituents. This is also part of the leader's ability to "tweak the vision"—to remain committed to the final destination but adapt the technique or roadmap to arrive there.

As in other areas, Moses learns from his mistake and shows greater flexibility with the second generation in the final months of his leadership. Several months after striking the rock, Moses, instead of flatly turning down the two tribes' request to settle on the east side of the Jordan River, negotiates with them and comes to a compromise solution.[37] Although Moses extracts a promise from both tribes that their men will participate in the forefront of the nation's conquest of the Promised Land, he agrees to allow their women, children, and cattle to stay behind on the east bank of the Jordan River, safely out of harm's way (Num. 32:25–27). He achieves the goal of communal solidarity and maintaining the nation's esprit de corps, while demonstrating admirable leadership elasticity in allowing the two tribes to settle in the verdant east bank of the Jordan River.

The final episode in the book of Numbers is a second example of this principle of how Moses learned to temper his firm resolve with pragmatic accommodation to the needs of the second generation. The five daughters of a deceased Israelite man named Tzelofchad come before Moses, requesting the right to inherit their father's portion of the land of Israel: "'Let our father's name not be lost to his clan just because he had no son! Give us a holding among our father's kinsmen!' Moses brought their case before the Lord" (Num. 27:4–5)

After consulting with God, Moses accedes to their request and in fact goes further, setting an unusual precedent in the patriarchal, ancient Near East: "Further, speak to the Israelite people as follows: 'If a man dies without leaving a son, you shall transfer his property to his daughter'" (Num. 27: 8).

The matter seems settled. The daughters are to inherit their father's portion once they settle in the Promised Land. But then, in the final episode of the book of Numbers, Tzelofchad's tribe brings forward a legal appeal:

> *The family heads in the clan of ... Manasseh, one of the Josephite clans, came forward and appealed to Moses and the chiefs, tribal heads of the Israelites. They said, "The Lord commanded my lord to assign the land to the Israelites as shares by lottery, and my lord was further commanded by the Lord to assign the share of our kinsman Tzelofchad to his daughters. Now, if they marry persons from another Israelite tribe, their share will be cut off from our ancestral portion and be added to the portion of the tribe into which they marry; thus our allotted portion will be diminished." (Num. 36:1–3)*

The tribe of Manasseh is concerned about losing the plot of land that will be divided among the daughters of Tzelofchad; they are worried about having the tribe's territorial integrity violated by these woman marrying members of other tribes who will bequeath the woman's land to their sons who will follow the father's tribal affiliation and poke permanent holes in their tribal territory.

Moses could have been rigid and held to his original decision. After all, he had consulted with God, who had rendered the original decision granting the daughters' request. Relying on divine authority, he could have been unyielding and refused to hear the tribal appeal. But Moses does not do this. Instead, after further consultations with God, he amends the original decision as follows:

> *So Moses, at the Lord's bidding, instructed the Israelites, saying: "The plea of the Josephite tribe is just. This is what the Lord has commanded concerning the daughters of Tzelofchad: They may marry anyone they wish, provided they marry into a clan of their father's tribe. No inheritance of the Israelites may pass over from one tribe to another, but the Israelites must remain bound each to the ancestral portion of his tribe. Every daughter among the Israelite tribes who inherits a share must marry someone from a clan of her father's tribe, in order that every Israelite may keep his ancestral share." (Num. 36:5–8)*

While guarding the principle laid down in the earlier decision protecting the rights of daughters to inherit their fathers' land, God and Moses amend their decision to protect the property rights of the tribe as well. Henceforth, women who wish to inherit their father's real property can still do so, but they must marry within the tribe so that the inherited land will not transfer to another tribe. By doing so, they can inherit their father's property and yet safeguard the territorial integrity and contiguity of their tribe. By finding a clever way to protect both the women's and the tribe's rights, Moses defuses a potentially explosive situation from unfolding. By being responsible to both the women's and the tribes needs—a classic case of effectively managing conflicting responsibilities— Moses builds on the success he established in apportioning land to the two tribes on the eastern side of the Jordan River.

When viewed with a wide-angle lens, these two episodes regarding Moses's leadership and judgment at the end of the book of Numbers act as bookends to two earlier episodes regarding Moses's leadership and judgment at the beginning of the book of Exodus. There, in his first recorded acts of leadership, Moses had intervened in a dispute between two Israelites to halt their internecine squabbling and had later rescued the unmarried daughters of Jethro from abuse by the shepherd bullies of Midian. In each of those episodes, Moses uses his imposing physical presence in an attempt to lead. In parallel fashion, Moses here, too, adjudicates a dispute that threatens to split the Israelites (the two and a half tribes), and he protects the daughters of one of the tribes from economic abuse (Tzelofchad's daughters). Yet in both of the latter episodes, he also reflects on the interests of the other side and, using the power of thoughtful reflection and words rather than mere physical force and authority, grants them some part of what they sought: allowing the two tribes to settle in their own chosen territory while preventing the demoralization of the other ten tribes in the former; and protecting the tribe's economic rights as a whole even as he guards the women's economic rights in the latter. Moses learns from his error at the "Waters of Contention" to make greater use of his powers of persuasion and lesser use of his powers of coercion to lead his people.

Moses certainly made mistakes along the way, some earlier in his leadership journey, some later on. But he proves himself at the very end to have actualized and refined the leadership potential that he precociously exhibited at the beginning of his leadership journey. Moses's leadership at the conclusion of his stewardship of the people was no longer that of the young zealot who acted righteously but impulsively in Egypt to intervene forcefully at every turn. Rather, it was that of a mature, principled leader who kept his eye on the larger vision of leading his people but also mastered the fine art of compromise and self-control. By remaining focused on enabling the Israelites to achieve their mission of becoming a holy, self-reliant people, Moses does not permit himself to get distracted either by those who attempt to resist him or by becoming a prisoner of his own previous decisions. By being reflective and compromising on the small things that were less essential to the people's mission and by standing firm on the large matters that were essential and nonnegotiable, Moses regained his leadership traction and put the people on a winning course before his departure. In becoming a listening, learning, and persuasive leader, Moses became what the Israelite tradition affectionately refers to him as: *"Moshe Rabbenu,"* "Moses our teacher," the teacher of all future leaders.

The story of Numbers takes place entirely in the desert—no-man's-land. What it teaches about leadership is therefore not limited to a particular man (Moses) in a particular place (the wilderness of Zin), but is true of all leaders who guide the journeys of their people in all of life's places on God's good earth. Just as the book of Exodus constitutes a timeless template for the principles that leaders need to internalize and faithfully follow, the book of Numbers encapsulates a universal cautionary tale of what perils and pitfalls, scorpions and poisonous snakes, leaders are likely to be challenged with as they attempt to guide their followers to their "promised land." From the temptation to break the people's trust by abandoning them physically or emotionally when they are not yet ready to stand on their feet; to the failure to communicate, motivate, and inspire rather than manage by command and control; to abusing position and authority by creating the appearance of nepotism and self-righteousness, Moses teaches us in the book of Numbers what *not* to do as leaders. By allowing the narrative of the Bible to do what it is designed to do—to teach by example—the book of Numbers empowers us, its readers and leaders, to learn and to change. And never-ending learning and changing is what life and leadership are all about.

Book IV

THE LEGACY OF LEADERSHIP

Once leaders have followed the principles of leadership, survived the inevitable challenges of detractors, and have achieved a modicum of success, they need to consider planning and implementing an exit strategy. For leaders who really care about the welfare of their current and future constituents, how and when they leave an organization is as important a concern as how they lead that organization during their tenure. The impact of the changing of the guard can be a seismic one for an organization, depending on how well leaders manage and execute the transition process.

The threshold issue that leaders need to consider is whether they have achieved what they set out to do—that is, have they been successful?

Evaluating Leadership Success

How do we measure successful leadership? How do we know whether we have fulfilled our leadership potential? After all is said and done, were God and Moses successful leaders? In the book of Exodus, God and Moses led an amazing process of national change, moving the Israelite nation from the miserable depths of Egyptian slavery to political freedom and spiritual redemption. In the first half of the book of Numbers, much of the forward progress made during the Exodus was reversed when God sentenced the people to thirty-nine years of aimless wandering in the desert and the people repeatedly yearned to return to Egypt. Moses himself was sentenced to die in Numbers, rather than leading the people into the Promised Land. Only the second generation, led by Joshua, enjoyed the fruits of the land flowing with milk and honey. How to judge, then, whether God and Moses were successful?

One way to measure success is to measure the final results against the initial vision. Another way is to evaluate whether the leader has been able to make his or her own physical presence superfluous to the continued success of the people. Finally, we might compare the leader to another leader of a similar type, to see how they measure up against each other. We will examine each in turn.

Moses's initial vision, we recall, took place at the burning bush. The vision consisted of three parts:

1. Freeing the people from Egypt
2. Worshipping God at Mount Sinai
3. Bringing the people to the Promised Land

In Exodus, the leadership team of God, Moses, and Aaron succeeded in freeing the people from Egypt and bringing the people to worship and declare their fealty to God at Mount Sinai. This fulfilled the first two parts of Moses's leadership vision. The book of Numbers began at the point when the people, under the leadership of God and Moses, were supposed to march triumphantly into the Promised Land, fulfilling the third and final part of Moses's leadership vision. But of course that did not quite happen. First, the people sinned and were sentenced to die in the desert; later, Moses and Aaron sinned and were also sentenced to die in the desert. Only 66 percent of the vision seems to have been actualized, barely a passing mark.

In light of these apparent failures, it is interesting to look more precisely at the three ways God referred to the land during the vision of the burning bush: "I have come ... to bring them ... to a good and spacious land, a land flowing with milk and honey, to the region of the Canaanites ... " (Exod. 3:8). The terms "good and spacious" and "land of milk and honey," aside from their poetic content, mean a well-irrigated, fertile land that would produce abundant vegetation (date honey) and provide ample room and grass for pasture of the cattle (milk).[1] In Numbers 32, when the two tribes of Gad and Reuben approached Moses and requested to remain on the eastern side of the Jordan River in the lands that the people conquered under Moses's leadership, they did so because they had much cattle and the eastern side of the Jordan River, just like the western side, was green and fertile territory, ideal for grazing cattle (see Num. 32:1–4). Right off the bat, the land that the people succeeded in conquering under Moses's leadership met two of the three descriptions presented to Moses at the burning bush.

Although Moses may not have brought the people into the land of the patriarchs, he did succeed in bringing them to the mirror image of that land on the other side of the Jordan. Moreover, because of the wars that took place under Moses's watch, those lands were in effect annexed onto and became part of the Land of Israel for some five hundred years. From the perspective of the tribes that settled there, the east bank of the Jordan River was every bit as good and spacious—perhaps even more so—than the lands they would have inherited on the Jordan River's western bank.

As for the land on the east bank meeting the third description as "the region of the Canaanites" and the other indigenous nations, it apparently met that criteria as well. Indeed, the first war that the Israelites fought on the eastern bank of the river was against the Canaanite king of Arad:

> *When the Canaanite king of Arad, who dwelt in the Negev, learned that Israel was coming by the way taken by the scouts, he engaged Israel in battle and took some of them captive. Then Israel made a vow to the Lord and said, "If You deliver this people into our hand, we will utterly destroy their towns [reserving no booty except what is deposited in the sanctuary]." The Lord heeded Israel's plea and delivered up the Canaanites; and they and their cities were utterly destroyed ... (Num. 21:1–3)*

These three verses, which begin the twenty-first chapter of Numbers, clue us into one of the most overlooked yet pivotal leadership chapters in the entire Bible. It is the chapter par excellence that demonstrates how Moses fared using both the first and the second standard for evaluating successful leadership.

In the three verses cited above, what makes the reader sit up and take notice is that the Israelites, without Moses, negotiate a deal directly with God for divine assistance in their military challenge. This is the first time that the Israelites engage in a dialogue with God and embark on such a military expedition on their own initiative. And they are successful in their battle, despite Moses being nowhere to be found.

To appreciate the leadership significance of this story, it is useful to contrast this battle with the battle against the Amalekites in the book of Exodus (Exod. 17:9ff.). As with the Amalekites, the Israelites are attacked first and caught off-guard. In both cases, vows are taken. In the war against the Amalekites, God takes the vow to wage eternal war against Amalek on behalf of Israel; in this war, the Israelites take their own vow to proscribe the spoils of war to God if God assists them in battle. Although the victory against the Amalekites required Moses to be the medium of God's miraculous assistance, here the Israelites are victorious and presumably gain divine assistance even though Moses is strikingly absent.

Numbers 21 goes on to describe a second battle in which the Israelites are victorious. Preceding the second battle, the Israelites initiate their own foreign policy negotiations. Again we find that the Israelites are victorious and Moses is nowhere to be found:

> *Israel now sent messengers to Sihon, king of the Amorites, saying, "Let me pass through your country. We will not turn off into your fields or vineyards and we will not drink water from your wells. We will follow the king's highway until we have crossed your territory." But Sihon would not let Israel pass through his territory. Sihon gathered all his people and went out against Israel in the wilderness. He came ... and engaged Israel in battle. But Israel put them to the sword, and took possession of their land ... Israel took all those towns. And Israel settled in all the towns of the Amorites....* (Num. 21:21–25)

This victory against an "Amorite" king and nation is significant because the Amorites were not just one of the indigenous nations of the Promised Land. Rather, *Amorite* (like the word *Canaanites*) was a generic name for all the indigenous inhabitants of the Promised Land.[2] To be victorious over a Canaanite and an Amorite king, and to conquer their land, is to be the victor and conqueror—symbolically, at least—of the Promised Land.

The third and final war in which the Israelites engage in Numbers 21 confirms the symbolism that the Bible is intending to convey just beneath the surface:

> *They [the Israelites] marched on and went up the road to Bashan. King Og of Bashan, with all his people, came out ... to engage them in battle. The Lord said to Moses, "Do not fear him, for I will give him and all his people and his land into your hand. You shall do to him as you did to Sihon, king of the Amorites, who dwelt in Heshbon." They defeated him and his sons and all his people, until no*

remnant was left and they took possession of his country. (Num. 21:33–35)

The Israelites are confidently marching forward. Moses, however, is frightened. Why? Because when the ten spies returned from their advanced scouting mission, they reported that giants dominated the landscape of the Promised Land (Num. 13:28, 32–33). Og is one of those giants.[3] Moses, the last member of the previous generation, remembers their report and is haunted by it—so much so that God has to comfort and reassure him that all will be well. The Israelites, in contrast, need no such reassurance. They take on Og, the "giant king," and defeat him as handily as they defeated their first two adversaries. By defeating the Canaanite, Amorite, and giant kings without Moses's assistance, the people fulfill the third part of Moses vision—that of "bringing the people to the land of the Canaanites ... Amorites ... " They prove that Moses was a highly successful leader using the first standard of evaluating leadership success: that of comparing Moses's results to his original leadership vision at the burning bush.

Numbers 21 tells the attentive reader that Moses succeeded in bringing the people to a good and spacious land, a land dripping with milk and honey, the region of the Canaanites (and Amorites, and giant kings). While he does not complete the job, the people under his leadership have begun it—they have regained their traction and begun a new winning streak of significant proportions. Moses's successor, whom he grooms over the entire forty-year period of desert wandering, completes the job of conquering the good and spacious land that Moses envisioned and whose conquest was begun during Moses's leadership tenure. Measuring Moses's original vision against his results, Moses is a far more successful leader than appeared at first glance.

Paradoxically, by proving to themselves, to their leadership, and to the Canaanite/Amorite nations, who dreaded the Israelites' coming invasion, that they had achieved the strength and independence to succeed without Moses, the people also proved that Moses was a successful leader using the second standard of leadership success: that of making our physical presence as a leader superfluous.

A fourth episode in Numbers drives home this latter point. In Numbers 20, the Israelites found themselves without water, and Moses struck a rock twice, causing it miraculously to burst forth with plentiful water. Finding themselves again without water in chapter 21, the people, rather than have Moses perform another miracle with his staff, instead have their leaders dig a well with their own staffs and provide water for all the people. They then sing a song of praise about their leaders, a song of praise about water, which they lead themselves, without Moses conducting the chorus:

> Then Israel sang this song: Spring up, O well—sing to it—
> The well which the chieftains dug,
> Which the nobles of the people started
> With maces, with their own staffs,
> From the desert, a gift ... (Num. 21:17–18)

Unlike the song at the sea that "Israel and Moses sang," the Israelites have found their voice and are now able to sing their own song, a song that extols the natural gifts of the desert oasis to which God has led them. By making the people militarily independent and making his services largely redundant and superfluous, Moses has succeeded in his leadership mission using the second standard for measuring leadership success.

Moses made himself superfluous in another area, too: the need to stand up to the spiritual challenges of the people. As we saw in Books II and III, back at the episode of the golden calf, when the generation that left Egypt was worshipping an Egyptian deity, tottering on the verge of total chaos and social anomie, it was Moses who stood up to the people, brought them back from the brink of implosion, and rescued them from God's wrath.

In chapter 25 of the book of Numbers, in contrast, when the second generation was seduced into the worship of a Canaanite idol, Baal Peor, Moses was paralyzed into inaction and weeping. But his great-nephew Pinchas follows Moses's example of forty years earlier and does exactly what Moses did for his own generation: he rescues them from spiritual oblivion and from God's wrath. Pinchas does this of his own accord and on his own initiative as a concerned member of the Levite community, without Moses explicitly instructing him to do so.

Just as Moses has groomed a political leader to take the people to the Promised Land, so, too, has he groomed a spiritual leader to guide the people on the straight and narrow during their journey and after their arrival (see Num. 31; Josh. 22). Both militarily and spiritually, Moses's physical presence was no longer necessary.

Finally, using the third standard for evaluating leadership success, we might want to compare Moses to his prophetic counterpart among the nations, Balaam ben Beor. Balaam was commissioned by the king of Moab to act as the spiritual counterweight to Moses and the Israelites. By neutralizing Moses's spiritual power, the Moabite king hoped to penetrate the spiritual force field around the Israelite people and thus emerge victorious from war. Balaam, like Moses, was a prophet of obvious stature, and their basic stories—coming as outsiders with a sojourn in Midian to play a role with the Israelite people—were also alike. But when it came to identity, character, and results, Balaam proved to be just the opposite of Moses. While Moses's task was to rescue the Israelites, as his name, Moshe ben Amram, which means "the extractor, son of a great nation," implies, Balaam's task was to curse the people, as his name, Balaam ben Beor, which means "swallower of the people, the son of conflagration," implies. Moses was a modest man. The Bible tells us he was the humblest man on the face of the earth, too modest initially to undertake God's mission. Balaam, in contrast, was repeatedly self-promoting, eager to embark on his nefarious mission to thwart the Israelites in order to obtain the accolades that the Moabite king has promised him: "Here is the word of Balaam son of Beor, the word of the man whose eye is true, the word of him who hears God's speech, who obtains knowledge from the most high, and beholds visions of the Almighty … "(Num. 24:3–4, 15–16).

But in the end it was Moses, the modest leader, who fulfilled his mission and is remembered for all generations, while Balaam failed in his mission and met an ignoble end.[4] The entire story of Balaam is included in the Bible precisely to act as a standard of comparison for Moses's prophetic leadership. When compared to his prophetic counterpart, Moses's leadership comes through with flying colors.

As contemporary leaders approach the end of their tenures, these three criteria of success by which we evaluated Moses's leadership can help them evaluate their own —and others'—leadership success. Have they actualized much of the original leadership vision? If so, have they succeeded in raising their followers and successors to be independent of them, thus making their own physical presence superfluous? Do they measure up well to similar leaders of other organizations? If they can honestly give affirmative answers to these three questions, then they can rest easy in implementing their exit strategy and handing over the leadership reins, knowing they have accomplished their leadership mission.

Ceding Power and Appointing Successors

For a change effort to be successful, it must have longevity beyond the leadership of the original change agent. This, in turn, requires that leaders transcend the insecurity of their own egos and begin the process of grooming their potential successors as early as possible.

The issue of succession is intertwined with the issue of ego transcendence—of leaders being able to overcome their inner anxiety about their futures after they no longer occupy their current leadership role. The importance of leaders doing so cannot be overemphasized. The desire to lead and be viewed as a hero is very powerful. Leaders, like all human beings, want to continue feeling the respect and deference that others give them because of their positions. If the greatest danger of leadership is being "assassinated" by those who resist change, then the second greatest danger of leadership is of leaders confusing their own selves with the leadership roles they occupy. I have seen too many leaders abuse their leadership authority and hang on to their positions long after it would have been better for them to leave. Power corrupts; absolute power corrupts absolutely. The danger of self-aggrandizement compounds the danger of leadership.

In the Bible, leadership is stewardship. Leadership is a sacred trust between followers and the person(s) whom God and they agree to have lead them. If leaders confuse their own egos and inflated sense of self-importance prompted by their leadership roles, with the important leadership job with which they have been entrusted by God and their followers, then they almost always overstep their boundaries and sever the relationship of trust they have built with their constituents. They may then end up leading themselves and perhaps a few faithful yes-men that surround them, but they will have forfeited the basis for leading the great majority of their followers.

Moses's epitaph at the end of his life was not to be called the great redeemer, the great lawgiver, or even the great leader. Rather, despite the miraculous power that the Bible acknowledges he wielded against

Pharaoh and his legions, personally witnessed by the Israelites, the Bible simply refers to him as "God's servant" (Deut. 34:5; Josh. 1:1):

> *So Moses, the servant of the Lord, died there, in the land of Moab, at the command of the Lord ... Never again did there arise in Israel a prophet like Moses—whom the Lord singled out, face to face, who could perform all the signs and wondrous miracles that the Lord sent him to display in the land of Egypt, against Pharaoh, all his servants and his whole country, and for all the great might and awesome power that Moses displayed before all Israel. (Deut. 34:5, 10–12)*

Despite the awesome miracles that he was able to affect, Moses, with one exception already discussed, did not let his power go to his head. Even after his death, he remained God's humble servant. Instead of having colossal structures built to mark his tomb, as did the Egyptian Pharaohs, the Bible tells the reader: "No man knows his place of burial until this day"(Deut. 34:6).

Jim Collins, in his book *Good to Great* (HarperCollins, 2001), describes this typology of selfless leadership as "Level V leadership." Level V leaders, Collins maintains, combine ferocious resolve on behalf of the group with deep personal modesty and humility. According to Collins and his research team, having a Level V leader at the helm is what distinguishes a merely good institution from a truly great one. Moses was just the kind of leader that Collins and his team learned to extol: a Level V, self-effacing yet passionate leader, who was responsible for co-leading with God a civilization that remains alive and impactful to this very day.

Assuring Multigenerational Leadership

Every generation has people who perform great deeds or lead great movements. Such people usually get the adulation and the admiration of their communities, nation, and sometimes, even the entire world. That's why the Bible says that Noah was a great person *b'dorotav*, "in his own generation." He was a hero because he saved the human race and the animal kingdom of his time.

But there's a difference between being a hero and being a leader. A leader's ultimate concern is not his or her own fate or fame. It's not achieving greatness or hero status in one generation. A leader's ultimate concern is the well-being of the followers—this generation, and the next generation, and the one after that. That is true, biblical leadership. If we think in the short term, if we don't plan for succession in terms of who is going to lead our project, our program, our institution after us, and in terms of who is going to be led after we are long gone, then, in my book, and in the book of the Bible, we have failed as leaders.

Now, the Mosaic genius, and it was truly genius, is that he worked in two directions at the same time. On the one hand, he groomed a successor over a long period of time, and that was Joshua. On the other hand, he also made sure there would be a people to be led.

As far as succession was concerned, Joshua was very different from Moses. Joshua was a military leader. Moses was not. Moses was a visionary. Joshua was not. Nevertheless, they shared a value system. In fact, Joshua complemented Moses's weaknesses. Consequently, Joshua was able to complete the implementation of the vision that Moses originally formulated of bringing and settling the people in the Promised Land.

The selection of Joshua as Moses's successor teaches us that we don't have to find a clone of ourselves to succeed us, we just have to find somebody who shares our values and our vision. If we don't, then all the work that we put into our project, all the work that we are investing through our leadership, will ultimately fall apart.

Moses's grooming of Joshua is a wonderful example of how a conscientious and caring senior leader can shape the thinking and leadership of a junior subordinate with the potential to succeed him. From the get-go, Moses placed Joshua at his side and he stood there, ready to be called on, through some of the most difficult crises that challenged Moses's leadership. It was Joshua whom Moses asked to lead the battle against Amalek;[5] it was Joshua who met and accompanied Moses down the mountain when, having received the Ten Commandments, Moses confronted the revolt of the golden calf;[6] it was Joshua who stood by his side when there was a potential threat to Moses's life after his slaying of the three thousand idol worshippers[7] and when there was a danger to Moses's prophetic authority;[8] and it was Joshua, who, along with Caleb, led the failed mission of the spies, confronting the angry mob and endangering his life in an (unsuccessful) attempt to accomplish his mentor's mission.[9]

The manner by which Moses appointed Joshua is a great example of how succession ought to be done. Although it took him a few months to do so, Moses initiated the conversation with God regarding his successor, not the other way around. Moses, in other words, broached the issue of succession willingly out of his genuine caring and concern for his embattled nation:

> *Moses spoke to the Lord, saying, "Let the Lord, Source of the breath of all flesh, appoint someone over the community who shall go out before them and come in before them, who shall lead them in all matters and whom they shall follow in all matters so that the Lord's community may not be like sheep that have no shepherd." And the Lord answered Moses, "Single out Joshua, son of Nun, an inspiring man, and lay your hand upon him. Have him stand before Elazar the priest and before the whole community, and commission him in their sight. Invest him with some of your authority, so that the whole Israelite community may obey. He shall present himself to Elazar the priest, who shall on his behalf seek the decision of the Urim before the Lord. By such instruction they shall go out and by such instruction they shall come in, he and all the Israelites, the whole community." Moses did as the Lord commanded him. He took Joshua and had him stand before Elazar the priest and before the whole community. He laid his hands upon him and commissioned him—as the Lord had spoken through Moses. (Num. 27:15–23)*

Moses publicly appointed Joshua in the presence of the highest official in the nation (in biblical times, the high priest) and in the presence of all the people. He also received independent confirmation of his choice through the high priests' *Urim V'Tumim,* a "divine transmitter," which informed the people of God's will and gave the decision visible legitimacy, just as an election might in contemporary times.

Moses goes one step further. Although God tells him to place one hand on Joshua to invest him with some of Moses's spiritual authority, Moses places both hands upon him, thereby investing Joshua with his full spiritual authority. By unequivocally endorsing Joshua's leadership in this public and physical manner, he squashes any potential rumors of Moses's reticence to appoint his successor, which could have potentially undermined Joshua's future leadership.

The Bible tells us just how effective his transfer of leadership was in the closing verses of Deuteronomy. Following Moses's death, the Bible states: "And Joshua, the son of Nun, was filled with the spirit of God because Moses had placed [both] of his hands upon him. And the Israelite People listened to him [Joshua] and they acted as God had commanded Moses" (Deut. 34:9). The transfer of power to Joshua from Moses resulted in Joshua's authority being established and Moses's legacy being continued.

Following President Franklin Delano Roosevelt's death during the final stages of World War II, Walter Lippman wrote, "The final test of a leader is that he leaves behind him in other men the conviction and the will to carry on. The genius of a good leader is to leave behind him a situation which common sense, without the grace of genius, can deal with successfully." Moses's genius lay in appointing a successor who, while not his spiritual equal, could nevertheless carry on and fulfill his vision of bringing the people to the Promised Land. He also left behind self-sustaining systems of governance (see below) and a generation of people prepared to follow their new leader and fight for their future in their own land.

Establishing Self-Sustaining Systems of Governance

Aside for grooming and then appointing his second in command to succeed him, Moses also created the framework of a just political system to govern the people once they entered the Promised Land. It included, first and foremost, the creation of a judicial system and law enforcement mechanism. The judicial system, like the one that Moses established in the desert, had multiple levels to deal with both local and national issues of contention and to permit a de facto system of judicial appeal (Deut. 16:18–17:13). Moses also carefully worked out rules of civil procedure and verification of witness testimony (Deut. 19:15–21).

Second, Moses established the institution of kingship, an executive branch of government to parallel his own leadership role among the people. However, unlike other kings in the ancient world, Moses's institution of kingship was replete with checks and balances on the king's power:

If, after you have entered the land that the Lord your God has assigned to you, and taken possession of it and settled in it, you decide, "I will set a king over me, as do all the nations about me," you shall be free to set a king over yourself, one chosen by the Lord your God. Be sure to set as king over yourself one of your own people; you must not set a foreigner over you, one who is not your kinsman. Moreover, he shall not keep many horses or send people back to Egypt to add to his horses, since the Lord has warned you, "You must not go back that way again." And he shall not have many wives, lest his heart go astray; nor shall he amass silver and gold to excess. When he is seated on his royal throne, he shall have a copy of this Teaching written for him on a scroll by the Levitical priests. Let it remain with him and let him read in it all his life, so that he may learn to revere the Lord his God, to observe faithfully every word of this Teaching as well as these laws. Thus he will not act haughtily toward his fellows or deviate from the instruction to the right or to the left, to the end that he and his descendants may reign long in the midst of Israel. (Deut. 17:14–20)

Unlike the kings of the ancient Near East, who had absolute power to do as they pleased, the biblical monarchy that Moses made allowances for was circumscribed by and subject to the rule of law. No one was above the law, not even the king. He was to write his own copy of the Bible and have that Bible with him at all times. Moreover, there were limits placed on his ability to wage war (horses, the engines of military chariots, were the ancient equivalent of tanks), to establish treaties with foreign countries (in the polygamous ancient Near East, wives were often taken to establish political alliances with foreign monarchies), and to tax his constituents ("nor shall he amass silver and gold to excess"). The point of all these laws was to assure that the king would not abuse his leadership position and forget that he was merely one of the Israelite people.

Third, Moses set up a civil service system consisting of the Levites and priests that would administer to the religious and educational needs of the people. Like the king, the priests and Levites' power was severely restricted. They were not entrusted with a single, large contiguous parcel of land that could function as a power base. Instead, they were dispersed in forty-eight small Levite cities throughout the entire Israelite nation. This restriction reduced the likelihood of priestly corruption, a common occurrence in ancient as well as in contemporary times. It also made them geographically mobile to serve the people wherever they were most needed.

At the same time, the priests and Levites were awarded a small but not insignificant percentage of the people's agricultural income, to allow them to live in dignity rather than in penury among the Israelite people (Deut. 18:1–8).

Fourth, Moses established standards by which the people could judge the veracity of those who aspired to be their spiritual leaders—the "prophets." Any prophet who attempted to overturn the foundational status of the Bible was immediately to be considered suspect. Ultimately, if the prophet failed to prove his credibility by correctly predicting how positive events would unfold, he was to be removed (Deut. 18:9–22).

Fifth, because military warfare was to be a pivotal part of the nation's near-term future, Moses established rules to limit the temptation to go to war and to prevent abuses. These included the duty to seek a peaceful resolution to the conflict before going to war, the prohibition against wanton destruction of the enemies' natural resources, and rules governing the treatment of female captives to make it less likely that male soldiers caught in the heat of battle would engage in rape and plunder (Deut. 20–21).

By establishing the institutions and rules of governance for the people before taking leave of them, he assured that Joshua, his successor, and the Israelites, his disciples, would be able to fulfill his vision of becoming a special people in their own land.

Recording Your Legacy

As leaders prepare to leave their leadership roles or, depending upon circumstances, shortly after departing, they have the responsibility of leaving behind a distillation of the wisdom and experience they have amassed in the course of their tenure. The purpose of such a distillation is to strengthen the ability of the leader's successor and followers to build on the accomplishments of the leader. Without the fruits of the leader's experience being recorded in some permanent and accessible form, the lessons learned by the leader and by the leader's generation will be forgotten and will have to be relearned over and over again at considerable cost to the organization in subsequent generations.

Yet recording the legacy is not enough. Ideally, "replaying" what is recorded must itself be institutionalized by the outgoing leader in such a way that the future successors and followers will be receptive to, learn from, and incorporate what was experienced during the leader's steward-ship of the organization. This replaying, like the communication of the original vision, needs to be not merely communicated but overcommu-nicated in as many media and on as many occasions as possible.

The book of Deuteronomy, which is described in the Bible as Mish-neh Torah, the "reiteration or repetition of the Torah" (Deut. 17:18; Josh. 8:32), is the embodiment of Moses's personal, recorded legacy to his own generation and to all future generations of his people; it is Moses's ethical will. Deuteronomy is not Moses's review of the Bible's previous four books. Anyone who even cursorily reads the book knows how dras-tically it differs from the previous books of the Bible, both in content and in style. Much of it is written in the first person while the rest of the Bible is written in the third person—it is Moses's voice that we hear rather than the voice of the detached narrator. Upon more careful reading of the book, many of the stories recounted by Moses, and a substantial por-tion of the laws, differ in important respects from the versions found in the first four books of the Bible. The legal experts of Judaism in the early centuries of the Common Era also read its content as having indepen-dent legal value and information not contained in the previous four books. Therefore, the meaning of Mishneh Torah, literally, "the review of the Bible," is directed not at the object, the text itself; rather, it is an imper-ative to the subject, the reader and particularly the leader, to review over and over the essential principles contained therein.[10] Moses, the great edu-cator and leader of the Israelites, knew that repetition is an important key to effective communication and long-term memory for leader and fol-lower alike.

No wonder, then, that there are devices built into Deuteronomy that make it incumbent on the people to recall and "replay" essential parts of the book's message at given times in their lives. The twice daily read-ing of the passage of the shema, the Jewish credo, by all the people was one such "replaying" device.[11] The pilgrim's yearly retelling of the people's history upon bringing the first fruits to the Temple was a second.[12] The king's duty to consult Deuteronomy "all the days of his life" and to read publicly from the book at the conclusion of every seventh (Sabbatical) year as all the people stood before him in solemn assembly were a third and fourth.[13] Moses's re-covenanting ceremony in the plains of Moab before he took leave of the second generation and they entered the land was a fifth.[14] The command to Joshua to rewrite the Bible on the plaster painted cliffs of the Promised Land upon entry and to hold there a dramatic reconfirmation of the people's fealty to the covenant was the sixth.[15] The seventh was the teaching of Moses's poem to the people at the very end of his life.[16] These were all attempts at institutionalizing the replaying of the leader's final message to the people so that it would be remembered. Finally, Moses handed a definitive written version of his legacy over to the Levites for safekeeping in the holy of holies, next to the Ark containing the Ten Commandments. Recording his legacy in written form and safeguarding it in the equivalent of the national archives ensured that his message would not be forgotten.

When a leader leaves a legacy, an organization's ethical will, it should include a reiteration of the organization's mission statement, norms, and historical experience (including the mistakes made during the leader's term both by the leader and by the followers, and their respective consequences); the leader's vision for the future if the mission is adhered to— or not; and the leader's parting blessings for success.

In the book of Deuteronomy, Moses leaves a one-volume summary of the key events that took place under his leadership watch;[17] the fundamental principles and practices of the Bible to prepare the people for dealing with life on the land (Deut. 6–26); his vision of the people's future, witnessed by the entire Israelite nation, both if the people followed the covenant and if they did not (Deut. 27–32); and a parting set of blessings to the individual tribes and to the nation as a whole (Deut. 33–34). The purpose of Deuteronomy was to offer the people a benchmark to which they could easily refer, to evaluate where their society was in relationship to their founder's vision, so as to make the appropriate corrections in the nation's course. In fact, in Kings II, chapters 22 and 23, the apparently long-lost book of Deuteronomy, served this evaluative and corrective function in 622 BCE, during the reign of King Josiah.

Moses concludes the book with a song (easily remembered) and a blessing. The latter is the fitting conclusion to the Bible, in which human beings begin life with blessing (Gen. 1:28), the Israelites' story begins with blessing (Gen. 12:3), and now their story, as a full-fledged nation, concludes with blessing.

The Bible teaches us that the job of a leader is to take leave of his people with blessing. That is the way God took leave of the world at creation (Gen. 2:4). It is the way God took leave of Abraham (Gen. 22), the way Jacob/Israel took leave of his children (Gen. 49), and the way Moses, too, leaves his people. To use Max Depree's parallel insight in his classic book *Leadership Is an Art*, the final job of a leader is to leave gracefully and to say thank you.[18]

By concluding with a blessing, Moses also models for his readers what it means to be "a kingdom of priests" (Exod. 19:6). One of the main functions of the priesthood was to bless the people (Num. 6:22–26). At the peak experiences of the year, the priesthood, representing God's overflowing love, would bless the people.[19] So, too, is it the responsibility of God's kingdom of priests to bring blessing to all the peoples of the world.

Conclusion

It is fitting that the fifth and final of the Five Books of Moses is called "words" in Hebrew. The man who said to God as he was recruited to be the Israelites' leader, "I am not a man of words, not today, yesterday, nor the day before" (Exod. 4:10), learns to become the quintessential man of words at the end of his leadership reign. He begins the book of Deuteronomy with: "These are the words that Moses spoke to all the Israelites … " (Deut. 1:1) and ends the book thirty-three chapters later with inspired words of poetry and blessing. Indeed, almost the entire book of Deuteronomy consists of Moses using his newfound power of words to persuade his people to remain fiercely committed to their vision and faithfully loyal to their values—and to each other.

In his final book, Moses displays no miraculous show of force, only an eloquent and forceful choice of language to convince the new generation to learn and follow all that he has learned—from God and from them—in the Promised Land that they are about to conquer and settle. With his brother Aaron no longer alive to be his spokesman, Moses incorporates into his own self Aaron's power of speech to communicate passionately his life's vision, values, and mission to his people. By using his words and committing them to writing, he provides an inspiring legacy of leadership for his successor, Joshua, and all the leaders who follow in his wake.

Moses retells and records the story of his nation in Deuteronomy and in so doing puts his final stamp of leadership on his people. It is not leaders like the Pharaohs, who accumulate the most wealth or power before they die, or who have the largest, well-attended funerals, or the most impressive pyramids erected, who succeed in defeating death and achieving leadership immortality. Rather, it is leaders who author the foundational story of their group, which is retold from generation to generation, who succeed in defeating death and assuring their own and their people's eternity. Moses's people survived 3,200 years and are alive today because Moses authored their foundational story, taught them his vision, and left them his legacy.

This, too, is the key to our own immortality as leaders. To share and record our leadership story—from its genesis to its conclusion—with our people is to embed life-affirming values and a hopeful vision of our future in their hearts and minds. To help them learn from our mistakes and to leave them with a legacy fortifies them to face life's many opportunities and challenges with confidence and blessings. To paraphrase the penulti-mate verse of the book of Ecclesiastes, "When all is said and done, that is the final word."

Notes

Introduction

1. For my purposes, I have dated the beginnings of contemporary leadership and management theory to the writings of John Gardner, Peter Drucker, and James MacGregor Burns. See John Gardner, *On Leadership* (New York: Free Press, 1989). Peter Drucker, *The Practice of Management* (New York: HarperCollins, 1954); *Management: Tasks, Responsibilities, Practices* (New York: Harper Collins, 1999). James MacGregor Burns, *Leadership* (New York: HarperCollins, 1978).
2. Isaiah 11:9.
3. The third book of the Bible, the book of Leviticus, contains almost no narrative and with three exceptions will remain outside the purview of this study. By focusing on the Bible's narrative, this study does not mean to discount the importance of the other literary genres in the first five biblical books, whether they concern law, temple ritual, or genealogy. Rather my work emphasizes how life stories—"narratives"—whether of an individual or of a nation, provide the ground from which relationships and leadership emerge.
4. In a recent interview, Yann Martel, author of *Life of Pi*, winner of the Man Booker Prize in 2002, said the following about the primacy of stories: "Yes, we're all made of stories, whether it's personal stories like the stories of your grandmother, your parents, you, or national stories or invented stories, that's really what makes a life, the story we tell. And religion does the same thing, it's a grand story and if we trust it it becomes faith and it changes our reality. The tragedy of secularism is that it has no stories ... " (Interview by Shiri Lev-Ari, "Writing Is a Kind of Happiness," published in *Ha'aretz*, October 7, 2005.)
5. Noel M. Tichy, "The Mark of a Winner," *Leader to Leader* 6 (Fall 1997): 24–29.
6. See also the biblical commentary of Shlomo Yitzchaki, known by the acronym Rashi, on Genesis 1:1, who asks precisely why the Bible does not begin with the first biblical laws, found in Exodus 12.
7. See Yochanan Muffs, *The Personhood of God* (Woodstock, Vt.: Jewish Lights, 2005), 63, 87.
8. Genesis 3:24, 4:12, 11:8; Exodus 33:1–3; Numbers 17:27.

9. Genesis 12:1–3; Exodus 19:1–8.
10. See Muffs, *The Personhood of God*, 89–94.

Book I: In the Beginning … : Relationships, Responsibility, and the Primacy of Values in Leadership

1. See John Kotter, "Leadership at the Turn of the Century," in *What Leaders Really Do* (Cambridge, Mass.: Harvard Business Review Press, 1999), 10–14. See also Warren Bennis and Burt Nanus, *Leaders: The Strategies for Taking Charge* (New York: Harper and Row, 1985).
2. In the Bible, trustworthiness and truth are interlocking concepts. See Yoram Hazony, "Truth in the Hebrew Bible," unpublished common Judaism manuscript (February 6, 2005).
3. See Stephen Covey, *The Seven Habits of Highly Effective Leaders* (New York: Simon and Schuster, 1989), 81ff. for a similar, but not identical, division. See also four types of responsibility in Jonathon Sacks, "Covenant and Conversation," *Parshat Noach* (October 16, 2004).
4. Genesis 38:26.
5. Genesis 43:8–10, 44:18–34.
6. Similarly, in the early part of the book of Exodus, Moses's coming to the aid of seven previously unknown shepherdesses who are being bullied by the local shepherds is another example of adopting this third circle of responsibility.
7. On how the status quo is changed see Genesis 3:7, 22.
8. I am again indebted to Yoram Hazony for this insight.
9. See Book III, Challenge 8.
10. See Psalm 115.
11. See the book of Daniel, chapter 3. The leadership of this earlier Babylonian edifice was interested only in its own self-aggrandizement.
12. Percy B. Shelley's poem "Ozymandias" was written perhaps with these type of self-aggrandizing edifices, and the leaders who built them, in mind:

> *I met a traveller from an antique land,*
> *Who said—two vast and trunkless legs of stone*
> *Stand in the desert … near them, on the sand,*
> *Half sunk a shattered visage lies, whose frown,*
> *And wrinkled lips, and sneer of cold command,*
> *Tell that its sculptor well those passions read*
> *Which yet survive, stamped on these lifeless things,*
> *The hand that mocked them, and the heart that fed;*
> *And on the pedestal these words appear:*

> *"My name is Ozymandias, King of Kings,*
> *Look on my Works ye Mighty, and despair!"*
> *Nothing beside remains. Round the decay*
> *Of that colossal Wreck, boundless and bare*
> *The lone and level sands stretch far away.*

13. "Unless God builds the house, its builders labor in vain over it" (Ps. 127:1).

14. See the commentary of the thirteenth-century Spanish biblical exegete, Nachmanides on Genesis 12:10, who takes Abraham to task for leaving God's land and exposing Sarah to moral compromise.

15. Later on, in the books of Exodus and Numbers, we will see similar instances of leadership on the basis of the willingness to risk oneself and cross over to protect one's brother. Moses puts his own life at risk by rescuing his endangered "Hebrew" brother (Exod. 2:11–15). In the book of Numbers, Moses demands the same of the two tribes who seek to settle in what is today the kingdom of Jordan. He conditions their being granted their request on their "crossing over" (the Jordan River) as a vanguard force to fight with their "brethren" for the Promised Land (Num. 32:6ff.).

16. My brilliant colleague, Dr. Avi Hilbuch, has pointed out that the contemporary Hebrew word for responsibility, *achrayut*, contains within it the word *ach*, meaning "brother"; *ach(e)r*, meaning "other"; and *ach(a)ray*, meaning "follow me." Abraham's persuading his allies and friends to follow him in rescuing his estranged "brother" is the full actualization of *achrayut*—taking responsibility.

17. See Covey, *The Seven Habits of Highly Effective People*, 188–190.

18. Sarah ends up using her free hand to abuse Hagar, a morally problematic outcome to Abraham's gesture to his wife. This episode will be morally compounded in Genesis 21, when Sarah insists on the banishment of both Hagar and her son Ishmael. See pp. 79.

19. In the second chapter of Exodus, a later leader, Moses, is faced with a trilogy of leadership situations, each of which he responds to differently: using commensurate force to halt an Egyptian taskmaster who was using lethal force against an Israelite slave, intervening with words to halt a clash between two fellow Israelites, and using his physical presence to side with the vulnerable shepherdesses against their bullying shepherds. The point of that chapter is also to highlight the discernment and the full repertoire of responses that leaders need to possess in order respond to different situations.

20. This testing of sacrificial commitment may also be the deeper meaning of the strange incident found in Exodus 4:24–26 in which Moses, before he can assume the leadership of his people, must have his son circumcised.

21. See, for instance, Leviticus 19:33–34; Deuteronomy 10:19, 24:17.

22. See Genesis 11:29. The spiritual masters of early Judaism interpret Sarai as being identical with Yiskah (Sarai and Yiskah having similar meanings: i.e., princess), the daughter of Abraham's brother, Haran, and therefore the granddaughter of Abraham's father, Terach.

23. Later on, the Jewish tradition developed a thoughtful and thorough process of personal change precisely from this recognition of human nature. See Maimonides, Mishneh Torah, "The Book of Knowledge—Laws of Repentance."

24. In Genesis, God's self-reflective learning is made explicit; see Genesis 8:31. In Numbers, God's learning curve is implicit in God's absence from the narrative for a thirty-eight-year period (cf. Num. 10:11 and 20:1). It is as if God has taken a time-out to reflect on what has gone wrong in God's leadership strategy with the first generation before reestablishing communication with the second generation.

25. This was obviously the case in the leadership life of President Bill Clinton, an otherwise successful and popular leader, whose tendency to philander, which repeatedly marred his political career, nearly cost him his presidency.

26. I am indebted to my colleague Rabbi David Silber for this important insight.

27. See Devora Steinmetz, *From Father to Son: Kinship, Conflict, and Continuity in Genesis* (Louisville, Ky.: Westminster John Knox Press, 1991).

28. As to the later patriarchs, Isaac does better but does not completely succeed with his two sons, Jacob and Esau. Jacob, despite major mistakes along the way, ultimately ends up being the most successful of all the patriarchs in taking responsibility for his twelve sons and his two grandsons, who were at the highest risk of being left out of the family's covenantal future. Jacob fails to take responsibility, however, for his daughter—see Genesis 34. The Bible attempts, at least partially, to deal with parental responsibility for daughters in Numbers 30:2ff.

29. In fact, in a commentary of the spiritual masters of early Judaism on the story, when Sarah finds out that Abraham has taken Isaac to be slaughtered, she dies of a heart attack before hearing that Abraham did not go through with the act (Bereshit Rabbah, 5).

30. This is what Abraham apparently did later on in his life when he sent away the children of his third wife, Keturah, with "presents" (Gen. 25:6).

31. This refusal to slaughter one's children in the service of God becomes normative in the Bible through the prohibition of Molech worship. See Leviticus 18:21, 20:1–5.

32. See the section "The Crucible of Leadership: Joseph in Egypt" for how Joseph plays the role of God in testing his brothers' willingness to abandon Benjamin to a life of slavery in Egypt, as they had abandoned Joseph years earlier. There, too, an act of substitution, with Judah offering his service in place of Benjamin, allows the brothers to pass the test.

33. A contemporary theory of leadership known as "polarity management" explains how this process works. See Barry Johnson, *Polarity Management: Identifying and Managing Unsolvable Problems* (Amherst, Mass.: HRD Press, 1996).

34. While it is true that Abraham's covenantal blessings of fertility and possession of the land were given by Isaac to Jacob later on before sending him off to find a wife, the ability to be a source of blessing to the world was also part of Abraham's legacy; see Genesis 12:1–3; 22:17–18. Had Rebecca not acted, Abraham's blessings would have been split into two, with the covenantal blessings becoming subordinate to the material blessings. I am indebted for this insight to an unpublished manuscript by my friend and colleague Joseph Rackman.

35. The later hostility between Jacob's descendants, the Israelite people who leave Egypt, and one of Esau's descendants, the marauding tribe of Amalek, is prefigured in this contention over their father's blessing (see Gen. 36:12; Exod. 17:9ff.; Deut. 25:17ff.). Note also the similarities of language between Esau's coming from the field (Gen. 25:29) and the coming of Amalek (Exod. 17:9) and the "measure for measure," karma-like comeuppance between Jacob's taking advantage of Esau's fatigue (Gen. 25:32) and Amalek's taking advantage of the Israelites' fatigue (Deut. 25:18). Edom, another of Esau's descendants, refused to allow the Israelites to traverse his territory, and this is probably also linked to Jacob's refusal to follow Esau to his territory after their apparent reconciliation (cf. Num. 20:14ff.; Gen. 32:12ff.).

36. In all fairness to Rachel, Jacob had already set the precedent for the commoditization of their spousal status by agreeing to Lavan's proposal that Jacob purchase Rachel's services as a wife. See Genesis 31:15.

37. See Genesis 24:3–4, 26:34–35, 27:46–28:9 and Leviticus 18.

38. Including Reuben should be contrasted to Ham's being disowned by Noah for his sexual indiscretion; including Shimon and Levi is noteworthy because Ishmael and Esau may have disqualified themselves from being carriers of God's covenant precisely because of their violent natures—Ishmael was an archer and a plunderer (Gen. 21:20, 25:18), and Esau was a hunter and military strongman (Gen. 25:27, 32:6).

39. Shimon's tribal territory in the Promised Land will be surrounded by the tribe of Judah, who will keep them in line, and the tribe of Levi will be scattered among the twelve tribes.

Book II: The Ten Guiding Principles of Leadership

1. Michael Hammer, "The Hardest Part of Reengineering," in *The Reengineering Revolution* (New York: HarperCollins, 1995), 117–136.

2. Ibid.

3. John Kotter, "Leading Change: Why Transformation Efforts Fail," in *What Leaders Really Do* (Cambridge, Mass.: Harvard Business School Press, 1999), 76–77.

4. In Genesis 13:10, the Bible compares the fertility of Egypt to the fertility of the Garden of Eden. The setting for the comparison is Lot's appraisal of the western side of the Jordan River, which appears to him as being as extraordinarily fertile, "as the Garden of God, as the Land of Egypt." Lot chooses to settle there in the ill-fated cities of Sodom and Gomorrah. Apparently, the Bible is telegraphing the reader that Sodom and Egypt, despite their shared Shangri-la appearance, will end up being experienced by their Abrahamic relatives the way that Adam and Eve experienced Eden—as seductive environments from which they will be expelled, with no possibility of return.

5. *The New York Times,* July 15, 2003, F3.

6. Or, as the sages state, remarrying (Shmot Rabbah 1:19).

7. Numbers 32.

8. See Genesis 15:13, where God uses the double verb for "knowing" in the promise to Abraham to redeem Abraham's descendants from slavery.

9. See Ronald A. Heifetz, *Leadership without Easy Answers* (Cambridge, Mass.: Belknap Press, 1994), 269ff.

10. These twin attributes of caring and courage explain the double use by the Bible of a "coming of age" metaphor regarding Moses in the second chapter of Exodus: *Vayigdal Moshe,* literally, "and Moses grew up" (Exod. 2:10–11). The first "growing up" in his parents and stepmother's home refer to his physical development from an infant to a young child to a man. The second "growing up," in which Moses goes out to witness and intervene in the plight of his brothers, refers to the qualities of empathy and responsibility that he developed—the "coming of age" of Moses's moral character and compass. Moses was fortunate enough to have several significant parental figures early in his life who modeled and imbued him with a sense of security, empathy, courage, and responsibility.

11. Peter Koestenbaum, *Leadership: The Inner Side of Greatness* (San Francisco: Jossey-Bass, 2002), 186–218.

12. See Michael Walzer, *Exodus and Revolution* (New York: Basic Books, 1985) for the impact of Moses's leadership on subsequent human history.

13. See chapter 4, "Confront the Brutal Facts (but Never Lose Faith)," Jim Collins, *Good to Great* (New York: Harper Collins, 2001).

14. James S. Kouzes and Barry Z. Posner, *The Leadership Challenge* (San Francisco: Jossey-Bass, 1987), 95–96.

15. See John Keegan's *Winston Churchill: A Penguin Life* (New York: Viking, 2002).

16. This is what Ron Heifetz of Harvard's JFK School of Government refers to as adaptive change rather than just technical change. See *Leadership without Easy Answers,* 30ff.

17. Kotter, *What Leaders Really Do.*

18. In the book of Genesis, Jacob knows that he must recruit others to actualize his vision as a patriarch of his nation. At the outset, he makes a bargain with God, promising to tithe his resources and to build a household for God that is capable of developing into a nation if God will enable him to survive. To help actualize his vision for building a large, extended family, he recruits his wives, Leah and Rachel, for whom he labors a total of fourteen years and who bear his sons. Later on, in the midst of a regional famine that threatens their continued survival, Jacob recruits his son Judah to present the family's case before the Egyptian viceroy and to make preparations for their immigration to Egypt. To guarantee his burial in the ancestral grave back in Canaan, he recruits Joseph, who has the ear of the Egyptian court and the authority to execute his final wishes. (For God, see Gen. 28:20–22; for Rachel and Leah, see Gen. 31:4–16; for Judah, see Gen. 43–44, 46:28; for Joseph, see Gen. 46:29–31, 50:4–14.)

19. It is unclear from the passage and the verses that precede it whether the "him" who God tries to kill refers to Moses or to their own, previously uncircumcised son. See David Gelernter, "Orim," *Yale Student Journal,* 1986.

20. See Exodus 4:26, where there is no mention of Tziporah, and Exodus 18:2—*After She Was Sent Away* and Rashbam, op. cit., indicating that Tziporah was sent away by Moses shortly after the circumcision episode.

21. It may be that the words God instructed Moses to use were a code established by Joseph with his brothers and handed down from generation to generation as the words that the future redeemer would actually use. Moses, however, was not yet aware of the significance of God's words (cf. Exod. 3:16–17 to Gen. 50:24–25, plus the commentaries of Rashi and Nachmanides on Exod. 3:17).

22. Pharaoh releases the Israelites not because of any genuine change of heart on his part but because his nation will not let him do otherwise; they fear they will all die (Exod. 12:33). Indeed, at the first available opportunity, Pharaoh will resume his hardheartedness and seek to re-enslave the Israelites (Exod. 14:5). Still, the plagues break the chains of bondage and allow the Exodus from Egypt to get under way.

23. See Exodus 7:5, 17; 8:6, 18; 9:14–16; 10:2.

24. Kotter, *What Leaders Really Do,* 82–85.

25. For a penetrating analysis of the power of winning and losing streaks to become self-fulfilling prophecies, see Rosabeth Moss Kanter, *Confidence* (New York: Random House, 2004).

26. Abraham Maslow, *Motivation and Personality* (New York: Harper and Row, 1987).

27. See Stephen Covey, *The Seven Habits of Highly Effective People* (New York: Simon and Schuster, 1989), 185–203.

28. It is interesting to note that although God tells Moses about the double portion of Manna that will fall on Fridays to make unnecessary the gathering of the manna on the Sabbath, Moses does not initially tell the people about this special, extra pre-Sabbath provision. He instead waits until the people themselves discover the double portion of heavenly food that has fallen on the first Friday and come to him seeking an explanation. By managing the people's expectations to only anticipate the single portion of Manna to fall, and then producing double the amount every Friday, Moses underpromises and overdelivers, a favorite leadership strategy of former mayor of New York, Rudolph Giuliani (see Rudolph W. Giuliani, *Leadership* [New York: Hyperion, 2002], 155–170).

29. See Deuteronomy 25:17–19.

30. See Aaron Wildavsky, *Moses as Political Leader* (Lanham, Md.: Shalem Press, 2005), 22–29.

31. The latter consideration, while not mentioned in the Bible in this episode, seems to have been the thinking behind the investment of spirit in seventy additional leaders that takes place about one year later (Num. 11:16ff.).

32. The view of the thirteenth-century biblical exegete Nachmanides.

33. The opinion of the eleventh-century biblical commentator Rashi.

34. See Leviticus 18, 20.

35. See, for instance, Moshe Greenberg, "Some Postulates of Biblical Criminal Law," *The Jewish Expression,* edited by Judah Goldin (New Haven: Yale University Press, 1976). See also Neal M. Soss, "Old Testament Law and Economic Society," *Journal of the History of Ideas* 34, no. 3 (July–September 1973).

36. Either the feast of weeks, as traditionally understood or, as I have argued elsewhere, the day of Rosh Hashanah (see my essay, "Rosh Hashanah and Revelation," *Jewish Spectator* [Summer 1999]).

37. Edgar Schein, *Organizational Culture and Leadership* (San Francisco: Jossey-Bass, 1997), 106–115.

38. The holiday of Shavuot was also celebrated to mark the giving of the Bible.

39. Quoted in Walzer, *Exodus and Revolution,* 56, 159.

Book III: The Challenges of Leadership

1. See Eliyahu Goldratt, *The Goal: A Process of Ongoing Improvement* (Great Barrington, Mass.: North River Press, 1984).

2. This may, in part, account for the attempt by the rabbinic interpretative tradition, cited in the Babylonian Talmud, Tractate Shabbat 89a, to argue that Moses did, in fact, tell the people how long he would be away but that the people miscalculated by one day. Nevertheless, the plain meaning

of the text does not indicate this to be the case. Because the sin committed was so egregious and so affected the future course of the people, one expects that the Bible would be very precise in saying exactly what was and was not communicated. Moreover, it is highly unlikely, if not physically impossible, that the forming of the golden calf took place in one day.

3. When Moses is met by Joshua during his descent, Joshua mistakenly believes from the shouting below that another war has broken out in their absence (Exod. 32:17).

4. We will see exactly this situation developing in Numbers 11 after Aaron's leadership is discredited and Hur disappears from the biblical narrative—possibly the result of being assassinated by the unruly mob during the episode of the golden calf (see *Midrash VaYikra Rabbah* 10:13). Without his supporters, Moses complains that the weight of "holding" the people is simply too much for him to bear alone.

5. See Tosefta, Tractate Sotah, chapter 4, law 3 (Lieberman edition).

6. See Exodus 19:5–7.

7. Those ten instances were: the rebellion at the Sea of Reeds, *Marah, Midbar Sin, Massah-Umeriva*, the golden calf, *Ketoret Zarah, Tavayrah, Kivrot Ha-Taavah, Odot Miriam*, and *Meraglim*.

8. See also David Noel Freedman, *The Nine Commandments*, (New York: Doubleday, 2000), 10ff.

9. See chapter 6, "The Turnaround Challenge," in Rosabeth Moss Kanter, *Confidence: How Winning Streaks and Losing Streaks Begin and End* (New York: Crown Business, 2004). Jeffrey Lurie's moving his residence from Hollywood to Philadelphia upon purchasing the then-losing Philadelphia Eagles is an inspiring contemporary example of a leader symbolically throwing in his plight with his group.

10. *Midrash Vayikrah Rabbah* 10:3.

11. See Rashi on Numbers 25:6, "and they were crying."

12. Ironically, in this sense, as we will see in Book IV, Pinchas is proof positive of Moses's success as a spiritual leader. Moses has made himself superfluous by raising from among the people leaders who are ready to do the right thing on their own initiative rather than waiting for Moses to act alone or tell them what to do.

13. See the commentary of Rabbi Isaac Arama in *Akeidat Yitzchak*, chapter 85. See also the analysis that supports the position of Rav Elchanan Samet on *Parshat Matot-Masei*, http://www.VBM-torah.org/parsha.60/42mm.htm.

14. See Nachmanides on Numbers 32:5 and the commentary of Abravanel, ad. loc.

15. As we noted in Genesis, the story of Moses confronting the two seceding tribes serves as a corrective not merely for Moses's failure to confront courageously the people in the book of Numbers but also for Abraham's initial failure to take responsibility for his "brother" Lot in the book of

Genesis. In Genesis 13, the Bible describes how the great number of cattle owned by Abraham and Lot caused their shepherds to quarrel and led Abraham to suggest that they ought to separate, implicitly agreeing to Lot's settling in the evil city of Sodom. When Lot was taken as a prisoner of war in the victory of the four kings over the five kings, Abraham, called for the first time by the surname Ivri, the one who "crossed over," did an about-face and rescued him in a daring nighttime raid (Gen. 14).

16. On the need for leaders to assert themselves, see also the biblical commentary of Rashi on Deuteronomy 3:28 and 31:7.

17. This is precisely the argument made by Rabbi Abraham Isaac Kook, see *War and Peace*, David Samson and Tzvi Fishman, editors (Jerusalem: Torat Eretz Yisrael Publications, 1997), 116–118.

18. Indeed in the Book of Joshua, immediately prior to the people's first battle to conquer the city of Jericho, Joshua has an encounter that proves this angel was not just a figure of God's speech:

> *When Joshua was near Jericho, he looked up and saw a man standing before him, drawn sword in hand. Joshua went up to him and asked him, "Are you one of us or of our enemies?" He replied, "Neither; I am captain of the Lord, God's forces. Now I have come!" Joshua threw himself face down to the ground … (Josh. 5:13–14)*

The miraculous conquest of Jericho, with the walls tumbling down by themselves, indicate that God's angelic captain did the job that the Israelites expected.

19. Cf. Numbers 1:1 and 9:1.

20. Another way of reading what Moses was asking his father-in-law to do was to act as his in-house consultant in managing the people, as he did back in Exodus 18. To be "eyes for us" may reflect back on Jethro's "seeing," that is, "recognizing," what Moses was inadvertently doing to the people. Jethro provided an outsider's perspective on managing the volatile, anxiety-ridden Israelite camp that Moses lacked.

21. See Exodus 18:14ff.

22. I am indebted to my colleague, Daniel Polisar, president of the Shalem Center, for this insightful reading.

23. My teacher, professor Uriel Simon, has argued that once the Israelites were set free, they were expected to participate in their own defense. This may be true but, if so, then the repeated communications regarding the role of an angel in the book of Exodus engendered a set of false, unrealistic expectations among the people.

24. It may well be that the Bible, in the only instance in the Five Books of Moses, explicitly goes out of chronological order and separates the two episodes by several chapters (putting the military census and organization of the camp at the beginning of the book (chapters 1 and 2) and "bury-

ing" the subject of the second Passover in the middle of chapter 9) to try to hide the connection between these two events from the average reader. Nevertheless, careful readers of the text, who rearrange the events chronologically and imagine themselves in the time and place of these events immediately see a possible connection between the delay of the makeup Passover and the already discussed, unanticipated decision to count and arrange the people in military formation.

The similarity in language between this episode of the makeup Passover and the query that the five daughters of Tzelofchad will bring to Moses forty years later (see Challenge 8) may be noteworthy in this regard. Both episodes begin with the complaint "Why should we be barred" (Num. 9:7 and 27:4), indicating some sort of archetypal symmetry between the petition of the small group in the first generation, who sought to remain spiritually connected to God through God's commanded ritual of the Passover offering, and the petition of the small group in the second generation, who sought to remain geographically connected to God through the laws regulating inheritance rights of God's chosen land. Unlike in the first generation, when God and Moses's ruling in favor of the few (those who were ritually impure) at the expense of the many (the overwhelming majority of the people) was their first and final decision, in the second generation, as we will see, there is a legal appeal and a corrective to the original decision rendered by the leadership team. The corrective, found in the final text of the book of Numbers, protects the rights of the many—in this case, the territorial integrity of the tribe of Manasseh—while still addressing, albeit in more limited fashion, the rights of the few—the inheritance rights of the five daughters of Tzelofchad. This gives further credence to the view that the decision to have a makeup Passover at Sinai went too far in protecting minority rights at the expense of the majority.

The silver lining in comparing the cases of the makeup Passover offering and the inheritance rights of the daughters of Tzelofchad is that it shows that the leadership team of God and Moses continued to be learning leaders. They learned from the consequences of their leadership miscues with the first generation how to deal more effectively with the leadership challenges of the second generation.

25. See Ronald A. Heifetz and Marty Linsky, *Leadership on the Line* (Cambridge, Mass.: Harvard Business School Press, 2002), 13–14.

26. See Warren Bennis and Burt Nanus, *Leaders: The Strategies for Taking Charge,* (New York: Harper and Row, 1985).

27. See the section "God, Adam, and Eve," in Book I.

28. See Nachmanides, Numbers 16:1.

29. See Nathan Laufer, *Leading the Passover Journey: The Seder's Meaning Revealed, the Haggadah's Story Retold* (Woodstock, Vt.: Jewish Lights, 2005), 70–75.

30. See the eleventh-century biblical commentary of Abraham Ibn Ezra to Numbers 16:1.
31. This characteristic of the permanent and the unchanging was endemic to ancient Egyptian culture, in which the immutable sun was worshipped and monumental buildings of massive stone meant to convey the sense of unalterable permanence dominated the country's physical landscape. Israelite culture, in contrast, organized itself around the lunar calendar and had a portable, movable sanctuary at the center of its camp.
32. Since God is also referred to as the "Rock of Israel," it may be that Moses was symbolically striking out in grief and anger at God.
33. See chapter 2 of Maimonides, *Eight Chapters* (New York: Moznaim Publishing Corp, 1994), in which he takes Moses to task for his display of anger toward the people.
34. Cf. Exodus 15:26, where, following the miraculous provision of water to the people at Marah and prior to the miraculous provision of manna in the "Wilderness of Sin," God says that "if the Israelites obey God's commands … all the diseases that God set upon Egypt will not be set upon the Israelites because I am God your healer." Moses, by crediting himself and Aaron with the miracle of providing water for the second generation of Israelites, has failed to sanctify God as the provider and, by extension, the healer of Israel.
35. God's decree after the incident at the "Waters of Contention" brings us to another failure of Moses. Once God informs Moses that he will not lead his people into the Promised Land, it would have been proper for Moses to address the issue of his replacement immediately and assure the appointment of his successor. Instead, several chapters and months go by before Moses has the courage to initiate this discussion with God. One of the fallouts of this delay, and of Moses's faltering leadership, is the idolatrous celebration and worship of Baal Peor that results in 24,000 dead Israelites. It is not surprising that, almost immediately after that incident, God tells Moses to respond to the idolatrous seduction by going to war against the Midianites, who seduced the Israelites, and then to prepare to leave his people on earth and be gathered up to his people in heaven.

It is only after Moses is commanded to prepare for war against the Midianites, and after he conducts a second census of the military-age men to prepare for that battle, that Moses raises the issue of succession. Once he does, as we will soon see in Book IV, he does so wholeheartedly and in exemplary fashion. But like most leaders, he is hesitant to leave his position even when it should have been obvious to him that it was time to do so.

Moses is normal in that way, but normal is not what the Bible is trying to teach. The Bible is striving mightily to reach toward the ideal, and the ideal is for leaders, once they have been informed that they are being relieved of their leadership roles, to hand over the reins of leadership as soon as possible and bow out graciously.

36. Deuteronomy 17:14–20.
37. It is noteworthy that Moses comes to this compromise on his own, without consulting with God. See also Joshua 1:14.

Book IV: The Legacy of Leadership

1. See Deuteronomy 8:7–10.
2. See, for example, Genesis 15:16 and 48:22.
3. Deuteronomy 3:11.
4. Numbers 31:8.
5. Exodus 17.
6. Exodus 32.
7. Exodus 33:11.
8. Numbers 11:28.
9. Numbers 13–14.
10. For this insight, I am indebted to Menachem Liebtag, Introduction to Deuteronomy, VBM Internet archives, http://www.tanach.org/dvrint.htm.
11. *Vesheenantom Levanecha*, "and you shall repeatedly educate your children," Deuteronomy 6:4–9.
12. Deuteronomy 26:1–11.
13. Deuteronomy 17:19, 31:10–13
14. Deutronomy 28.
15. Deuteronomy 27.
16. Deuteronomy 31:14–32:47.
17. Deuteronomy 1–5; 9.
18. Max Depree, *Leadership Is an Art* (New York: Dell Publishing, 1989).
19. See, for instance, Leviticus 9:22; see also the Day of Atonement supplemental service in the High Holiday prayer book. The priestly blessing concludes "with love."

About the Author

Nathan Laufer is president emeritus of Wexner Heritage, a leadership education foundation established in 1985 by Leslie H. Wexner, founder and chairman of Limited Brands Inc. In his seventeen years of leadership at the foundation, including nine as president and CEO, he developed the foundation's two-year intensive leadership education program in thirty-one cities across North America, empowering more than 1,300 influential community leaders.

The Genesis of Leadership was written while Rabbi Laufer was a senior fellow at the Shalem Center, a Jerusalem think tank that addresses social, religious, and political issues of leadership in Israel and the world.

Rabbi Laufer received his Leadership Educator Certification from the John F. Kennedy School of Government at Harvard University, his law degree from the Fordham University School of Law, and ordination from Yeshiva University. He writes, teaches, and lectures throughout North America and Israel regarding leadership, education, identity, meaning, and the Bible's lessons for contemporary times. He is also the author of *Leading the Passover Journey: The Seder's Meaning Revealed, the Haggadah's Story Retold* (Jewish Lights).

Nathan Laufer, a member of the New York State Bar Association, is married to Sharon Laufer and is the father of four children, including triplets.

Spirituality/The Way Into... Series

The Way Into... Series offers an accessible and highly usable "guided tour" of the Jewish faith, people, history and beliefs—in total, an introduction to Judaism that will enable you to understand and interact with the sacred texts of the Jewish tradition. Each volume is written by a leading contemporary scholar and teacher, and explores one key aspect of Judaism. The Way Into... enables all readers to achieve a real sense of Jewish cultural literacy through guided study.

The Way Into Encountering God in Judaism By Neil Gillman
6 x 9, 240 pp, Quality PB, ISBN 1-58023-199-3 **$18.99**; Hardcover, ISBN 1-58023-025-3 **$21.95**

Also Available: **The Jewish Approach to God: A Brief Introduction for Christians**
By Neil Gillman 5½ x 8¼, 192 pp, Quality PB, ISBN 1-58023-190-X **$16.95**

The Way Into Jewish Mystical Tradition By Lawrence Kushner
6 x 9, 224 pp, Quality PB, ISBN 1-58023-200-0 **$18.99**; Hardcover, ISBN 1-58023-029-6 **$21.95**

The Way Into Jewish Prayer By Lawrence A. Hoffman
6 x 9, 224 pp, Quality PB, ISBN 1-58023-201-9 **$18.99**; Hardcover, ISBN 1-58023-027-X **$21.95**

The Way Into Judaism and the Environment By Jeremy Benstein, PhD
6 x 9, 225 pp (est.), Hardcover, ISBN 1-58023-268-X **$24.99**

The Way Into Tikkun Olam (Repairing the World) By Elliot N. Dorff
6 x 9, 320 pp, Hardcover, ISBN 1-58023-269-8 **$24.99**

The Way Into Torah By Norman J. Cohen
6 x 9, 176 pp, Quality PB, ISBN 1-58023-198-5 **$16.99**; Hardcover, ISBN 1-58023-028-8 **$21.95**

Bible Study/Midrash

Hineini in Our Lives: Learning How to Respond to Others through 14 Biblical Texts and Personal Stories By Norman J. Cohen 6 x 9, 240 pp, Quality PB, ISBN 1-58023-274-4 **$16.99**
Hardcover, ISBN 1-58023-131-4 **$23.95**

Ancient Secrets: Using the Stories of the Bible to Improve Our Everyday Lives
By Rabbi Levi Meier, PhD 5½ x 8½, 288 pp, Quality PB, ISBN 1-58023-064-4 **$16.95**

Moses—The Prince, the Prophet: His Life, Legend & Message for Our Lives
By Rabbi Levi Meier, PhD 6 x 9, 224 pp, Quality PB, ISBN 1-58023-069-5 **$16.95**

Self, Struggle & Change: Family Conflict Stories in Genesis and Their Healing Insights for Our Lives By Norman J. Cohen 6 x 9, 224 pp, Quality PB, ISBN 1-879045-66-4 **$18.99**

Voices from Genesis: Guiding Us through the Stages of Life By Norman J. Cohen
6 x 9, 192 pp, Quality PB, ISBN 1-58023-118-7 **$16.95**

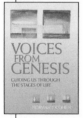

Or phone, fax, mail or e-mail to: **JEWISH LIGHTS Publishing**
Sunset Farm Offices, Route 4 • P.O. Box 237 • Woodstock, Vermont 05091
Tel: (802) 457-4000 • Fax: (802) 457-4004 • www.jewishlights.com
Credit card orders: (800) 962-4544 (8:30AM–5:30PM ET Monday–Friday)
Generous discounts on quantity orders. SATISFACTION GUARANTEED. Prices subject to change.

Spirituality

Does the Soul Survive? A Jewish Journey to Belief in Afterlife, Past Lives & Living with Purpose *By Rabbi Elie Kaplan Spitz. Foreword by Brian L Weiss, MD*
Spitz relates his own experiences and those shared with him by people he has worked with as a rabbi, and shows us that belief in afterlife and past lives, so often approached with reluctance, is in fact true to Jewish tradition.
6 x 9, 288 pp, Quality PB, ISBN 1-58023-165-9 **$16.99**; Hardcover, ISBN 1-58023-094-6 **$21.95**

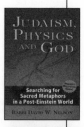

First Steps to a New Jewish Spirit: Reb Zalman's Guide to Recapturing the Intimacy & Ecstasy in Your Relationship with God
By Rabbi Zalman M. Schachter-Shalomi with Donald Gropman
An extraordinary spiritual handbook that restores psychic and physical vigor by introducing us to new models and alternative ways of practicing Judaism. Offers meditation and contemplation exercises for enriching the most important aspects of everyday life. 6 x 9, 144 pp, Quality PB, ISBN 1-58023-182-9 **$16.95**

God in Our Relationships: Spirituality between People from the Teachings of Martin Buber *By Rabbi Dennis S. Ross*
On the eightieth anniversary of Buber's classic work, we can discover new answers to critical issues in our lives. Inspiring examples from Ross's own life—as congregational rabbi, father, hospital chaplain, social worker, and husband—illustrate Buber's difficult-to-understand ideas about how we encounter God and each other. 5½ x 8½, 160 pp, Quality PB, ISBN 1-58023-147-0 **$16.95**

Judaism, Physics and God: Searching for Sacred Metaphors in a Post-Einstein World *By Rabbi David W. Nelson*
In clear, non-technical terms, this provocative fusion of religion and science examines the great theories of modern physics to find new ways for contemporary people to express their spiritual beliefs and thoughts.
6 x 9, 352 pp, Quality PB, ISBN 1-58023-306-6 **$18.99**; Hardcover, ISBN 1-58023-252-3 **$24.99**

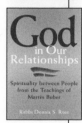

The Jewish Lights Spirituality Handbook: A Guide to Understanding, Exploring & Living a Spiritual Life *Edited by Stuart M. Matlins*
What exactly is "Jewish" about spirituality? How do I make it a part of my life? Fifty of today's foremost spiritual leaders share their ideas and experience with us.
6 x 9, 456 pp, Quality PB, ISBN 1-58023-093-8 **$19.95**; Hardcover, ISBN 1-58023-100-4 **$24.95**

Bringing the Psalms to Life: How to Understand and Use the Book of Psalms
By Dr. Daniel F. Polish
6 x 9, 208 pp, Quality PB, ISBN 1-58023-157-8 **$16.95**; Hardcover, ISBN 1-58023-077-6 **$21.95**

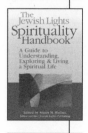

God & the Big Bang: Discovering Harmony between Science & Spirituality
By Dr. Daniel C. Matt 6 x 9, 216 pp, Quality PB, ISBN 1-879045-89-3 **$16.99**

Godwrestling—Round 2: Ancient Wisdom, Future Paths
By Rabbi Arthur Waskow 6 x 9, 352 pp, Quality PB, ISBN 1-879045-72-9 **$18.95**

One God Clapping: The Spiritual Path of a Zen Rabbi *By Rabbi Alan Lew with Sherril Jaffe*
5½ x 8½, 336 pp, Quality PB, ISBN 1-58023-115-2 **$16.95**

The Path of Blessing: Experiencing the Energy and Abundance of the Divine
By Rabbi Marcia Prager 5½ x 8½, 240 pp, Quality PB, ISBN 1-58023-148-9 **$16.95**

Six Jewish Spiritual Paths: A Rationalist Looks at Spirituality *By Rabbi Rifat Sonsino*
6 x 9, 208 pp, Quality PB, ISBN 1-58023-167-5 **$16.95**; Hardcover, ISBN 1-58023-095-4 **$21.95**

Soul Judaism: Dancing with God into a New Era
By Rabbi Wayne Dosick 5½ x 8½, 304 pp, Quality PB, ISBN 1-58023-053-9 **$16.95**

Stepping Stones to Jewish Spiritual Living: Walking the Path Morning, Noon, and Night *By Rabbi James L. Mirel and Karen Bonnell Werth*
6 x 9, 240 pp, Quality PB, ISBN 1-58023-074-1 **$16.95**; Hardcover, ISBN 1-58023-003-2 **$21.95**

There Is No Messiah ... and You're It: The Stunning Transformation of Judaism's Most Provocative Idea *By Rabbi Robert N. Levine, DD*
6 x 9, 192 pp, Quality PB, ISBN 1-58023-255-8 **$16.99**; Hardcover, ISBN 1-58023-173-X **$21.95**

These Are the Words: A Vocabulary of Jewish Spiritual Life *By Dr. Arthur Green*
6 x 9, 304 pp, Quality PB, ISBN 1-58023-107-1 **$18.95**

Holidays/Holy Days

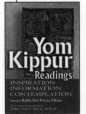

Yom Kippur Readings: Inspiration, Information and Contemplation
Edited by Rabbi Dov Peretz Elkins with section introductions from Arthur Green's These Are the Words
An extraordinary collection of readings, prayers and insights that enable the modern worshiper to enter into the spirit of the Day of Atonement in a personal and powerful way, permitting the meaning of Yom Kippur to enter the heart.
6 x 9, 348 pp, Hardcover, ISBN 1-58023-271-X **$24.99**

Leading the Passover Journey
The Seder's Meaning Revealed, the Haggadah's Story Retold
By Rabbi Nathan Laufer
Uncovers the hidden meaning of the Seder's rituals and customs.
6 x 9, 208 pp, Hardcover, ISBN 1-58023-211-6 **$24.99**

Reclaiming Judaism as a Spiritual Practice: Holy Days and Shabbat
By Rabbi Goldie Milgram
Provides a framework for understanding the powerful and often unexplained intellectual, emotional, and spiritual tools that are essential for a lively, relevant, and fulfilling Jewish spiritual practice. 7 x 9, 272 pp, Quality PB, ISBN 1-58023-205-1 **$19.99**

7th Heaven: Celebrating Shabbat with Rebbe Nachman of Breslov
By Moshe Mykoff with the Breslov Research Institute
Explores the art of consciously observing Shabbat and understanding in-depth many of the day's spiritual practices. 5⅛ x 8¼, 224 pp, Deluxe PB w/flaps, ISBN 1-58023-175-6 **$18.95**

The Women's Passover Companion
Women's Reflections on the Festival of Freedom
Edited by Rabbi Sharon Cohen Anisfeld, Tara Mohr, and Catherine Spector
Groundbreaking. A provocative conversation about women's relationships to Passover as well as the roots and meanings of women's seders.
6 x 9, 352 pp, Quality PB, ISBN 1-58023-231-0 **$19.99**; Hardcover, ISBN 1-58023-128-4 **$24.95**

The Women's Seder Sourcebook
Rituals & Readings for Use at the Passover Seder
Edited by Rabbi Sharon Cohen Anisfeld, Tara Mohr, and Catherine Spector
Gathers the voices of more than one hundred women in readings, personal and creative reflections, commentaries, blessings, and ritual suggestions that can be incorporated into your Passover celebration.
6 x 9, 384 pp, Quality PB, ISBN 1-58023-232-9 **$19.99**; Hardcover, ISBN 1-58023-136-5 **$24.95**

Creating Lively Passover Seders: A Sourcebook of Engaging Tales, Texts & Activities
By David Arnow, PhD 7 x 9, 416 pp, Quality PB, ISBN 1-58023-184-5 **$24.99**

Hanukkah, 2nd Edition: The Family Guide to Spiritual Celebration
By Dr. Ron Wolfson. Edited by Joel Lurie Grishaver.
7 x 9, 240 pp, illus., Quality PB, ISBN 1-58023-122-5 **$18.95**

The Jewish Family Fun Book: Holiday Projects, Everyday Activities, and Travel Ideas with Jewish Themes *By Danielle Dardashti and Roni Sarig. Illus. by Avi Katz.*
6 x 9, 288 pp, 70+ b/w illus. & diagrams, Quality PB, ISBN 1-58023-171-3 **$18.95**

The Jewish Gardening Cookbook: Growing Plants & Cooking for
Holidays & Festivals *By Michael Brown* 6 x 9, 224 pp, 30+ illus., Quality PB, ISBN 1-58023-116-0 **$16.95**

The Jewish Lights Book of Fun Classroom Activities: Simple and Seasonal
Projects for Teachers and Students *By Danielle Dardashti and Roni Sarig*
6 x 9, 240 pp, Quality PB, ISBN 1–58023–206–X **$19.99**

Passover, 2nd Edition: The Family Guide to Spiritual Celebration
By Dr. Ron Wolfson with Joel Lurie Grishaver 7 x 9, 352 pp, Quality PB, ISBN 1-58023-174-8 **$19.95**

Shabbat, 2nd Edition: The Family Guide to Preparing for and Celebrating the Sabbath
By Dr. Ron Wolfson 7 x 9, 320 pp, illus., Quality PB, ISBN 1-58023-164-0 **$19.99**

Sharing Blessings: Children's Stories for Exploring the Spirit of the Jewish Holidays
By Rahel Musleah and Michael Klayman
8½ x 11, 64 pp, Full-color illus., Hardcover, ISBN 1-879045-71-0 **$18.95** *For ages 6 & up*

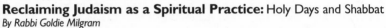

Theology/Philosophy

Aspects of Rabbinic Theology
By Solomon Schechter. New Introduction by Dr. Neil Gillman.
6 x 9, 448 pp, Quality PB, ISBN 1-879045-24-9 **$19.95**

Broken Tablets: Restoring the Ten Commandments and Ourselves
Edited by Rachel S. Mikva. Introduction by Lawrence Kushner. Afterword by Arnold Jacob Wolf.
6 x 9, 192 pp, Quality PB, ISBN 1-58023-158-6 **$16.95**; Hardcover, ISBN 1-58023-066-0 **$21.95**

Creating an Ethical Jewish Life
A Practical Introduction to Classic Teachings on How to Be a Jew
By Dr. Byron L. Sherwin and Seymour J. Cohen
6 x 9, 336 pp, Quality PB, ISBN 1-58023-114-4 **$19.95**

The Death of Death: Resurrection and Immortality in Jewish Thought
By Dr. Neil Gillman 6 x 9, 336 pp, Quality PB, ISBN 1-58023-081-4 **$18.95**

Evolving Halakhah: A Progressive Approach to Traditional Jewish Law
By Rabbi Dr. Moshe Zemer
6 x 9, 480 pp, Quality PB, ISBN 1-58023-127-6 **$29.95**; Hardcover, ISBN 1-58023-002-4 **$40.00**

Hasidic Tales: Annotated & Explained
By Rabbi Rami Shapiro. Foreword by Andrew Harvey, SkyLight Illuminations series editor.
5½ x 8½, 240 pp, Quality PB, ISBN 1-893361-86-1 **$16.95** (A SkyLight Paths Book)

A Heart of Many Rooms: Celebrating the Many Voices within Judaism
By Dr. David Hartman 6 x 9, 352 pp, Quality PB, ISBN 1-58023-156-X **$19.95**

The Hebrew Prophets: Selections Annotated & Explained
Translation & Annotation by Rabbi Rami Shapiro. Foreword by Zalman M. Schachter-Shalomi
5½ x 8½, 224 pp, Quality PB, ISBN 1-59473-037-7 **$16.99** (A SkyLight Paths book)

Keeping Faith with the Psalms: Deepen Your Relationship with God Using the
Book of Psalms By Daniel F. Polish 6 x 9, 320 pp, Quality PB, ISBN 1-58023-300-7 **$18.99**
Hardcover, ISBN 1-58023-179-9 **$24.95**

The Last Trial
On the Legends and Lore of the Command to Abraham to Offer Isaac as a Sacrifice
By Shalom Spiegel. New Introduction by Judah Goldin.
6 x 9, 208 pp, Quality PB, ISBN 1-879045-29-X **$18.95**

A Living Covenant: The Innovative Spirit in Traditional Judaism
By Dr. David Hartman 6 x 9, 368 pp, Quality PB, ISBN 1-58023-011-3 **$20.00**

Love and Terror in the God Encounter
The Theological Legacy of Rabbi Joseph B. Soloveitchik
By Dr. David Hartman
6 x 9, 240 pp, Quality PB, ISBN 1-58023-176-4 **$19.95**; Hardcover, ISBN 1-58023-112-8 **$25.00**

The Personhood of God: Biblical Theology, Human Faith and the Divine Image
By Dr. Yochanan Muffs; Foreword by Dr. David Hartman
6 x 9, 240 pp, Hardcover, ISBN 1-58023-265-5 **$24.99**

The Spirit of Renewal: Finding Faith after the Holocaust
By Rabbi Edward Feld 6 x 9, 224 pp, Quality PB, ISBN 1-879045-40-0 **$16.95**

Tormented Master: The Life and Spiritual Quest of Rabbi Nahman of Bratslav
By Dr. Arthur Green 6 x 9, 416 pp, Quality PB, ISBN 1-879045-11-7 **$19.99**

Your Word Is Fire: The Hasidic Masters on Contemplative Prayer
Edited and translated by Dr. Arthur Green and Barry W. Holtz
6 x 9, 160 pp, Quality PB, ISBN 1-879045-25-7 **$15.95**

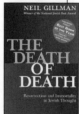
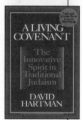

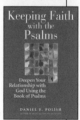

I Am Jewish
Personal Reflections Inspired by the Last Words of Daniel Pearl
Almost 150 Jews—both famous and not—from all walks of life, from all around
the world, write about Identity, Heritage, Covenant / Chosenness and Faith,
Humanity and Ethnicity, and *Tikkun Olam* and Justice.
Edited by Judea and Ruth Pearl
6 x 9, 304 pp, Deluxe PB w/flaps, ISBN 1-58023-259-0 **$18.99**; Hardcover, ISBN 1-58023-183-7 **$24.99**
Download a free copy of the *I Am Jewish Teacher's Guide* at our website:
www.jewishlights.com

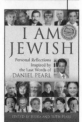

About Jewish Lights

People of all faiths and backgrounds yearn for books that attract, engage, educate, and spiritually inspire.

Our principal goal is to stimulate thought and help all people learn about who the Jewish People are, where they come from, and what the future can be made to hold. While people of our diverse Jewish heritage are the primary audience, our books speak to people in the Christian world as well and will broaden their understanding of Judaism and the roots of their own faith.

We bring to you authors who are at the forefront of spiritual thought and experience. While each has something different to say, they all say it in a voice that you can hear.

Our books are designed to welcome you and then to engage, stimulate, and inspire. We judge our success not only by whether or not our books are beautiful and commercially successful, but by whether or not they make a difference in your life.

For your information and convenience, at the back of this book we have provided a list of other Jewish Lights books you might find interesting and useful. They cover all the categories of your life:

Bar/Bat Mitzvah	Life Cycle
Bible Study / Midrash	Meditation
Children's Books	Parenting
Congregation Resources	Prayer
Current Events / History	Ritual / Sacred Practice
Ecology	Spirituality
Fiction: Mystery, Science Fiction	Theology / Philosophy
Grief / Healing	Travel
Holidays / Holy Days	Twelve Steps
Inspiration	Women's Interest
Kabbalah / Mysticism / Enneagram	

Stuart M. Matlins, Publisher

Or phone, fax, mail or e-mail to: **JEWISH LIGHTS Publishing**
Sunset Farm Offices, Route 4 • P.O. Box 237 • Woodstock, Vermont 05091
Tel: (802) 457-4000 • Fax: (802) 457-4004 • www.jewishlights.com
Credit card orders: **(800) 962-4544** (8:30AM–5:30PM ET Monday–Friday)
Generous discounts on quantity orders. SATISFACTION GUARANTEED. Prices subject to change.

For more information about each book, visit our website at www.jewishlights.com